INDIA'S DEVELOPMENT AND PUBLIC POLICY

Dedicated to the development
of the great potential of India
through better public policy

India's Development and Public Policy

Edited by

STUART S. NAGEL
University of Illinois

LONDON AND NEW YORK

First published 2000 by Ashgate Publishing

Reissued 2018 by Routledge
2 Park Square, Milton Park, Abingdon, Oxon OX14 4RN
711 Third Avenue, New York, NY 10017, USA

Routledge is an imprint of the Taylor & Francis Group, an informa business

Copyright © Stuart S. Nagel 2000

All rights reserved. No part of this book may be reprinted or reproduced or utilised in any form or by any electronic, mechanical, or other means, now known or hereafter invented, including photocopying and recording, or in any information storage or retrieval system, without permission in writing from the publishers.

Notice:
Product or corporate names may be trademarks or registered trademarks, and are used only for identification and explanation without intent to infringe.

Publisher's Note
The publisher has gone to great lengths to ensure the quality of this reprint but points out that some imperfections in the original copies may be apparent.

Disclaimer
The publisher has made every effort to trace copyright holders and welcomes correspondence from those they have been unable to contact.

Typeset by Manton Typesetters, Louth, Lincolnshire, UK.

A Library of Congress record exists under LC control number: 97037211

ISBN 13: 978-1-138-70636-1 (hbk)
ISBN 13: 978-1-138-70634-7 (pbk)
ISBN 13: 978-1-315-20185-6 (ebk)

Contents

Notes on the Contributors	ix
Introduction: Super-optimizing Analysis and India's Industrial Policy	1
Stuart S. Nagel	
Background and Trends	1
Alternatives, Goals and Relations	3
A Super-optimum Solution	5
Finding Other Super-optimum Solutions	6

PART I   ECONOMIC POLICY

1 India's Textile Policy and the Informal Sectors	9
Sanjiv Misra	
Introduction	9
The Textile Industry	10
Textile Policy	15
Impact of Policy	19
Policy Making in the Textile Sector	23

PART II   SOCIAL POLICY

2 Women's Rights in India: a Socioreligious Perspective	31
Kunja Medhi	
Rights of Women Through the Ages	31
The Era of Social Reform and Indian Women	32
Social Legislations and Women	39
Political Consciousness and Indian Women	39
Human Rights vis-à-vis Women of India	41
The UN Conferences on Women and the Steps Taken in India	42
Steps Taken by India	43

3 Political Education and Political Socialization in a Pluralistic Society: a Case Study of Two Generations of Women in India   47
Vijay Laxmi Pandit

Political Socialization   47
Political Socialization and Political Education   48
Changes in the Political Socialization and Political Education of Indian Women   49
The Views of Indian Women on their Place in Society   51
Family, Education and Political Socialization   54
The Relationship Between Political Socialization and Political Participation   57
Political Education, Political Socialization and Role Perceptions   60
Concluding Observations   63

PART III ENVIRONMENTAL AND HEALTH POLICY

4 Gender Dimensions of the Environment and Development Debate: the Indian Experience   69
Hem Swarup and Ram Rajput

Destroyers of the Environment or Victims of Development: the Case of Women at Survival Levels   73
Forest Policies and Grass-roots Women's Movements   78
Mega-dams, Rehabilitation and Women   84
Population Explosion and the Environment   85
Urbanization and Women in Slums and Squatter Settlements   88
Concluding Remarks   91

PART IV SCIENCE AND TECHNOLOGY POLICY

5 Science, Technology and National Goals: a Study of the Role of the Indian Council of Agricultural Research in the Agricultural Development of India   97
O.P. Sharma

Mandate   99
Organization   100
The Headquarters   101
Autonomy   103
ICAR and the National Agricultural Research System   104
Research Planning   107
Financing Agricultural Research   108
Human Resources   109
Research Monitoring and Evaluation   109

	Agricultural Community Outreach	110
	Concluding Observations	111

6	**The State and Information Technology in India: Emerging Trends**	115
	Pradip Thomas	
	The State: Continuity and Change	116
	The State in Crisis	118
	The Monopoly Capitalist State	121
	Information Technology and the State in India	124
	The Myth of Self-reliance	126
	A Captive Labour Pool	128
	Conclusion	131

7	**Administering Electronics: the Experience of India and Brazil**	137
	Jørgen Dige Pedersen	
	Introduction	137
	Some Theoretical Considerations	138
	Managing 'the Electronics Revolution': the Experience of India and Brazil	141
	The Role of Political and Administrative Structures	149
	Conclusion	157

PART V POLITICAL REFORM

8	**Panchayati Raj: the Indian Model of Local Self-government**	169
	Madan Sankhdher	

9	**General Elections in India, 1989**	181
	M.V. Pylee	

Index 191

Notes on the Contributors

Kunja Medhi, Gauhati University, India.

Sanjiv Misra, Centre for Policy Research, Dharma Marg, Chanakyapuri, New Delhi, India.

Stuart S. Nagel, University of Illinois and the Developmental Policy Studies Consortium, USA.

Vijay Laxmi Pandit, Maitreyi College, University of Delhi, India.

Jørgen Dige Pedersen, Institute of Political Science, University of Aarhus, Denmark.

M.V. Pylee, University of Cochin and Asian Institute of Development and Entrepreneurship, Cochin University, India.

Ram Rajput, Women's Studies and Development, Panjab University, Chandigarh, India.

Madan Sankhdher, University of Delhi, India.

O.P. Sharma, Shaheed Bhagat Singh College, University of Delhi, India.

Hem Swarup, All India Women's Studies and Development Organization, Kanpur, India.

Pradip Thomas, World Association for Christian Communication.

Introduction: Super-optimizing Analysis and India's Industrial Policy

Stuart S. Nagel

Super-optimizing refers to a new and useful form of public policy evaluation which seeks to find solutions to policy problems whereby conservative, liberal and other major viewpoints can all come out ahead of their best initial expectations simultaneously. The problem of industrial policy can serve as an illustration, including the more specific problem of hand-crafted work versus assembly line in India.

Background and Trends

India's textile policy and the informal sectors are almost an emotional topic in India because they relate to a key part of Gandhiism. Gandhi is often pictured making things at a handloom in the informal sector in order to counter the idea of people working in textile factories like the ones that exist in North Carolina. There are statistics which measure how well the handlooms are competing with the mills in India. If one compares 1912 with 1939, the mills went from about a million yards to about four million yards of output. The handlooms went from a million yards to a million and half. However, if one looks at the more recent figures, something has changed. By 1989, the mills were producing less than they were in 1939. Production had dropped from about four million to 2.6 million yards, while that of the informal sector had shot up from 1.5 million to 10.7 million yards. Yet the data show that in 1980 there were 452 power looms (there were only 15 in 1942) and in 1989 there were 944. If the mills have so many more power looms, why are they not producing more cloth?

The answer is partly that Gandhiism is working psychologically. There has been a phenomenal expansion of informal handloom output, partly for ideological reasons. Probably no other developing nation has experienced that kind of development, which shows that people can get satisfaction out of things that may not be so productive but are probably more fun to do. Working on a textile mill assembly line in North Carolina is pictured in a recent movie, *Norma Rae*, as being very depressing, as contrasted to being one's own boss with the family loom. This could be generalized a little. There is no question that highly mechanized collective farms in Russia are not as productive as a bunch of farmers working their own plots as their own boss on into the night. Certain occupations or industries in certain cultures may be more productive because they try to take into consideration individual psychology, instead of treating people like machines.

If the mills were capable of running solely by themselves, like Japanese mills where there is no dehumanizing because there are not many humans around, one would get a kind of super-optimum solution of high productivity and no dehumanizing. The North Carolina mills, which are like the India mills, may give the worst of both possible worlds. They may be an example of a super-malimum, where productivity is down through lack of incentive, and dehumanizing is up owing to regimentation. The Indian handloom is very humanizing, but it is not as productive as the Japanese automated factory.

This is also relevant to African business development. At the 1991 conference of the Association of Management Training Substitutes of East and South Africa (AMTIESA) held in the Seychelles, that was one of the best debated subjects. Some people lauded the informal sector. Others said that it was only justifiable as a means towards more efficient factories and should be considered, not as an end in itself, but just as a stepping-stone.

There has been a big increase in the total productivity of household looms in India, as compared with factory looms. At first it may seem strange that handlooms could outproduce power looms, even if there are a lot of handlooms. The explanation is that the household looms are not handlooms: they are machines, like sewing machines, which run on electricity. They constitute a compromise between home handicrafts and factory machines. These home machines may seem like an ideal compromise. They may, however, sacrifice some potential productivity that could come from more factory automation. There may be greater fairness among family members than there is among strangers in a factory. Likewise, home may sometime be a better quality workplace than a dirty factory.

Alternatives, Goals and Relations

Table I.1 is a super-optimizing or SOS table. SOS stands for 'super-optimum solutions'. The table shows goals to be achieved in the columns, alternatives available for achieving them in the rows, and indicators of relations between goals and alternatives in the cells. It also shows neutral, liberal and conservative totals in the columns at the right. Those totals reflect neutral, liberal and conservative weights for the goals. This is a simplified SOS table. It only involves two goals and four alternatives. Other SOS tables may involve more goals and more alternatives. This Indian problem lends itself well to a simplified SOS. The conservative alternative is hand-crafted work by artisans, or just hand-crafted work. The liberal approach is a kind of Eli Whitney–Henry Ford assembly line that at one time was considered, and was indeed, such a technological advance. The compromise is the current Indian situation which involves cottage industry using small machines.

We should say 'home' industry rather than 'cottage' industry, although both may suggest sweatshops. That is one of the drawbacks to this kind of compromise: it easily leads to people working at home, but they are not their own bosses. They may be more wage slaves than if they worked in a factory; they do piecework and someone shows up every day or so to pick up what they have done; they are paid a pittance and work very long hours. Just because they are at home does not mean that they have much quality of life or control over their working hours. The Indian data do not say anything about the quality of life of these people working at home. They just say that they are producing a lot of cloth, which may also have been true of the sweatshops in the New York garment industry in the early 1990s.

The conservative goal is productivity: turning out a lot of cloth at a relatively low price. The liberal goal is a quality workplace, in terms of one which is safe, psychologically pleasant, not polluted and with work that is not drudgery. The hand-crafted work involves a quality workplace: it is pretty hard to do much polluting when one works with needle and thread; it is also pretty hard to get an arm chopped off by a power tool. On the productivity side, though, needle and thread are not so productive. One would expect that assembly line work would be more productive than 'cottage' industry with small machines. However, if there are a lot of homes with a lot of small machines, they will out-produce a small number of assembly lines, even though one assembly line produces a lot more than one home. It depends on how we define productivity: if it is defined in terms of effectiveness or total output, then the Indian data show that the home industry is doing better; if productivity means output divided by some kind of input of money and effort, then the assembly line probably does better.

Table I.1 Handwork versus assembly lines in Indian clothmaking

Alternatives \ Criteria	C Goal Productivity C=3 N=2 L=1	L Goal Quality workplace L=3 N=2 C=1	N Total (neutral weights)	L Total (liberal weights)	C Total (conservative weights)
C Alternative Hand-crafted work	2	4	12	10	14*
L Alternative Assembly line work	4	2	12	14*	10
N Alternative Cottage industry with small machines	3	3	12	12	12
S Alternative Highly automated assembly plant	>3.5 ~5	>3.5 ~5	>12	>14**	>14**

Notes for SOS tables in general:
1. Symbols: C = conservative, L = liberal, N = neutral, S = super-optimum, #1 = group 1, #2 = group 2.
2. The 1–5 scores showing relations between alternatives and goals have the following meanings: 5 = the alternative is highly conducive to the goal; 4 = mildly conducive; 3 = neither conducive nor adverse; 2 = mildly adverse; 1 = highly adverse.
3. The 1–3 scores showing the relative weights or multipliers for each goal have the following meanings: 3 = this goal has relatively high importance to a certain ideological group; 2 = relatively middling importance; 1 = relatively low but positive importance.
4. A single asterisk shows the winning alternative on this column before considering the SOS alternative. A double asterisk shows the alternative that simultaneously does better than the conservative alternative on the conservative totals and better than the liberal alternative on the liberal totals.

Notes:
1. The conservative Gandhi position is to emphasize hand-crafted work. Doing so may not be high in productivity, but it provides quality workplaces in terms of safety, dignity and being free of pollution.
2. The liberal position is to emphasize assembly-line work associated with industrialized societies. Doing so may be high in productivity, but often lacks safety, dignity and cleanliness.
3. The compromise is working at home but with machines that work off electric outlets. Such machines are more productive than handlooms while at the same time not so unsafe, undignified or unclean as factories.
4. The SOS alternative might be to have highly automated assembly plants like Japan. Such plants do even better on productivity than traditional assembly lines, and generally better on safety, dignity and cleanliness than electric machines.

A Super-optimum Solution

The super-optimum solution is to strive for the kind of factory that Japan has pioneered that is highly productive and not-dehumanizing because it involves only highly skilled humans in the form of executives and engineers, and nobody on an assembly line except robots. Somebody may be on a console platform watching the robots; he or she may also be watching television, just like farmers in big harvesters having televisions in their cabs – very different from working with a scythe to harvest wheat.

We can refer to these factories as highly automated assembly plants. Japan does not even like to use the word 'factory' because it implies something that is belching smoke. They call their car manufacturing plants assembly plants. (General Motors frequently calls its car factories forges, which really sounds like some place belching smoke.) Although the word 'assembly' makes one think of assembly lines, it is possible to have things being assembled without a line of people turning a bolt, like Charlie Chaplin in the movie on the dehumanizing Ford automobile company.

Highly automated assembly plants achieve better than a 3.5 score on productivity, maybe even a 5. They are quality workplaces with very few injuries or unhappy employees. The energy source is likely to be reasonably clean, rather than coal-burning. It may be nuclear energy, although that raises safety issues for people outside the assembly plant and inside. The safety of nuclear energy is a separate issue; one could have a highly automated assembly plant that does not use nuclear energy or coal. It could even use solar energy, although that is not so likely with the current solar technology. It probably uses electricity and, if there are any chimney's belching, they are over at the power company, not in the assembly plant.

'Conservative' in the present context does not mean pro-business. It means preserving traditions and old ways of doing things. Likewise, liberal does not mean pro-labour. It means pro-technology and industrialization, rather than non-industrial lifestyles. This is different from African business development, although related. The African problem is basically large business versus small business, rather than factory versus home. To put it in a way that brings out the distinction, the Indian problem is handicrafts versus machines, while the African problem is small business (regardless of whether the businesses are handicrafts or use machines) versus big business (regardless of whether handicrafts or using machines). One could conceivably have a big business that employs a lot of people who work with their hands.

There are two different SOS solutions. One involves a technological fix with machines that do not involve assembly line workers, so that there is the productivity of machines without the dehumanizing of an assembly line. The other, addressing the African problem, involves a sequential SOS where small business leads to big business and is not an end in itself. This requires consciously encouraging small businesses that are not dead-ends, but are likely to be capable of expansion. It especially means small businesses that manufacture something, rather than small businesses that sell groceries.

Finding Other Super-optimum Solutions

Finding SOS solutions is facilitated by the use of spreadsheet-based decision-aiding software, which allows one to work simultaneously with many goals, alternatives and relations, including missing information and goals that are measured in multiple ways. Such software also allows for 'what if' analysis, to see how the tentative conclusions change as a result of changes in the inputs.

SOS solutions are also facilitated by having checklists based on generalizing from previous examples. Such checklists and examples can be found in the growing literature on super-optimizing, which includes win–win dispute resolution, growth economics and non-zero-sum games. For further details, see 'Super-Optimizing Analysis and Development Policy', in S.S. Nagel, *Global Policy Studies: International Interaction Toward Improving Public Policy* (St Martin's Press/Macmillan, 1991) and 'Improving Public Policy Toward and Within Developing Countries', in S.S. Nagel, *Public Administration and Decision-Aiding Software: Improving Procedure and Substance* (Greenwood Press, 1990).

It is the purpose of this book to apply related policy analysis ideas to public policy problems in India that include economic, social, technological and political problems. The book is a key volume in a multiple-volume set. The other volumes deal with Africa, Asia, East Europe and Latin America. This volume is the first one dealing with a single country, rather than a region: India is an important enough country to merit a volume of its own. It is hoped that the total set will help in the development of these regions and countries through better policy analysis and better public policy.

PART I
ECONOMIC POLICY

1 India's Textile Policy and the Informal Sectors

Sanjiv Misra

Introduction

India's textile industry has been characterized by a distinct, secular trend towards informal, small-scale production of cloth. This has, over time, led to an overwhelming dominance of the informal sectors which at present account for nearly four-fifths of total cloth output. This process has been accompanied by a corresponding decline in the formal manufacture of cloth, not only in relative terms, but in absolute terms also.

Although dualistic structures are fairly common features of many developing economies – a relatively modern, capital-intensive sector coexisting with a traditional, technologically backward, labour-intensive sector – it is usually the growth of the modern sector that threatens the existence of its backward counterpart. The Indian experience has, obviously, been quite contrary to the archetypal developmental pattern as far as the manufacture of cloth is concerned.

While informal-sector production has certain manifest advantages such as low wages and overheads, these are often offset by poor technology, lack of institutional credit, costlier raw materials and marketing problems. It is therefore doubtful whether, without the state interventions that severely handicapped the organized mills, the informal sector would have reached the position of unqualified dominance that it has today. It is the purpose of this chapter to analyse the causes and consequences of such state interventions in India's textile industry, focusing in the process on the key ideas, issues and interests that have motivated policy outcomes. We plan to proceed as follows. The first section gives a brief overview of the textile industry: its historical growth, structure and main forms of organization. The second section outlines the evolution of state policy towards the textile industry, focusing particularly on the issue of small versus large that has been one of its dominant themes. The impact of policy on intersectoral competitiveness and, concomitantly, on the relative growth of formal and informal production, is critically assessed in the third section. In a final section we attempt a conceptual framework to explain policy outcomes in the context of India's historical orientation, stemming from its colonial past, the ideological predilections of its policy makers and the liberal democratic framework within which such exercises take place.

The Textile Industry

History

The textile industry is India's oldest industry. While the tradition of hand spinning and hand weaving is many centuries old, the first mechanized spinning mill was started in Bombay in 1854. Thereafter, the organized industry grew rapidly as the result of certain obvious advantages: the easy availability of indigenously grown cotton, a plentiful supply of unskilled labour and a large and growing domestic market for yarn and cloth. By 1914, India already had the fourth or fifth largest cotton textile industry in the world,[1] and at Independence in 1947, it was the largest organized industry, spread across Bombay and Ahmedabad in the west, Kanpur in the north and Coimbatore in the south. While the majority of the mills in the north and west were of the composite type (those which combined spinning, weaving and processing in the same unit), the mills in the south were predominantly spinning units supplying yarn to the traditional handlooms.

What is indeed remarkable and not very well known is that the rapid growth of the formal or organized sector of the Indian textile industry during the four decades preceding World War II did not (except for a brief period following World War I) imply a decline in the traditional, informal mode of production. On the contrary, handloom output continued to expand (Table 1.1) and satisfied a significant proportion of the incremental demand for cloth of the growing population. Two major factors were probably responsible for this: one was the underdeveloped communications structure, which limited the penetration of formal-sector manufacture and imports into the hinterland; the other was the product specialization of handlooms in coarse cloth, in the manufacture of which they faced little competition from the textile mills.

The achievement of independence saw immediate curbs on imports of cloth and an active pursuit of a policy of import substitution. At this time the mill sector was without doubt the dominant producer of cloth, accounting for almost four-fifths of total cloth production (Table 1.2). In fact, between

Table 1.1 Production and availability of cotton cloth, 1900–39 (million yards)

Years	Indian mills	Handlooms	Imports	Total	Exports
1900–1903	482.8	792.8	1 967.7	3 243.3	113.3
1912–1915	1 187.0	1 048.5	2 738.7	4 974.2	121.7
1918–1920	1 575.8	712.4	1 132.0	3 420.2	220.0
1927–1930	2 195.6	1 155.5	1 916.3	5 267.4	171.7
1936–1939	3 629.6	1 420.5	654.7	5 704.8	173.3
Change in production:					
1900–1915	+704.2	–255.7	+771.0	+1 730.9	+8.4
1917–1939	+2 058.8	+708.1	–477.3	2 284.6	–46.7

Source: Mazumdar (1984), Table 1:1, p.7.

1951 and 1957, mill cloth production increased by over a billion metres, reaching a peak total of 4862 million metres in 1957.

In the immediate post-Independence period, then, India started out with a textile industry that was essentially 'dualistic': a modern, urban mill sector and the traditional, non-mechanized handloom industry that was almost entirely rural. A new actor was to gain prominence on the Indian textile scene around this period – small-scale, mechanized weaving units, commonly referred to as power looms. Although firm evidence on the number of power looms in the pre-Independence period is not available, their number was put at around 15 000 in 1942.[2] By 1956, this had increased remarkably, to around 27 000.[3] This increase was partly due to handloom weavers switching over to a more efficient and productive mode of production to improve their earnings. These units used discarded looms from the mills and they developed in areas where electric power was readily available. Partly, the growth of power looms was spurred by the indigenous manufacture and improved availability of rayon filament yarn. There was a growing demand for pure non-cotton fabrics woven from filament yarns (or 'art silk' fabrics) and their manufacture was extremely cost-effective in such small-scale, mechanized weaving units.[4] In fact, power loom concentrations in certain areas, such as Surat in western India, had begun to specialize almost exclusively in their manufacture.

The period 1956–7 marks, in some sense, a watershed as far as organized or formal manufacture of cloth is concerned. Mill weaving capacity was

Table 1.2 Production of cloth, 1948–89 (million metres)

Year	Mill sector		Informal sectors	Total
1948	3 949	(77.4)	1 151	5 100
1951	3 727	(78.6)	1 014	4 741
1957	4 862	(72.9)	1 811	6 673
1961	4 703	(61.5)	2 942	7 645
1966	4 252	(51.8)	3 963	8 215
1971	4 107	(47.9)	4 470	8 577
1976	4 226	(44.2)	5 325	9 551
1981	4 073	(36.5)	7 072	11 145
1982	3 035	(28.9)	7 479	10 514
1985	3 411	(27.4)	9 016	12 427
1987	3 114	(23.7)	10 003	13 117
1989	2 674	(19.9)	10 778	13 452

Note: Figures in parentheses indicate percentage of total production.

Source: *Handbook of Statistics on Cotton Textile Industry*, Indian Cotton Mills Federation, Bombay (various editions).

frozen at existing levels as a matter of conscious industry policy, with expansion permitted only for exports. Although the share of mill output in total cloth production had begun to decline from 1951, in absolute terms too, a decline set in from 1957. Between 1957 and 1966, mill output fell by over 600 million metres. After a periods of relative stagnation which lasted until around the end of the 1970s, the decline was particularly sharp during the 1980s: between 1980 and 1989, mill output of cloth fell by more than 1500 million metres.

The fall in the formal production of cloth was accompanied by a rapid inflationary expansion of the power loom sector (Table 1.3). By 1964, the number of power looms had already increased sixfold over their 1951 figure, to around 146 000. By 1977, this had risen further, to around 350 000, and by 1990 their number was estimated to be over a million looms. From a small beginning around three and a half decades before, the power loom sector had grown, in a manner that can only be described as phenomenal, to a level where it stands today as the principal clothier of the nation: at the very least, around 60 per cent of all the cloth produced in the country originates from power looms, the balance being shared in almost equal proportion by the organized mill sector and the traditional informal sector,

Table 1.3 Number of power looms (thousands)

Year	Power looms
1942	15
1956	27
1964	146
1977	348
1980	452
1981	499
1982	573
1983	605
1985	639
1988	873
1989	944

Note: The figures for the period 1977–85 indicate only the number of authorized power looms, since official policy did not permit the setting up of new power looms – only those set up prior to 1.1.1981 were to be regularized. It is estimated that, on 1.1.1985, there were at least 200 000 power looms which were unauthorized. Similarly, the figure for 1989 indicates only the officially registered power looms. The total number of applications filed for registration was close to 1.1 million. The latter figure better approximates the total number of power looms in the country.

Source: GOI (1964); GOI (1985–90).

the handlooms.[5] What is also remarkable is that, despite substantial productivity handicaps, the handloom sector has been largely able to maintain the share of total cloth production that it had around four decades ago.[6] The only real loser in the bargain has, quite unambiguously, been the formal, organized, composite mill sector.

Structure and Organization

As will be evident from the foregoing historical résumé, for purposes of analytical convenience, India's textile industry can be subdivided into two distinct segments on the basis of whether manufacture is formal and organized or informal and unorganized. This distinction is based on the scale of operations and the nature of industrial organization although, as in the case of the non-mechanized handlooms, the technology employed may also be different. In contrast with the formal segment, which is typically organized on a factory basis, with a complement of largely permanent and usually unionized wage labour, units in the informal sector work with mainly pre-industrial forms of organization. While setting up units in the formal sector needs a licence or registration, informal-sector units may or may not be registered. As a consequence, reliable statistics of employment and output in the latter are generally not available and usually have to be estimated only indirectly.[7]

The spinning operation takes place almost exclusively in the organized sector, in independent spinning mills or in the spinning sections of composite mills (where the spinning, weaving and processing stages of textile manufacture are combined in a single composite unit). While some hand spinning does take place for the manufacture of hand-spun yarn which is used in the production of 'khadi' cloth,[8] its output is relatively insignificant.

In the organized sector, the weaving operations take place almost entirely in the composite mills, since independent weaving units imply loss of economies of integration, with no corresponding benefits. The technology preponderantly consists of the plain, non-automatic shuttle loom (also known as the 'Lancashire' loom) although automatic shuttle looms and, to a lesser extent, shuttle-less looms are also used. As we have seen, the informal weaving sector has two distinct sub-sectors on the basis of whether production is mechanized or not: the power looms and the handlooms. The former is the archetypal informal sector, consisting of power-driven weaving units operated by sweated labour located in urban or semi-urban shanty towns. Apart from the fact that the composite mills may often use newer and, in some cases, more modern equipment, the technology of weaving in the power looms and the mills is essentially the same: that is, the non-automatic shuttle loom. What places them apart is the scale of operations and the manner in which the production process is organized. Most power loom units operate on a small scale, typically using three or four looms per unit, which places them outside the ambit of the state's licensing and labour welfare regulations.[9]

There are essentially two forms of organization prevalent: the master-weaver system which is a form of the classical 'putting out' system with the master-weaver providing the raw materials to the loom owners, who in turn are paid conversion charges according to the quantity of cloth produced; and the owner–entrepreneur who undertakes all the investment and consequently bears the entire risk. The looms may be operated by family or hired labour, or a combination of both. In contrast with the organized mill sector, almost the entire requirement of working capital as well as fixed capital is met from non-bank sources, at higher than institutional lending rates of interest, from the large quantum of undeclared, untaxed and, often, illegal income which is perpetually in circulation in the 'black' or underground economy. One major source of labour for this sector is the migrants from the surrounding countryside; another is workers from the composite mills, laid off as a result of partial or complete closures. In the absence of unionized labour, wage rates are market-determined and are often half the level prevailing in the composite mills. The working hours are invariably longer. In fact, this constitutes one of the major sources of competitiveness of informal against formal production.

The handloom sector is the traditional weaving sector using manually operated looms. Although there are some large production units or 'Karkhanas' usually located close to urban consuming centres, weaving is normally carried on in small household units located in the rural areas, often as an activity ancilliary to agriculture. The organization of production is generally of the master-weaver type. Around 70 per cent of the output of this sector is sold in the rural areas.[10] However, a significant number of handlooms, particularly in north-east India, operate on a non-commercial basis, the production being primarily for domestic or local consumption only.[11] Many of the credit requirements of handlooms are met from non-institutional sources such as village money lenders, although, unlike the case of power looms, these do not form part of the underground economy.

The Indian textile sector, at first sight, represents a good example of the dualism that is usually characteristic of the economic structure of developing economies: the coexistence of a relatively modern, capital-intensive sector with a traditional, technologically backward, labour-intensive sector. There are, however, obvious departures from the classical archetype. First, as we have seen, the informal 'backward' sector is itself dualistic, with power looms and handlooms representing different degrees of 'backwardness'. Second, as already mentioned, contrary to the typical developmental experience in which the growth of the modern sector threatens the existence of its relatively 'backward' counterpart, in India the trend has been in the opposite direction as far as the production of cloth is concerned. Finally, while the formal and the informal sectors complete with each other in the production of cloth, the latter is almost wholly dependent on the former for the supply of the basic raw material, that is, yarn. Similarly, a part of the processing of cloth produced in the unorganized sector is done in the organized sector, so emphasizing the intimate linkages that exist between the two.

Textile Policy

There is no denying the fact that, excepting the centrally planned economies, the Indian textile industry has been one of the most tightly regulated in the world. There are several reasons for this. First, to an extent state controls were inevitable given the highly interventionist industrial policy enunciated in the Industrial Policy Resolution of 1948. The textile industry was one of 18 basic industries whose regulation and control was considered necessary in the national interest. It thus became subject to a complex regime of licensing and controls implied by the Industries (Development and Regulation) Act of 1951. Second, the textile industry being an item of mass consumption satisfying, as it were, a basic human need, it seemed necessary, given the imperatives of the prevailing development ideology, for the state to ensure adequate production and its proper distribution. Thus textiles became subject to a wide-ranging array of regulations and controls embodied in the Cotton Textiles (Control) Order, 1948. Although the sweeping regulatory powers vested in the state under the latter derived their original justification from the need to deal with the shortages at the end of World War II, they were retained substantially unaltered for almost four decades. They empowered the state to regulate and control every conceivable aspect of textile manufacture, from the installation and disposal of machinery to the production, packing, distribution and pricing of yarn and cloth.

While these factors were undoubtedly very important, the unusual degree of state intervention and regulation in the textile sector, to a large extent, stemmed also from policies that attempted to 'harmonize' or balance the often sharply conflicting economic interests of producer and consumers and, more importantly, to regulate competition between different sub-sets of producers. The most visible outcome of this was the plethora of restraints imposed on the organized mill sector, ostensibly to protect the traditional non-mechanized modes of production.

In the initial flush of independence and the considerable influence of Gandhian ideology at that time, the dominant opinion on the choice of technology for cloth manufacture was that the promotion of handlooms could achieve, at one stroke, the twin objectives of generation of employment and the production of cloth for mass consumption. The brutal devastation of the traditional Indian textile industry by imported mill-made cloth in the 19th century being firmly imprinted in nationalist perceptions, it was easy to stretch the argument to emphasize the vulnerability of the handloom sector to competition from the growing indigenous mill sector. It was therefore considered necessary, not only to physically restrict the output of the mills, but also to make mill-made cloth considerably more costly by the imposition of fiscal levies. Thus, in 1950, the government reserved certain areas of production, comprising a wide variety of items of common use, for exclusive manufacture by the handlooms, mills being legally prohibited from producing these items. This was followed up with a cess on all mill-made cloth in 1953 to fund the subsidies for the handloom and khadi sectors. The severity and scope of levies on mill-made cloth were to increase progressively over the years.

While there was near-unanimity in the view that the composite mills had to be physically restrained to protect the handlooms, there was considerable divergence of opinion on whether the latter could, in fact, effectively fulfil the role of meeting the entire future clothing needs of a growing population that was being thrust upon them. The Kanungo Committee (GOI, 1954) was of the opinion that for ordinary cloth 'the pure and simple handloom is, and must be, a relatively inefficient tool of production'. With the exception of those textile items which required an 'intricate body pattern' there seemed 'to be no variety of fabric which the handloom industry could produce in a better quality or at a lower price (consistent with a reasonable wage being paid to the handloom weaver and his assistants) as compared to the mill or the powerloom industry'. The Committee thus recommended a progressive conversion of handlooms into power looms through organized effort over a period of 15–20 years.

These views were sharply opposed by another official committee, the Karve Committee (GOI, 1955) which was concerned with the role of the village and small industries in the Second Five Year Plan. Not only did this Committee recommend the freezing of both mill and power-loom output at existing levels, so that the entire incremental demand for cotton cloth during the second plan period (1956–7 to 1960–61) was to be met by handlooms, but it also recommended the deferment of any proposals for additional spinning capacity in the mill sector, in order to promote the hand spinning sector. The recommendations of the Karve Committee represent perhaps the most extreme ideological position in favour of small, hand-operated technology vis-à-vis power-aided production. It was evident, however, that any curbs on spinning capacity would run counter to the interests of the handlooms, which were critically dependent on the spinning mills for their supply of yarn. Ultimately, therefore, it was the narrow band of convergence of views between the Kanungo and Karve Committees on restraining mill capacity that became official policy: weaving capacity in the mill sector was frozen at the existing level in 1956, with expansion permitted only for exports. Strong theoretical justification for such a policy approach towards the mills was also provided by the development paradigm current at that time, epitomized by the so-called 'Mahalanobis model', which emphasized the development of heavy industry for the achievement of the growth objective and small-scale, labour-intensive production of essential consumer goods for promoting employment.

With the mills physically restrained, a wide area was created for the power looms to grow. Much of this expansion was due to extraneous factors such as excise exemption which made power loom cloth cheaper than mill-made cloth. It was also aided by the considerable ambiguity on the precise role of power looms that was to characterize policy over the next few decades. While curbs on capacity expansion in this sector had been retained along with the freeze on the mills, the benefits of reservations of certain items for handlooms had also been extended to small power-driven units so as to encourage handloom weavers to upgrade to mechanized production.

In fact, in 1964, the report of the Asoka Mehta Committee (GOI, 1964) resurrected the views of the Kanungo Committee put forward a decade earlier; it recommended that the power loom sector be allowed to acquire a paramount position in the decentralized sector of the textile industry. Seriously questioning the long-term viability of handlooms, it further urged that the regulatory provisions regarding acquisition and installation of power looms should be done away with since they had not only proved ineffective but had also given scope for serious malpractices. Though the regulations on power looms were retained on the grounds of administrative necessity, the acceptance of the recommendation of the Asoka Mehta Committee on permitting a planned expansion of this sector seemed to signify an official recognition of the role of the power looms in the textile economy.

With the unabated, rapid growth of power looms and the inherent conflict of interests with handlooms, however, it was only a matter of time before serious concern began to be voiced about the latter's survival prospects. In its report submitted in July 1974, the Sivaraman Committee (GOI, 1976) was of the view that government support for the handlooms had been inadequate and that product reservation meant for the protection of the handloom sector had in fact benefited the power looms. Apart from recommending the creation of a comprehensive institutional framework for the promotion of handlooms, it also urged a set of wide-ranging fiscal measures to reduce the considerable cost advantages that the power looms had over the handlooms. Although complete parity in the matter of excise duty between mills and power looms as recommended by the Committee was not accepted, the government took steps to reduce considerably the disparity in the incidence of excise duty between the power loom and the mill sectors. A decision was also taken not to permit any further expansion of the power loom sector.

The continuing concern at the rapid growth of the power loom sector and its detrimental impact on handlooms again found reflection in the textile policy of 1978 (GOI, 1978), which reiterated the government's resolve to freeze power loom capacity at existing levels. To this end, it envisaged the introduction of legislation to prevent statutorily the growth in the number of power looms. The proposed legislation, however, never saw the light of day. In fact, only three years later, in 1981, the government announced a fresh textile policy which allowed a marginal expansion of this sector, limited to cooperatives of handlooms wishing to install power looms. As in the previous policy, the existing unauthorized power looms, of which there were a substantial number, were to be regularized on the payment of a fee.

However, it was becoming increasingly apparent that the growth of the power loom sector could not be checked through administrative fiat. Moreover, this sector had emerged as, virtually, the exclusive producer of non-cotton cloth, by which reckoning alone it had become an integral segment of the textile economy. Even if it were administratively possible, its expansion could be curbed only with serious consequences for the availability of such cloth, for which there was a marked consumer preference. Also this facet of the growth of power looms posed no direct threat to the handlooms, which specialized almost entirely in the production of pure cotton cloth.

Taking a pragmatic cognizance of these ground realities, the textile policy of June 1985 (GOI, 1985) largely did away with the physical curbs on the growth of power looms. Only compulsory registration was required and looms could be set up as long as they did not violate the locational guidelines to be prescribed. The recognition that the sector required no protection from the composition mills was evident from the assertion in the policy itself that the mills and power looms would be treated on par for fiscal purposes. The 1985 textile policy made yet another major break from the past: it did away with the virtual freeze on weaving capacity of the mills that had existed since 1956, although replacement of looms had been permitted for purposes of technological upgrading since 1976. It was a belated recognition of the fact that the freeze had served no useful purpose apart from inhibiting the infusion of new entrepreneurship and, consequently, limiting competition within the mill sector itself. It had been evident for quite some time that the greater threat to the existence of the handlooms came from the power looms, rather than the mills. It is intriguing, therefore, that this policy survived, virtually unchanged, for as long as it did.

Impact of Policy

The impact of policy can be assessed at two levels: (a) the effect of the macroeconomic policy environment, and (b) the impact of sector-specific policies. There is little doubt that a relatively autarkic development strategy giving overwhelming priority to the growth of heavy industry had major implications for some of the older light industries such as textiles. Although World War II had left the composite mill sector in a run-down condition due to the overworking of machinery to cope with wartime requirements and the disruption in the supplies of spares and machinery which had to be imported, the issue of renovation and modernization of the industry was given a backseat, in accordance with the low priority accorded to investments in light industries in general. Further, the extreme 'export pessimism' of developmental economic thinking in India and the generally anti-export bias of policies precluded any major inroads into external markets. Instead, the highly protected nature of the domestic economy stemming from an open-ended commitment to import substitution had opened up other, more lucrative, avenues for investment. Many of the prominent textile companies were thus encouraged to diversify into fresh areas, instead of ploughing back into the industry capital for renovation and modernization.

Coming to sector-specific policies, apart from the virtual freeze on mill weaving capacity and fiscal discrimination against mill-made cloth, there were other aspects of policy which had major adverse implications for this sector. To meet the clothing needs of the economically weaker sections of society, the government had, in 1964, introduced statutory price controls for certain commonly used varieties of cloth. Under this dispensation, all composite mills were required to produce, at least, the stipulated minimum amounts of such cloth (commonly referred to as 'controlled cloth') to be sold at prices fixed by the government. The mills were permitted to sell the non-controlled varieties in the open market. The stipulated amount was originally fixed at 45 per cent of total mill production, was raised to 50 per cent in 1965 and finally was reduced to 25 per cent in 1968, as a result of representations from the mills.

Since the prices of controlled cloth fixed by the government usually did not cover production costs, mills were forced to raise the prices of the non-controlled varieties sold in the open market to offset the losses incurred in the production of the 'controlled' ones, thereby adding to the uncompetitiveness of mill-made cloth vis-à-vis the output of the power looms. The fact that this measure was, without doubt, a major contributory factor to the poor state of health of the composite mill sector was taken cognizance of in the textile policy statement (GOI, 1978) itself.

Although this wholly irrational obligation was removed in 1978, the combined effect of the sustained anti-mill bias of policies had left the composite mill sector in much too weakened a state to cope with the competitive onslaught of the burgeoning power loom sector. As early as 1968, 16 loss-making mills were taken under state management to prevent their closure. By 1973, the number of such mills had grown to 103. In addition, around 73 privately managed textile mills were declared 'sick' by the banks in 1977.[12] A comprehensive census of textile machinery in the mill sector carried out in 1979 revealed that around 56 per cent of the installed ring frames (see GOI, 1979) and 85 per cent of the non-automatic looms (which constituted around 80 per cent of the total installed loomage) were more than 20 years old (GOI, 1979).

There was some softening of the stiff anti-mill policy stance from the mid-1970s. This was a belated attempt to counteract some of the deleterious effects of the earlier policies on the mill sector. Thus finance on concessionary terms was made available for modernization and installation of automatic looms permitted as replacements for ordinary non-automatic looms, even if, in the bargain, mill output was significantly augmented. The impact of these measures was, however, limited. First, the autarkic development strategy largely precluded technology imports, so that reliance necessarily had to be placed on domestically produced equipment which was not only technologically inferior but considerably more expensive. Second, with overall capacity frozen, superior technology could be brought in only via machine replacements. Since the new technology was invariably labour-saving, this implied reduction of labour, the costs of which, when added onto the already high capital costs of the superior technology, probably rendered the investment quite unattractive.[13] Finally, the overall policy bias against the composite mill sector and the unequal competition from the power looms almost certainly adversely affected entrepreneurial expectations and incentives to modernize.

It was the one and a half year-long strike by the workers of the Bombay textile mills commencing in 1982 which finally broke the back of the composite mill sector. Although almost 29 per cent of the country's mill-weaving capacity was shut down because of the strike, there was virtually no impact on cloth availability or prices, the loss of output being made good by the power looms. In fact, many of the affected mills, eager to retain their share of the cloth market, entered into clandestine sub-contractual arrangements with power loom owners in order to get cloth woven on power looms and stamped with their own brands. Such informal relationships between the mills and power looms were nothing new. Even in 1964, an official committee had estimated that around 25 per cent of the power loom units were owned by textile mills.[14] Such arrangements have only grown, not diminished, over the years and have provided a profitable avenue for the mills to circumvent capacity restrictions. By all accounts there is at present considerable involvement of the mills themselves in the financing and organization of power loom operations.

It seems fairly certain, then, that the consistent anti-mill bias of textile policy, which derived its rationale primarily from the protection of the traditional handloom sector, was in large measure responsible for the exponential growth of the mechanized informal sector, that is the power looms. The latter in some sense therefore is an unintended (and until 1985 largely illegitimate) offspring of government policy. According to an important World Bank Study (Mazumdar, 1984), however, the power loom sector would have out-competed the composite mill sector as a result of cost advantages stemming from substantially lower wages and lower overheads, so that, even without the capacity freeze on the mills, the former would in all probability have come to acquire a dominant position in the manufacture of cloth. This view has been questioned in a more recent study (Misra, 1991). The composite mills enjoy certain tangible economies of integration resulting in reduced raw material and transport costs, better marketing and, generally, a superior quality of output. Further, while capital costs per unit of output are certainly much higher in the mills than with the power looms, machinery is also utilized much more intensively and efficiently in the former than with the latter. Finally, the organized sector has access to bank credit which is usually substantially cheaper than that available for informal modes of manufacture. Although this issue is far from finally settled, it is extremely doubtful whether, in the absence of the sustained anti-mill policy stance, the power loom sector would have come to acquire the position of unqualified dominance that it has today.

Can it be said that this has been a desirable outcome? The power loom sector is decentralized and uses less capital and more labour per unit of output than the mill sector. It may appear that in a labour-surplus, capital-scarce economy this is adequate to justify its existence. However, the power looms also use inputs much more ineffectively than the mills, so that were the implicit tax on labour in the mills (which is what a higher wage rate effectively implies) removed, the existence of the power loom sector would become more difficult to justify in terms of the real costs and benefits (based on shadow prices of labour and capital) to the economy as a whole. The growth of the power loom sector therefore constitutes in some sense a 'social' loss.

Before concluding this section, some mention appears necessary about the state of the traditional informal sector, the handlooms. Although not a commercially viable technique for the production of ordinary cloth, handlooms have survived, on the one hand, by weaving high value-added, exotic varieties which cannot possibly be manufactured by mechanized means and, on the other, by producing extremely coarse cloth with very cheap labour for rural markets. Thus a differentiation of both products and markets has enabled this sector largely to retain the share of total cloth production that it had soon after Independence. Policy interventions have played, at best, a secondary role in this process.[15] It must be mentioned, however, that the spatial distribution of handlooms has undergone a significant change over the past four decades. Not unexpectedly, there has been a substantial decline in the number of handlooms located in areas close to power loom concentrations. This has been offset, to an extent, by the increase in the number of handlooms in east and north-east India where such concentrations are absent.[16]

In retrospect, it is doubtful, therefore, whether any equity objectives were served by the sustained anti-mill bias of state policy. On the contrary, these policies have had major adverse implications for international competitiveness in an area where India unquestionably possessed a comparative advantage. This is borne out by her miserable performance in the export of textile products, which contrasts sharply with that of other Asian textile exporters.[17] As a result, major opportunities for a 'textile-led' industrial growth on the patterns of Japan and, more recently, the newly industrialized countries (NICs) of Southeast Asia, were lost. Viewed in *toto*, there seems little doubt that the welfare implications of state interventions in the textile industry have been overwhelmingly in the negative.

Policy Making in the Textile Sector

Are any broad conceptual generalizations possible about policy making in the textile sector which could adequately explain the emergence of policies that resulted in the overwhelming predominance of informal production in the Indian textile industry? Viewed from an analytical perspective, at least three major factors, which are not mutually exclusive, seem to have crucially affected policy outcomes: ideology, the issue of equity, and the interplay of interests and populist imperatives.

Ideology was unquestionably the prime mover of economic policy in the first few decades after independence from colonial rule. Since the mid-1950s, planners in India had opted for an autarkic development strategy which gave emphasis to investments in heavy industry for achieving growth objectives and small-scale, labour-intensive manufacture of essential consumer goods for providing employment opportunities for the rapidly growing labour force. What came to be known as 'the Mahalanobis model' attempted, curiously, to combine essentially antithetical elements of the Soviet model of development, with its emphasis on comprehensive state planning and rapid industrialization, with Gandhian economic beliefs in the efficacy of essentially pre-industrial, non-mechanized techniques for the manufacture of yarn and cloth. In the words of Chakravarty (1987, p.16):

> In his famous four sector model, Mahalanobis wanted to define a 'dual development thesis' (which Mao Ze-dong called 'walking on two legs'), whose purpose was to combine high employment growth with building up a capital goods base. In the context of employment generation, he too assigned an important role to the highly labour intensive part of the textile sector. This precluded a fast rate of growth in a modern textile industry.

The Mahalanobis strategy obviously constituted a radical departure from the principle of 'comparative advantage' and deviated sharply from the textile-led pattern of industrial development followed so successfully by the late industrializers such as Japan. Thus vastly different strategies of development explain to a large extent the differential performance of the textile industry in India, in particular the poor state of the formal sector, vis-à-vis some of the Asian developing country textile producers.

Although India had opted for a mixed economy with ample scope for private initiative, the influence of the Soviet model and the 'socialist' preconceptions of policy makers led to the dominance of what Lal (1983) has termed the 'dirigiste dogma' in Indian economic thinking. Two of the major prescriptive elements emanating from such thinking which are particularly relevant to the issue of the small versus the large in the textile industry where (a) a preference for direct, discretionary physical controls over indirect, market-mediated ones operating through the price mechanism, and (b) the promotion of equity through direct state interventions in favour of traditional labour-intensive modes of production and price controls. Such postulates naturally exercised considerable influence on the evolution of policy.

A major offshoot of such beliefs was the continuation of a complicated web of regulations and controls on the textile industry which had been essentially devised to cope with the shortages of the post-World War II period. These regulations, which came to be embodied in the Cotton Textiles (Control) Order (CTCO) of 1948, vested the state with wide-ranging powers to regulate prices, distribution and production of textile products, including the installation of capacity to produce them. The CTCO, which represents perhaps the most elaborate system of regulation and control devised for any industry anywhere in the non-socialist world, was continued virtually unaltered both in form and in content long after its raison d'être had ceased to exist. In fact, its ambit was progressively widened to encompass newly emerging sectors (for example, man-made textiles) and to deal with changing contours of policy. Once introduced, these controls, with the passage of time, acquired an existence of their own, with powerful constituencies and strong justifications in favour of their perpetuation.

Although the straitjacket regime implied by the CTCO encompassed all mechanized production of textiles, its actual impact did not extend much beyond the formal sector, owing to the sheer administrative non-feasibility of enforcing these controls over a large number of tiny units spread across a number of locations all over the country. This stranglehold of controls was undoubtedly an important contributory factor in the decline in competitiveness of the formal textile-weaving sector. As a logical corollary, the power looms which, at least de facto, were largely outside their pale were able to thrive and flourish.

The issue of equity has always been in the forefront of the Indian economic policy agenda, although more often than not it has amounted to little more than populist rhetoric. This is scarcely surprising, given the vast number of the poor and unemployed in the economy and the limited resources at the disposal of the state to make any significant improvement in their economic condition. Thus the policy tilt in favour of traditional non-mechanized production of cloth, although initially deriving its impulse from Gandhian beliefs, was subsequently justified as an instrument for providing income and employment for the economically weak sections of the population. In a similar vein, the concern for meeting the clothing needs of the poor was the raison d'être of the controlled cloth scheme.

Whether any equity objectives were indeed served by these measures is another matter. What is significant for the purposes of the present discussion is that the costs of meeting these distributional objectives were imposed on other mechanized sectors of the industry (through fiscal instruments as well as physical controls) instead of the society at large. Overwhelmingly, the burden of such policies fell on the formal composite sector (where such measures were easier to enforce), adversely affecting its competitive strength vis-à-vis the mechanized informal sector.

In the final analysis, policy outcomes in India have to be viewed in the liberal democratic context in which the policy formulation exercises take place. From this viewpoint, the structural evolution of the Indian textile industry constitutes in some sense a paradox, for, while the mills collectively represent an 'interest' quite capable of influencing policy, and the protection of handlooms carries with it a certain emotional and populist appeal which cuts across the political spectrum, it is the power loom sector devoid of a political constituency which has shown the most rapid growth. A part of the explanation for this lies in the curbs imposed on mill weaving capacity which, although ostensibly working against mill interests, were in reality not entirely unwelcome since they served to limit competition within the mill sector. While the original rationale behind this measure was undoubtedly the protection of the traditional small-scale sector, the fact that it remained so long after it was overwhelmingly apparent that it served no useful purpose was almost certainly due to the existing mill interests not being averse to its continuation.

Capacity restraints on mills cannot by themselves provide us with a complete explanation for the spectacular growth of informal mechanized weaving since capacity expansion in the composite mill sector had always been allowed for export production. Further, since the mid-1970s, the introduction of sophisticated technologies via machinery replacements had been permitted, and these were capable of augmenting mill output several times over with the same physical number of looms. The fact that these strategies did not constitute feasible options was due to the unfavourable policy environment already described. Further, as mentioned earlier, to circumvent capacity restrictions and to take advantage of the substantially lower wages as well as lower excise levies, the mill sector has over time forged strong links with the informal sector. A large part of the power loom sector is thus run by the mills by proxy. While at one level the mill and power loom sectors appear competitive, at another their relationship is essentially symbiotic. As a result, the runaway proliferation of power looms is no longer an important issue with mill interests: it is an issue mainly with handloom activists, since it is the traditional weaver whose livelihood is most threatened by the growth of informal mechanized weaving.

In conclusion, there can be little doubt that the phenomenal expansion of the mechanized informal sector in textile weaving is overwhelmingly linked to the strong ideological bias against formal manufacture of cloth. Its remarkable growth has been sustained and aided by entrepreneurial initiative getting around government regulations in response to the growing demand for cloth.

Notes

1. See Morris (1983), p.553.
2. See GOI (1964), para.2.19.
3. Ibid., para.2.35.
4. Filament yarn is constituted of man-made fibres of indefinite length in continuous form, so that the spinning stage is rendered unnecessary. Such yarn can be used directly for weaving cloth. With the use of filament yarns, one of the major advantages that a composite mill has over independent weaving units (that is, integration of spinning and weaving) is lost.
5. See Misra (1991), ch.4.
6. Ibid., ch.5.
7. Cloth output of the informal sectors is estimated from yarn delivered in the market by spinning mills. There are no reliable estimates of employment.
8. Hand-woven cloth using hand-spun yarn is known as 'khadi' cloth. The manufacture of such cloth, and the wearing of apparel made from it, were important symbols of political resistance to colonial rule.
9. Two such regulations which are important are the Industries (Development and Regulation) Act, 1951, which applies to all units using power and employing 50 or more people, and the Factories Act, 1922 which is applicable to all units using power and employing 10 or more people. Units coming under the ambit of the former need a licence or registration to commence operations, while the latter lays down the minimum age and maximum permissible working hours for employees.
10. See IRMA (1989), para.3.02, p.6.
11. This is the finding of the national census of handlooms conducted by the Government of India in 1987–8. See also Misra (1991), ch.5.
12. According to the Reserve Bank of India, a unit may be considered as 'sick' if (a) it has incurred a cash loss for one year and is likely to continue to incur cash losses for the current year and the following year; and (b) it has an imbalance in its financial structure, such as a worsening debt–equity ratio (total outside liabilities to net worth).

13 See Misra (1991), ch.7.
14 See GOI (1964), para.2.41.
15 See IRMA (1989), para.3.01, p.6.
16 See Misra (1991), ch.5.
17 From a peak of 58 per cent of all developing country exports of textile products in 1953, India's share fell precipitously to a meagre 8 per cent by 1969 (Wolf, 1982, p.33). It currently lies in the vicinity of 4 per cent.

Bibliography

Chakravarty, Sukhamoy (1987), *Development Planning – The Indian Experience*, Oxford: Oxford University Press.

Government of India (GOI) (1954), *Report of the Textile Enquiry Committee*, Ministry of Industry (the Committee was headed by Nityanand Kanungo).

Government of India (1955), *Report of the Village and Small Scale Industries (Second Five Year Plan) Committee*, Planning Commission (the Committee was headed by D.G. Karve).

Government of India (1964), *Report of the Powerlooms Enquiry Committee*, Ministry of Industry.

Government of India (1976), *Report of Committee on Urban Waste*, New Delhi: Ministry of Works and Housing.

Government of India (1978), 'Statement on Textile Policy', Ministry of Industry, 7 August.

Government of India (1979), 'Census of Textile Machinery', *Indian Textile Bulletin*, Ministry of Industry.

Government of India (1981), 'Statement on Textile Policy', Ministry of Commerce, 9 March.

Government of India (1985), 'Statement on Textile Policy', Ministry of Textiles, 6 June.

Government of India (1985–90), *Annual Reports*, Ministry of Textiles.

IRMA (1989), *A Study of Interventions in the Handloom Industry*, Anand: Institute of Rural Management.

Lal, Deepak (1983), 'The Poverty of Development Economics', London: Institute of Economic Affairs.

Mazumdar, Deepak (1984), 'The Issue of Small versus Large in the Indian Textile Industry', *World Bank Staff Working Papers*, No.645, Washington, DC: World Bank.

Misra, Sanjiv (1991), *India's Textile Sector – A Policy Analysis*, New Delhi: Centre for Policy Research.

Morris, M.D. (1983), 'The Growth of Large-Scale Industry to 1947', *Cambridge Economic History of India*, vol. 2, Cambridge: Cambridge University Press, 553–676.

Wolf, M. (1982), 'India's Exports', Oxford: Oxford University Press.

PART II
SOCIAL POLICY

2 Women's Rights in India: a Socioreligious Perspective

Kunja Medhi

India is a sex-segregated traditional society whose deeply entrenched customs and practices are sanctioned by almost all the religions of India, namely Hinduism, Islam, Christianity, Sikhism, Zoroastrianism and Jainism. Even at the threshold of the 21st century, outdated customs, rites and rituals rule in such a way that the benefits accruing through liberal educational programmes and democratic political culture appear to be less than marginal. Surprisingly, the whole gamut of socioreligious practices run through women.

Rights of Women Through the Ages

The ancient texts of Hindu civilization painted a bright picture of women. Some of the texts of the Vedic and Upanishadic periods claimed that women occupied a very high position in society and enjoyed the right of access to education, agriculture and religious ceremonies. The celebrated names of a galaxy of women scholars of that time, such as Lopamudra, Gargi, Lilabati, Atreyi, Khana and Ghosa, confirmed the texts. In terms of inheritance and succession, familial and social duties and the use of bow and arrow also they were not lagging behind or discriminated against. The scriptures allowed the girls to be initiated in Vedic studies. Women played an important role in the family, society and religious ceremonies, along with men. This was the pre-Aryan era, calculated to be between 2500 to 1500 BC.[1] The society was matrilineal and the occupation of the people was mainly agricultural. The Indus Valley civilization of this period recorded the beginning of the cult of worshipping the Earth as the goddess. Religion was connected with the earth, fertility and the cycle of procreation. There were six ethnic types and nine sub-types of people and the mother goddess was the eternal symbol of life. The mother being the head of the clan life, her position was supreme.[2] The system of the girl choosing the groom and the remarrying of widows prevailed.[3] There was no reference to female infanticide, nor did the practices of purdah,[4] dowry[5] and child marriage prevail.

The later Vedic period saw the gradual deterioration of women's status, with various injunctions placed on women's rights and privileges by Manu.[6] These injunctions, surprisingly, came to form the basis of Hindu society for centuries to come.[7] The period was marked by one of the most heinous dispensations, suttee,[8] which required that a widow should burn to death on the pyre of her dead husband. The subsequent invasions of India by the Huns in the fifth century BC, Alexander in 320 BC, the Arabs and the Turks in the 11th and 12th centuries AD, respectively, reduced women to the position of 'war booty'. The women had to turn to their menfolk for protection. The gradual erosion of the position of women coincided with the increase in the authority of men, along with that of priests.[9] The Muslim invasion of India in the eighth and the 11th centuries brought the complete subordination of women to men. The Middle Ages saw women being oppressed in the feudal social order and patriarchal families. Certain social evils, such as child marriage and female infanticide made their appearance in this period. Women lost the rights to education and property and could worship only through the priests. The rituals of ancestor worship, the prohibition of inter-caste marriage and of the remarrying of widows, and the emergence of the dowry system also contributed to the oppression of women. The Mughal period, followed by the British periods witnessed the general practice of killing and abandonment of baby girls just after birth, the condemnation of widows, the practice of polygamy and the system of Devadasis,[10] in different parts of India.

The ideological rationale for subjugating women was provided in the name of religion in different epochs as well as societies. The two epics, the *Ramayana* and the *Mahabharata*, also depicted the lowly position of women. Consequently, the capacity of the male to defend the family property crystallized his position as the 'bread earner' and that of the woman as 'bread loser'. This led to the widespread practice of wearing charms or performing rituals to ensure the birth of a male child. Records of that period, including various books of the Indo-Iranian era, bear testimony to this.[11]

The Era of Social Reform and Indian Women

The trail of social reform in India was blazed by a group of social reformers led by Raja Ram Mohan Roy. Others to follow him were Dadabhai Naoriji, Swami Dayanand Saraswati, Iswar Chandra Vidyasagar, B.G. Tilak, Sri

Aurobindo and M.K. Gandhi. Before Independence, the reformers worked for the emancipation of women from the shackles of illogical orthodoxies, blind superstitions, unhealthy traditions and customs. Their approach was based on an integral synthesis of Vedantic and Buddhistic paradigms of reality. The Bhakti movement of the mediaeval period also projected a liberal attitude towards women and helped them to denounce unscientific rituals.[12] However, the Bhakti movement could not bring about radical change to restore the lost status of women.

The freedom struggle of India, fought on the synthesis of the western philosophy of scientific humanism and liberalism combined with the eastern wisdom of perennial values, heralded a new era of women's awakening. The struggle, which had a multidimensional objective to fight against all types of oppression, included issues such as the development of women, the creation of a new awareness based on equality, liberty and fraternity, and the equalization of opportunities for women at all levels. For this reason, Indian women did not have to launch a suffragist movement such as was necessary in some western countries. The outstanding women who played crucial roles during that period included Ms. Besant, Mother of Sri Aurobindo Ashram, Sister Nibedita, Sarojini Naidu, Sucheta Kripalani, Durgabai Deshmukh, Kasturba Gandhi and Vijoy Lakshmi Pandit.

The Changing Scenario and the Position of Women

After Independence, the constitution provided for the right to equality[13] for all citizens, irrespective of caste, creed, sex or place of birth. However, despite all this, the progress made by the mass of Indian women has been far below the level attained by men in the economic, literacy, employment and political fields, since the vast majority of them are still steeped in the traditional mediaeval prejudices and practices as well as the wife–mother role syndrome. The public–private dichotomy in the performance of traditional role models has also remained as strong as ever. Various social legislations passed and implemented to alleviate the sufferings of women have remained more or less beyond their grasp excepting the elite sections. Although there has been a steady rise in the number of educated women over the years, as seen in Table 2.1, the position of women, especially in the rural areas, has remained almost as grim as in the mediaeval period, so far as their family responsibility, social interaction and political participation are concerned. Sex discrimination and socio-religious prejudices are so deeply entrenched that an official document released to mark the South Asian Association for Regional Co-operation Year of the girl child has revealed that one-fourth of the 12 million girls born in India every year die before they are 15 years old and one-sixth of these deaths are due to sex

Table 2.1 Population and Literacy Rate by Sex in Different Years in India

Year	Population	Illiterates	Literacy Rate		
			Person	Male	Female
1901	238.4	225.8	5.3	9.8	0.6
1911	252.1	237.2	5.9	10.6	1.1
1921	251.3	233.2	7.2	12.2	1.8
1931	279.0	252.5	9.5	15.6	2.9
1941	318.7	267.4	16.1	24.9	7.3
1951	361.1	300.8	16.7	25.0	7.9
1961	439.2	333.8	24.0	34.4	12.9
1971	548.1	384.4	29.5	39.5	18.7
1981	683.3	435.9	36.2	46.6	24.8
1991	843.9	478.5	43.3	52.8	32.9

Notes:
1 Literacy rates for 1981 exclude Assam and they exclude Jammu and Kashmir for 1991.
2 Literacy rates refers to literates per 100 population of all ages.

Source: Census Report of India, 1991.

discrimination. Moreover, several studies conducted in this field have shown that poverty, undernourishment, sex-determination test and Medical Termination of Pregnancy (MTP) have wrought havoc as the most significant determinants of elimination of the girl child.[14] The prevailing complex socio-cultural scene, extremely diverse segments of caste system and economic standards, tribal, rural as well as urban background present a heterogeneous picture. For it the basic institutional complexes of religious traditions of the major religions, role of the family traditions and the general constraints faced by women in the traditional divisions of work vis-à-vis their adjustment in the context of social change, have put stumbling blocks in their way. The overall structural norms of the social framework limit women's activities and thus prevent them from participating in the works dominated by menfolk.

Even today as in earlier times, in Hinduism women are described by several derogatory terms such as fickle-minded, seducer, greedy, impure, brainless, cruel, trickster and the like. Women are identified by the father in childhood, by the husband after marriage and by the son in old age. In that sense, the present day Hindu women have not come far from the time of Manu.[15] Religious practices as well as socialization from early childhood, have continued to accord an inferior and dependent status to women. Exploitation of women in the name of religion, combined with poverty, has placed women in some parts of the country at an abysmal depth from which there is little chance of returning.[16] The concomitant emphasis on developing the feminine qualities of a girl instead of those as an individual, the custom of 'giving away' the girl in marriage, laying special emphasis on virginity and chastity, putting severe restrictions on menstruating women as periodical impurity and similar innumerable social customs are observed in bringing up the girl child from birth through youth to old age which exert a crippling effect on the development of mind and intellect and make them incapable of growing into independent personalities. Widows are prohibited from full participation in the socioreligious life. In some parts of India, like in Rajasthan, the Sati system is still adored.[17] Thus religion has been used as a double-faced weapon, an apparatus to eulogise the qualities of purity, sacrifice, spiritual power of motherhood on one hand and treating women as weak, wicked and dependent on menfolk on the other.

In the Mohammadan community of India Islam has accorded equal status to women, but the unequal rights given to men and women by the marriage contract and the legal sanction for polygamy have negated the rights of women. Moreover, women's right to inherit property is not often upheld in practice.[18] Excepting the elite section, the education of the girls of conservative families is restricted only to reciting the Quoran. The unilateral divorce system and seclusion of women have made the women's position distinctly inferior.[19]

In sharp contrast to this women belonging to Christianity have been accorded completely independent status and equal rights in the family and social life. It was possibly due to the philanthropic works initiated by the Christian missionaries in India in the late 19th century, for which the women of that religious community enjoyed the privilege of being as 'complete individual'. Since the people belonging to Jainism, Buddhism and Sikhism are governed by the Hindu Personal Law, the status of women belonging to these religious denominations invariably have similar status and position with that of the Hindu women.

The tribal religions do not constitute a homogeneous denomination. Some of the hill tribes of India, of whom there are around 200 different tribes with separate dialects, religious practices and traditions in the North-East India alone, present a completely diversified picture. Some of these with a matrilineal system like the Khasis, the Jaintias and the Garos of the Meghalaya State, although according women a higher status in family matters due to their privileged position in inheritance of family property, in social, religious and public matters or in the decision making, women's position is more or less similar to what it was in their primordial situation.[20] In the case of the plains tribal people like the Bodo Kacharis the custom of taking 'bride price' has put women in a somewhat better position, the overall conservative backdrop of the entire region continues to stalk womenfolk for which their effective functioning in the family, society or public sphere remains more or less as traditional and retrograde as before.

Emerging Trends

In India the number of educated women and their rate of participation in organized public and private sectors of jobs has increased gradually since Independence. Tables 2.2, 2.3 and 2.4 justify the findings respectively. However, women working in the formal and organized sector seldom get encouragement from their family members. For them the official work is an extra burden, since the same expectations from them remain in household activities.[21] Besides this, in the absence of a measuring yardstick of household

Table 2.2 Total Workers in India*, 1991

Population/Workers	Persons	Males	Females
1	2	3	4
Total			
Population	836 605 522	433 791 705	402 813 817
Workers	314 903 642	223 506 153	91 397 489
Percentage of workers	37.64	51.52	22.69
Rural			
Population	621 267 297	320 062 940	301 204 357
Workers	249 330 072	167 822 985	81 507 087
Percentage of workers	40.13	52.43	27.06
Urban			
Population	215 338 225	113 728 765	101 609 460
Workers	65 573 570	55 683 168	9 890 402
Percentage of workers	30.45	48.96	9.73

* Excludes Jammu & Kashmir where the 1991 Census has not been conducted.

Note: Workers include both main workers and marginal workers.

Table 2.3 Decadal Growth Rate of Main Workers, Cultivators, Agricultural Labourers, Household Industry Workers and Other Workers by Sex and Residence – India*, 1981–91

		Total Main Workers	Cultivators	Agricultural Labourers	Household Industry Workers	Other Workers
1	2	3	4	5	6	7
Total	Persons	26.12	16.92	33.01	33.90	82.19
	Males	21.51	10.74	30.12	29.41	29.70
	Females	44.24	48.85	37.85	46.13	52.67
Rural	Persons	23.03	16.44	31.99	24.30	26.93
	Males	17.57	10.26	28.66	17.96	24.98
	Females	41.78	48.08	37.47	40.83	40.41
Urban	Persons	37.98	35.06	52.49	56.83	36.00
	Males	34.74	28.07	55.41	55.70	33.00
	Females	62.41	94.04	46.29	60.27	64.52

* Excludes Assam and Jammu & Kashmir.

Source: Census Report of India, 1991.

Table 2.4 Work Participation Rate in India, 1971–91

Year	Total Rural Urban	Persons	Males	Females
1	2	3	4	5
1971	Total	34.17	52.75	14.22
	Rural	35.33	53.78	15.92
	Urban	29.61	48.88	7.18
1981	Total	36.70	52.62	19.67
	Rural	38.79	53.77	23.06
	Urban	29.99	49.06	8.31
1991	Total	37.68	51.56	22.73
	Rural	40.24	52.50	27.20
	Urban	30.44	48.95	9.74

Notes:
1. Excludes Assam where the 1981 Census could not be held and Jammu & Kashmir where the 1991 Census has not been held.
2. The 1971 Census figures include workers and non-workers with secondary work. The 1981 and 1991 Census figures include main workers and marginal workers.

works, in terms of monetary worth, the works of the housewives go unnoticed and unrecognized. The mythical superiority of the male buried deep in the Indian psyche, the process of socialization of the girl child and the strong patrilineal family structure have been such that even today irrespective of educational attainment or high-level jobs women face double standards in all spheres of social interactions. In the rural areas growing provisions of improved transport and communication, mass media and formal and informal educational and vocational facilities, have no doubt made their lives more comfortable, but it would take an indefinite period of time to free womenfolk from the bondage of unhealthy customs, traditions and obnoxious practices. It appears strange to note that even among some of the enlightened sections of urban societies, girls prefer to be prepared thoroughly for the feminine role. Recently a survey conducted among a group of post-graduate women students revealed the startling result that 99 per cent of them preferred to follow the traditional customs and traditions and perform the wife-mother role, although they would like to hold some paying jobs at the same time. It transpired that the respondents were not ready to work for effecting any radical change in the existing socio-religious scenario. The strong sense of responsibility towards family and an overwhelming concern for social approval inhibit women from self-assertion. A few non-conformists among them suffer.

Social Legislations and Women

A set of legislations bearing social importance have been passed[22] for the welfare of women. These Acts as a whole enforced monogamy, raised the marriageable age for girls to 18 years, permitted widow remarriage and inter-caste marriage. The Hindu Succession Act of 1956 brought radical and fundamental change by introducing equal rights of succession to both male and female heirs. Prior to the passing of the Act, the succession to property was governed by the Mitakshara system and Dayabhage systems in different parts of the country. Mitakshara succession was connected with the special incidence of copercenary properties. In copercenary, properties were acquired by a son, son's son and son's grandsons by birth. Thus only the male members of a family could be coperceners. The properties were managed by the eldest person and only in partition the share of a copercener could be ascertained. In the Dayabhage system the daughter had an equal share with the sons, as there was no right by birth for sons alone. In the matrilineal social system, although women enjoyed right to property, they could not have full ownership. Under the Hindu Succession Act Class 1 heirs of a man are his widow, mother, son, daughter, widow of a predeceased son and sons and daughters. These heirs get property in equal shares and as absolute owners.[23] However, for strong conservative ethos, the legislators did not hesitate to compromise and sacrifice uniformity by retaining Mitakshara system.

Political Consciousness and Indian Women

Over the years the number of women voters has increased. However, it does not indicate that political consciousness and level of participation of women in political affairs have been as expected in a democratic political society. Politics has remained almost outside the domain of women. Raising a handful of them to the topmost level in the Parliament, Cabinet or administrative jobs cannot be accepted as the index of general level of consciousness of women in political affairs. A gradual increase in the number of women voters as seen in the Table 2.5 is not the criterion to measure women's political participation. As a participant observer the author of this chapter saw in the rural areas that the voting days were regarded as the opportunities

Table 2.5 Census Population in India, 1901–81

Census Year	Total population (in lakhs)			Decennial change (per cent)	Geometric growth rate	Sex-ratio (females) per 1000 males	Density of population per Km²	Percentage of urban population to total population
	Persons	Males	Females					
1	2	3	4	5	6	7	8	9
1901	2384.0*	1207.9@	1173.6	—	—	972$	77	10.86
1911	2520.9	1283.8	1237.1	5.75	(+) 0.56	964	82	10.29
1921	2513.2	1285.5	1227.7	(−) 0.31	(−) 0.03	955	81	11.18
1931	2789.8*	1429.3	1357.9	11.00	(+) 1.06	950$	90	11.99
1941	3186.6*	1636.8	1546.9	14.22	(+) 1.34	945$	103	13.86
1951	3610.9	1855.3	1755.6	13.31	(+) 1.26	946	117	17.29
1961	4392.3	2262.9	2129.4	21.51	(+) 1.98	941	142	17.97
1971	5481.6	2840.5	2641.1	24.80	(+) 2.24	930	177**	19.91
1981@@	6851.8	3544.0	3307.8	25.00	(+) 2.28	933	216+	23.31

* The distribution of population by Sex of Pondicherry for 1901 (246 354), 1931 (258 628) and 1941 (285 011) is not available. The figures of these years are, therefore, exclusive of these populations so far as distribution by sex is concerned.
@ Sex-wise distribution of Chandannagar (26 831) of West Bengal and Gonda (18 810) of Uttar Pradesh is not available.
$ Excludes Pondicherry.
** Excludes Jammu & Kashmir.
@@ Includes projected population of Assam where the 1981 Census could not be conducted owing to disturbed conditions prevailing in that state then.
+ The density has been worked out on comparable data.

Source: Registrar General, India.

to go out in festive apparel. Newspapers of the election times also testify this statement.

Human Rights vis-à-vis Women of India

Human Rights as enshrined in the Charter of the United Nations numbering 30 Articles, provide civil, political and religious liberties. These rights are: right to freedom, right to equality, right to hold property, right to freedom of person, right to movement and association, right to take asylum after escaping from persecution, right to freedom of thought, conscience and religion, right to participate in free and fair elections, right to social security, right to education and agriculture. Since the Universal Declaration of Human Rights lays stress on material basis of rights, its aim has been to secure the benefits from social security, a decent standard of living and freedom from want in old age and infirmity.

The Constitution of India, in line with the UN Declaration has incorporated a Chapter on Fundamental Rights in Part III of the Constitution for the people of India irrespective of religion, race, caste, sex or place of birth. These rights can be classified as follows:

1. Right to Equality (Articles 14 to 18)
2. Right to Freedom (Articles 19 to 22)
3. Right against Exploitation (Articles 23 and 24)
4. Right to Freedom of Religion (Articles 25 to 28)
5. Cultural and Educational Rights (Articles 29 and 30).
6. Right to Constitutional Remedies (Articles 32 to 35)

Theoretically the women of India enjoy all these rights; but a world of difference lies between theory and practice. Conservative socio-cultural forces combined with lack of consciousness and literacy prevent women from enjoying fundamental rights in India. For the literate and well-informed women, however, the rights are not meaningless. Even in urban areas sex-determination test, medical termination of pregnancy, liabilities for dowry[24] have combined together to take away not only the fundamental rights but also the natural right of birth since all these have wrought havoc of unlimited dimension to the female embryo. The decreasing trend of female population is a pointer to it as seen in Table 2.5.

The UN Conferences on Women and the Steps Taken in India

The UN Conference of International Women's Year held in Mexico from 19 June to 2 July 1975 made as many as 23 recommendations directing the National Governments to:

1. Promote change in social and economic structures in order to make full equality of women and their access to all types of development without discrimination of any kind and to all types of education and employment; to take into account women's interests while implementing targets and priorities; to ensure national plans and strategies with special attention to the most disadvantaged in rural and urban areas; to establish interdisciplinary and multisectoral machinery for accelerating women's full integration in national life; to provide constitutional and legislative guarantees of the principle of non-discrimination on grounds of sex; to review and reform legislations affecting the status of women in the light of human rights, principles and internationally accepted standards; to encourage involvement of women in the promotion of international co-operation, peace, disarmament and in combating colonialism, neo-colonialism, foreign domination, apartheid and racial discrimination; to increase within 1975–1985 the number of women in elective and appointive public offices..; to provide equal opportunities for both sexes in education and training.
2. Formulate policies and action programmes to promote equality in work through legislation, equal pay, support for self-employment, providing multilateral approaches to combine family and work responsibilities; for elimination of exploitation of female labour; for elimination of discriminatory treatment of women in national security schemes; for protection of women's health, framing of marriage laws in conformity with international standards, establishing family courts.
3. Collect and analyse all census and survey data relating to characteristics of individuals, household and family composition to measure women's participation in local and national planning, economic and social contribution of household work and other domestic chores.
4. Encourage and support national, regional and international research to review the image of women portrayed by the media; report to Economic and Social Council about the implementation of plan and
5. Trade Unions to increase women's participation at all levels. The Conference also urged the International Agencies to assist the Governments to develop specific projects and programmes and facilitate free flow of information, experience and ideas; prepare an inventory of socio-economic indicators in co-operation with the interested specialised agen-

cies; UN Research Institute for Social Development, the regional Commissions and other agencies; proclaim 1975-1985 as the UN Decade for women; coordinate activities of various international agencies to improve situation of women through the existing machinery; increase women's involvement in policy making at the international level; undertake a comprehensive and thorough review and appraisal of progress made in meeting the goals at regular intervals.[25]

The Governments of the non-aligned countries responded to the recommendations of the Conference and subsequently a series of Ministerial Conferences were held at Lima in 1975; Colombo in 1976; New Delhi in 1977; Belgrade in 1978 and Baghdad in 1979. The last Conference identified the movement for women's equality and role in development as an integral aspect of the developing countries' struggle for a New International Economic Order.

The World Conference of the United Nations Decade for Women held in Copenhagen on 14-30 July 1980 laid stress on Equality, Development and Peace. It made as many as 51 recommendations urging the National Governments to legislate for involving women in national planning as well as for the all round development of women.

The Non-Aligned Movement High Level Experts Meeting held in Havana in 1981 laid stress for making efforts to connect the struggle for the advancement of women's role with all the basic activities of the movement for positive changes and development of the world.[26]

Steps Taken by India

The Committee on the Status of Women in India (CSWI) submitted its report in 1975 covering issues like: gainful employment, recognition of their substantial and even massive contribution to the national economy and families' survival which has been denied to them so long, to adequate rewards for their labour which they do not enjoy, and to a share of resources, benefits and decisions regarding development to which they are entitled as a citizen of a country which guarantees to them equality in all spheres of life. The Committee was appointed by the Government of India with members from the ruling party, social workers and social scientists.

Besides this, the cause of women's equal remuneration was taken up by the Empowered Committee, an internal Committee of the Government chaired by the Minister for Labour which also included senior bureaucrats.

The National Plan of Action prepared by the Department of Social Welfare of the Government of India in consultation with relevant Ministries and sent to various State Governments for implementation. It emphasized fuller economic participation, utilization of human resources, bridging economic disparities and providing the impetus for social and economic change towards an equality of status.

The Advisory Committee on Women's Studies in Indian Council of Social Science Research (ICSSR), consisting of eminent social scientists, a Judge of the Supreme Court of India and a senior officer of the Government of India was formed and it submitted a Memorandum to the Government of India on the measures to be adopted for employment of women in 1976.

The Working Group on Employment of Women was appointed by the Planning Commission which included bureaucrats, non-official social scientists and field activists and it suggested measures to increase women's employment through special provision in the annual plans for 1978–80.

The National Conference on Women and Development convened by the Government of India in which participants included women legislators from different parties of the country, civil servants, social workers, social scientists and field activists recommended formulation and implementation of development programmes so that women were not pushed out of economic activities.

The Working Group on Personal Policies, an internal Committee set up by the Government of India aims to increase women's involvement in science and technology and attempts to take follow-up action in a limited area initiated by the Government.[27]

Besides the above-mentioned steps non-Governmental voluntary social organizations have been formed in different levels in different parts of India to look after the welfare of women. The women's movements since 1976 onwards have consistently campaigned to create awareness among women, especially against femicide since the demographic, social, cultural and moral aspects of the society are connected with it.

There seems to be a link between over-population and lower status of women in India since one of the main drawbacks in women's development has been mainly their preoccupation with repeated pregnancies without respite in physical workload. Lack of formal and non-formal education and preponderance of social prejudices along with lack of independent economic generation activity or independent assets have also played their part in bringing down the status of women. Only a three-pronged strategy like education, employment and health as emphasized by the *Sixth Five Year Plan* of India could bring about total development.

The status of women in India is a serious problem which even after 44 years of independence has not improved. There has not been full mobilization of women who constitute half of the total population of the country. Gender prejudice is deeply entrenched in Indian psyche and women themselves are not free from it. The whole tenor of public life seems aimed at undermining rights, efficiency and forthrightness in women. Commodification and objectification of women, criminalization of politics, army atrocities on women whenever there is Presidential Rule or imposition of the Disturbed Areas Act and the like have continued to violate women's rights in India. Development of consciousness in women as 'individuals', encouraging them to change their outlook towards life and adoption of scientific measures for economic transformation, population control etc. are of imperative necessity. *The National Policy on Education 1986* aimed to promote national progress, a sense of common citizenship and culture as well as strengthen national integration. It covered more then 90 per cent of the country's rural population and tried to play a positive, interventionist role in the empowerment of women.

Women of India, by and large, are still the sacrificial goat at the crossroads of tradition and modernity for whom the social laws are yet to play a positive role. They have to go a long way before they can bridge the gap between legal norms and social practice.

Notes

1. R.C. Majumdar (1982), *Ancient India*, Motilal Benarasi Das, p.203. See also P. Thomas (1964), *Indian Women through the Ages*, Asian Publishing House, pp.43–54.
2. Tara Ali Daig (1976), *India's Women, Power* S. Chand & Co., pp.4–5. See also Manjushree, Chaki-Sircar (1984), *Feminism in a Traditional Society* (Shakti Books).
3. A.S. Altekar, *The Position of Women in Hindu Civilisation* (Motilal Banarasidas, 1983), pp.1–8.
4. A custom of covering the head of a woman in the presence of a male. See Frieda Hawswirth (1932), *Purdah: The Status of Indian Women* (London: Routledge and Kegan Paul), p.24.
5. The property which a woman brings to her husband's family at marriage.
6. Ancient law giver of Hinduism.
7. K.V.R. Aiyangar (1945), *Aspects of the social and political system of Manu Smriti*, p.164.
8. M. Fuller (1900), *The Wrongs of Indian Womanhood*, p.33. See A.L. Basham, *The Wonder that was INDI*, p.187.
9. Baig, *India's Women Power*, p.12.
10. Under the Devadasi system, parents donate their daughters to God in marriage. The girls afterwards become the object of sexual exploitation by priests and rich people.
11. David G. Mandelbaum (1974), *Human Fertility in India* (University of California Press, p.16. See also Doranne Jacobson and Susan S. Wadley (1977), *Women in India: Two Perspectives*, Monohar.
12. Neera Desai (1984), 'Women and Bhakti Movement', *Samya Shakti*, 1, *Journal of the Centre for Women's Development Studies*, New Delhi (II), 93.
13. *The Times of India*, National Daily, New Delhi, 28 December, 1990.

14 Pramilla Kapur (1970), *The Changing Status of Working Women in India*, New Delhi: Vikas Publishing House, p.27.
15 See Vimla Mehta (1979), *Attitudes of Educated Women Towards Social Issues*, New Delhi: National Publishing.
16 A Study conducted by the IHO in India has revealed that 15 per cent of the women in prostitution in the country come from the 'Devadashis', the women who are dedicated to goddess Yellamma-Renuka, in the border districts of Karnataka and Maharashtra. About 12,000 girls are dedicated to the goddess on the full-moon day of January every year and then they are 'put to auction'. *The Times of India*, New Delhi, 25 December, 1990.
17 A matriculate bride named 'Roop Kanwar' was burnt to death on the pyre of her dead husband in 1987 which started a countrywide turmoil of a socio-political nature and it was reported by almost all the leading newspapers and journals of India.
18 The controversy over the 'Shah Bano Case' demonstrated the rigidity of Muslim orthodox attitude towards reforming Muslim Personal Law. Ms. Shah Bano was granted maintenance by the Court after she appealed under the Criminal Procedure Code No. 125. It was challenged by her divorced husband as an interference in the Muslim Personal Law. It also invoked protest from the orthodox Muslims. The Government had to initiate a Bill, 'The Muslim Woman's (Protection of Rights) 1986' to appease the orthodox Muslims. See, Rafiq Zakaria (1986), 'In Defence of Shariat', in *The Illustrated Weekly of India*, 2 & 3 March, Bombay.
19 'Towards Equality', *Report of the Committee on the Status of Women in India* (1974), Government of India, pp.45–65.
20 *The Land of Seven Sisters* (1976), Government of Assam, Gauhati.
21 See *Women in Contemporary India and South Asia*, (ed.) by Alfred de Souza (1980), New Delhi: Monohar Publication. See Dr. Sushila Mehta (1982), *Revolution and Status of Women in India*, New Delhi.
22 The Sati Abolition Act 1829; The Widow Remarriage Act 1856; The Child Marriage Abolition Act 1860; The Civil Marriage Act 187; The Married Women's Act 1874; The Age of Consent Act 1881 etc.
23 The figure of the dowry death rose from 1912 in 1987 to 4006 in 1989.
24 *Towards Equality*, cited above, p.135.
25 *The Non-Aligned Movement and the International Women's Decade: A Summary of Decisions* (1983), Centre for Women's Development Studies, New Delhi, pp.1–4.
26 *CSWI Report* (1975), pp.6–7.
27 *Women's work and employment: Struggle for a policy* (1983), Selections from Indian Documents, Centre for Women's Development Studies, New Delhi, pp.1–32.

3 Political Education and Political Socialization in a Pluralistic Society: a Case Study of Two Generations of Women in India

Vijay Laxmi Pandit

Political socialization and political education have received much attention from political psychologists, political sociologists and political scientists during recent years. However, there seems to be a paucity of empirical studies examining the relationship between political socialization and political education; very few studies in India have examined the role of political education as an agent of political socialization. In this chapter an attempt is made to study the impact of political education on political socialization of two generations of women in a pluralistic society like India.

Before discussing the position of Indian women, it may be worthwhile to discuss, briefly, what we mean by 'political socialization' and the role of 'political education' as a socialization agent.

Political Socialization

Rosav,[1] Elkin and Handel[2] and Stacy[3] state that socialization refers to the development procedure whereby a person obtains knowledge, abilities, beliefs, values, attitudes and dispositions that make it possible to function as a more or less effective member of society. Thus socialization can be seen as a process whereby each society shapes its members and prepares them for successful incorporation in group life. Stacy takes the view that study of socialization should also take into account those people in society who are socialized to reject the conventional norms, values and behaviour and contribute to radical changes.

Writers like Greenstein,[4] Langton[5] and Nimmo and Bonjean[6] point to the fact that the study of political socialization includes the study of both individualistic orientations and system orientations. While the individualistic approach focuses on the individual as the main unit of investigation, the system approach inquires into the role of political socialization in a system's stability and maintenance.

Taking into account a variety of definitions, it seems that Greenstein offers both a narrow and a broad conception of the term. Narrowly speaking, political socialization is the deliberate inculcation of political values, information and practices by those in instructional agents who are formally given this responsibility. The broader aspect of Greenstein's definition focuses attention on the study of all political learning, formal or informal, deliberate and unplanned, at every stage of the life cycle, including political as well as non-political learning. Generalizing from different viewpoints, one can conclude that political socialization involves the study of individual roles, content and agents in a process of learning about politics.

Political Socialization and Political Education

One of the important issues of political socialization research is the impact of political education on political socialization. Basic political orientations are sometimes transferred by political education which is imparted in educational institutions in a society. Political education may help the members of a society in either forming or changing their views about politics. It can directly or indirectly influence eventual political orientations. Though it can be argued that political education plays a relatively limited role in socializing the people politically, its role must not be underestimated. Religious issues in India, such as Ayodhya[7] and Babari Masjid,[8] and social issues like regard for backward social groups, may change the attitudes of the members of society and especially of the new generation through political education. Though it may take a considerable period of time to socialize people politically, radical changes can be wrought in the political orientations of most of the people who are politically and otherwise uneducated.

Thus political education plays an important role in socializing the people. However, no serious attempt has been made so far to study it in India: only recently have scholars started looking into this field. Indian women, in spite of their importance in the transformation of Indian society, have not been the subject of study. In this chapter an attempt is made to fill this gap.

Changes in the Political Socialization and Political Education of Indian Women

In the classical Indian tradition, according to one point of view the various cults of the mother Goddess are believed to be the source of energy, power and fertility; a protector against all cruel and evil forces. This tradition believes that women are very powerful and can be dangerous as and when required, so a balance between the sexes is maintained.

The other viewpoint of the classical Indian tradition often presents conflicting opinions and pictures of women. Some believe that women were in no way made to live a life of subjugation in the family. They were paragons of beauty, wisdom and learning. They were politically socialized like men, even participating in decision making and exercising considerable power. Others believe in the supremacy of men. In case of conflict, it is the interest of men which has to be upheld. Women should accept the authority of men and should never disobey them. Women as a group thus had very little opportunity to participate in political affairs or to be politically educated.

Education of Women

During the first half of the 19th century, education for women was limited to only a small minority of aristocratic families who provided education for their women so that they could help them in the management of their huge estates. With the passage of time, and with the efforts of missionaries and social reformers, educational opportunities were opened to women and a large number of girls went to school. However, this advance was largely confined to urban areas.

The aim of education was not to prepare women to become literary luminaries and scientific prodigies so as to enable them to question the superiority of men and claim equal rights with them, but to make them loving, soft spoken and helpful companions to their husbands in passing through life's wilderness. Western education helped the upper middle-class Indians to play an important role in the Indian national movement. Women indirectly began to be politically socialized in the wave of support for the independence movement. Though their political education was informal during this period, they started to play an important role. Some men in India who believed in the philosophy of progressive liberals in the west also supported the view that women can play a role in public life.

Mahatma Gandhi added completely new dimensions to the debate on the role of women. He said that woman's subjugation and exploitation was the result of the 'teaching' which was based on the interest of males. He preached absolute equality of the sexes and stressed that women should participate directly in the nationalist struggle. The *Rama Rajya* (non-exploitative social order) which Gandhi visualized could only be achieved by the participation of both men and women. Women, he said, were better than men in waging non-violent protest because they have a greater capacity for love and sacrifice and have more moral courage. Women must become conscious of their historic role and should reject the disgraceful role of being 'man's plaything'. Equality of legal and political rights, freedom from any coercion, and autonomy to choose her own way of moral and other self-development were only basic conditions to enable the woman to play her destined role.[9] During the last phase of the national movement in India it was not merely the leaders of the Congress Party who pleaded for equality and education of women: the revolutionary leftists even gave major responsibilities and roles to women.

Modern education, with all its limitations, and women's participation in the national movement made them familiar with concepts like freedom and dignity of the individual. Along with the ideas of social reform, the ideas of social liberation also burgeoned among middle-class Indian women. During World War II, the political awakening of women increased. The leaders of the women's movement now pressed for the acceptance of the equality of women in all spheres and pleaded that women should not merely be considered as housewives and mothers, but also as citizens and active participants in the social, economic and political life of the country.

After Independence, in order to give special attention to the needs and problems of Indian woman and to enable them to be equal with men, the Indian constitution guaranteed certain fundamental rights and freedoms to all the citizens of India. To ensure that women are the beneficiaries of these rights in the same manner as Indian men, the constitution empowers the state to make any 'special provision for women and children' (Art. 15(3)).

With the constitutional pronouncements of equality of status of men and women and the declared state policy to encourage women to take their rightful place as equal partners with men in the cultural, economic, political and social life of the country, the question arises whether there has come a change in the attitudes, perceptions, status and role of Indian women. Are they different from those women who were born and brought up in the pre-independence period? If so, in what respect? Is there any change in the attitudes and perceptions of Indian society towards women? If so, what is the direction of this change? An examination of these questions will help us, not only in understanding the patterns of political socialization of Indian women, but also in evaluating the contribution made by them in the reconstruction of Indian society. Such an analysis may also help in reappraising policies and programmes aimed at women's development.

The present chapter makes an attempt to look into the political socialization of Indian women over a period of time. What role has political education played in this respect? In order to have a deeper insight into the continuities and discontinuities in their political socialization process, two generations of Indian women have been the subject of our investigation. By comparing and contrasting data from the two groups, we hope to have a somewhat better understanding of the political socialization process of Indian women and the role played by political education therein.

This being an exploratory study, we decided to limit it to only 50 women: 25 from each generation. Thus 25 were aged 41 years and above, and 25 were aged 20 to 40. All the women were residents of Delhi and were selected randomly. The data were collected by interviewing these women with the help of an open-ended questionnaire containing a series of questions pertaining to sources of political socialization, political attitudes and the political role. The objective was to find out whether the women show a consistency across generations in their thinking and whether there is a change in women's lifestyle over a period of time.

The socioeconomic characteristics of our sample are given in Table 3.1.

The Views of Indian Women on their Place in Society

The First Generation

It was noted that the first generation of women were brought up with a lot of restrictions. Their childhood lasted no more than seven to nine years and thereafter they had to behave like adults; those who were the eldest child in the family had to take charge of household activities from the age of 10. From the very beginning they were taught to be shy, reserved, modest and to observe the traditional values. For most of them, education was never considered at all important. No attempt was made to educate them.

Most of the women of this generation got married at an early age (12–15 years). They were socialized in such a manner that they could tolerate hardship. These women were taught to be obedient to their husbands and in-laws and were not expected to rebel against the authority of the elders in the family. They spoke highly of their elders and their ideals were duty, obedience and sacrifice for the members of the family. When asked if they would ever have liked to revolt against the authoritarian structure of the family, the answer was in the negative.

The family had been their priority and they never felt they were independent individuals. They found it easy to adopt their new roles as wives, mothers or mothers-in-law. Most of them were satisfied with their lives because of their faith in religion and fate. Only a few (2 per cent) showed dissatisfaction with the events in their lives. For most of these women,

Table 3.1 Socioeconomic characteristics

	First generation (41 years and above)	Second generation (20–40 years)
Education		
Above graduate	5(20)	8(32)
Graduate	1(4)	9(36)
High school	3(12)	4(16)
Literate	8(32)	1(4)
Illiterate	8(32)	3(12)
Religion		
Hindus	21(84)	20(80)
Muslims	1(4)	1(4)
Sikhs	2(8)	3(12)
Christians	1(4)	1(4)
Caste		
Upper caste	10(40)	14(56)
Middle caste	9(36)	6(24)
Lower caste	6(24)	5(20)
Occupation		
Business	1(4)	—
Service	4(16)	12(48)
Labourer	1(4)	3(12)
Housewife	19(76)	5(20)
Student	—	5(20)
Income		
Rs. 2001 and above	5(20)	12(48)
Rs. 1001–2000	—	—
Rs. 501–1000	—	3(12)
Rs. 100–500	1(4)	—
No income	19(76)	10(40)

Note: Figures in parentheses indicate percentage.

religion, religious practices and deep faith in the existence of God helped in coping with the problems in their lives. Rituals associated with various festivals added colour to their lives and they observed these religious rituals and customs compulsorily and even expected their daughters and daughters-in-law to observe them. They observed that the younger generation is not as duty conscious and responsible as they had been. In spite of the fact that they were happy because they had devotedly taken care of their in-laws, husbands and children, a sense of dissatisfaction and a desire for freedom were noticed among these women while they were being interviewed. Education had a very small role to play in their lives. Though 8 per cent of women in this age group had a chance to receive some education, their views on their place in society were not different from those who were illiterate.

Most of the women had no concept of health or hygiene and they suffered from many life-threatening diseases. No proper medical facilities were available to them. Elders in their family did not consider it worthwhile to provide them with medical aid. Strict seclusion was observed by upper-class women, Hindus and Muslims alike. The houses of the rich upper class had a separate *Zenana* (ladies) portion, which was like a prison to them. The position of Indian women was thus very bad from the point of view of literacy, individuality, health, social status and freedom of movement.

The Second Generation

The majority of the women belonging to this generation were brought up almost with the same restrictions as their predecessors, but they pointed out that in their childhood they enjoyed more freedom than their mothers or mothers-in-law. Adolescence meant curtailment of freedom and mobility. Married women felt that marriage gave them a status and some freedom in society, but at the same time it gave them more responsibilities also. Though their parents and in-laws expected them to give priority to their wishes, for this generation education, employment and economic independence also became important.

It is interesting to note that, though the younger women are coming out of the traditional purdah system, at the same time they want to be dutiful and responsible as daughters and married women. They are believers in religion and fate, like the women of the earlier generation. The similarity in the thinking of the two generations can be noticed when they say that they have adopted or would adopt new roles in life quite easily. Some of them said that, by nature and temperament, they found the best and happiest place for women is their household. The Indian woman is a mother first and last, but economic complexities have forced her to pursue a career outside the home. Her life has, therefore, become divided into two worlds: her career, where she has to work like a man, and her home, where she has to act as wife, mother or daughter-in-law. All this has affected her mentally and physically. Only 2 per cent of women felt that, because of the changing role of women, the complete transformation of values in Indian society is required so that they can perform their role more confidently, effectively and efficiently. For these women, education has a great role to play in the socialization process. Although a majority of this generation had shown a preference for education and changes in the attitudes of society, they accepted the same kind of social roles and more or less similar lifestyles as the earlier generation.

In a society like India, where cultural prescriptions have deep roots and political activism among women is allegedly discouraged, it will be interesting to study the socialization process of women which gives them a position of subordination. It is also interesting to study how this political subordination of women is rationalized, reinforced and transmitted from one generation to the next through the socialization process.

Family, Education and Political Socialization

The First Generation

The vast majority of Indian women belonging to this generation were not provided with socialization opportunities, and especially those opportunities which encouraged their active political participation. They were rather discouraged from forming any political opinion or expressing views on politics. Still, some of the women did develop an interest in the political affairs of the country during the last phase of the Indian national movement. To study their initiation into politics they were asked whether their family members encouraged them to discuss politics or to show interest in the political developments of the country. Their response was that they were not encouraged in this direction. These women pointed out that, whenever they tried to understand or ask about politics, the elders in the family (both males and females) said that 'politics is not meant for girls, you have to get married and go to your in-laws, so you had better learn about good housekeeping, cooking and sewing, rather than wasting your time on discussing matters which are not meant for you'. Some of the women of this generation did not even dare to open their mouths on the issue, though they had an interest in it. Many of them pointed out that, although the male member of their families (fathers, grandfathers, uncles, husbands) were either members of a political party or actively participated in demonstrations and so on, the women were not encouraged to express their views on these events.

A different picture was given by those women (8 per cent) whose profession is active politics. They reported intense political activity among the male members of their family, and one of them pointed out that her father-in-law, who was involved in active politics, encouraged her to play a similar role. Another active politician pointed out that 'my husband was a member of Parliament, I decided to perform my duty by continuing his work'. This role of the family as an agent of political socialization is atypical. The elite women were encouraged to be socialized politically by their family members, but the women belonging to the middle or the lower middle class did not get such opportunities.

Some of the women belonging to the first generation pointed out that they developed an interest in politics by listening to the discussions which took place among the male members of their family. They pointed out that the activities of the national movement and its leadership were discussed by the male members of the family and they were especially thrilled when the role of Mahatma Gandhi was being discussed. For these women, the nationalist movement under the leadership of Mahatma Gandhi was not merely a political movement, but a strong means of regenerating Indian Society.

These women thought that, in spite of the fact that their position might not change during this period, some of them, who could get out of their homes and could receive training and education, would be able to make a contribution in improving the position of the next generation of Indian women; and some of them might even become leaders and inspire others to follow them. During the national movement, Mahatma Gandhi either directly or indirectly educated and socialized the first generation of Indian women.

For the women of this generation, education did not play any role in making them politically socialized. Those who got a chance to study said that the objective of the women was not to imitate men but to make them better spouses. There was a very little chance of exposure to the mass media for these women. The majority of them (64 per cent) were illiterate or had very little knowledge and, therefore, were not able to read newspapers. Those who were educated sometimes did not get newspapers to read and those who read newspapers were interested in issues other than politics. Most of these women did not get a chance to listen to the radio.

The women of this generation had attended hardly any public meetings because they were not allowed to go out of their homes. They were not allowed by their families to become members of any political or social organization. There was also no desire in them to gain membership of such organizations because they were satisfied with their traditional roles within the family.

The Second Generation

The women belonging to the second generation specified that their schools rather than their families played an important role in socializing them politically. Like the older generation women, they pointed out, they were not encouraged by their family members to know or to talk about politics. One of these women remembered an incident when her brother and she asked their father almost the same question about politics. Her father discouraged her by telling her to go to the kitchen and help her mother with the cooking, while her brother's question was answered by her father very readily. These women pointed out that they wanted to learn about politics from their teachers, but the teachers took very little interest in making them politically aware. Their teachers, who happened to be females, did not impart political knowledge to their female students because for them learning about politics was not the business of girls: ultimately, a woman has to perform her household duties after finishing her education and so they should learn how to become good housewives rather than wasting their time on political matters. One of the young respondents pointed out: 'Once my grandmother asked me, "Do they teach you how to make pickles at school?" and I answered negatively and said that they teach us Indian politics. My grandmother answered, "This is not going to help you in future. You must learn household activities from your mother; after all, you have to get married".' The women of the younger generation feel that education and textbooks play very little part in socializing women politically, but at the same time they agree that they are better informed about politics than their earlier generation because of education.

A few women (20 per cent) pointed out that the chance of a modern education has helped them to learn about the concepts of freedom, equality and the dignity of the individual: women are not merely housewives and mothers, they are also citizens and equal participants in the socioeconomic and political life of the country.

The women of the second generation are more exposed to the mass media than the earlier generation. They read newspapers and magazines and listen to the radio, but the most important source of socialization identified by them is television. It is also disturbing to discover that these women like to watch programmes on television which are for entertainment rather than for political information. Some of the educated women pointed out that at the time of the news bulletins they either switch off the television or get busy with some household activity. But whatever information they get, they get it through television. Radio does not have any importance for them, except sometimes for listening to film music.

The women of this generation do not like to attend public meetings or to become members of sociopolitical organizations. A woman who earlier had been the convenor of the Young Women's Committee of a party said that she had resigned from this organization because all these activities, on the one hand, do nothing to help the women in poor communities and, on the other, membership of such organizations gets in the way of the proper performance of their household duties. They felt that, especially after getting married, women should devote themselves to their husbands and children. Elite women politicians provided the role model for middle-class women.

Thus it can be seen that, though the family does not play a very important role in making these women politically socialized, the right traditional norms are declining as they can sometimes discuss politics with their families. In the mass media, the television is the most important source of their political socialization. For some even political education and friends were important agents of their political socialization.

The Relationship Between Political Socialization and Political Participation

There is a direct relationship between political socialization and political participation. The more political socialized a person, the more he or she takes part in political activities. Let us look at this relationship in our sample respondents.

The First Generation

Only 10 per cent of women belonging to this age group admitted that they participated or participate in political activities such as public meetings, women's organizations and membership of political parties. If these women, who belonged to the upper or middle classes and were highly educated (postgraduates), 90 per cent were Hindus and only 10 per cent Muslims. This is due to the general trend of socialization among different castes and religions in Indian society.

Those who participated in politics pointed out that most of their participation coincided with the national movement because that movement, especially under Mahatma Gandhi's leadership, created opportunities for females' political socialization. According to these women, however, their political education and their participation never influenced them to deviate from the ideals of the Hindu culture. They pointed out that political participation during that time was necessary to uphold the ideals of the national movement and to protect the culture and moral superiority of Hinduism. The primary objective during that time was the nation's freedom and not the women's causes. Those who participated in any kind of political activity accepted the stereotypical image of women. Their participation in any political activity was supportive of the activity of their male family members. These women were generally hesitant to deviate from the acceptable norms of behaviour of Indian society and never tried to accept or do anything which would challenge or question the established norms. These women explained this stance by stating that even women leaders at that time were performing the role of a dutiful wife, sister or daughter and helping or supporting the male members of their family. This was significant in reassuring society about the rightness of females' participation in politics. The structure of authority within the family was such that women participated in politics only with the permission of the male members of the family. They believed that their participation in politics was a socially sanctioned activity. This explains their conventional attitude and their lack of anxiety over issues such as the emancipation of women.

They accepted the existing pattern of their sex-structured role and never found any forum to voice the demand for women's political participation on an equal basis with men. Almost all the women of this generation said that casting a vote in elections is their 'religious duty'. They therefore voted in each and every election. They considered the vote something very valuable and pointed out that that is why all political parties approach them. When asked whether they exercise their voting right independently, 50 per cent of them said 'yes'. They could not say, however, how their vote was valuable or how their participation at the time of elections can help to improve the status of women.

The Second Generation

The great majority of the women of this generation (80 per cent) do not want to become members of any political organization; nor do they like to participate in activities such as public meetings and demonstrations. Like the earlier generation, they do vote in the elections.

Those who participate in political activities say that they attend public meetings only of that political party whose leaders, policies and programmes they like. Some of them attended the public meetings just to see the party's local, national or state leaders. Some of them participated politically because they had nothing else to do and it helped them to pass the time. Those who participated, once or twice, in demonstrations declared that they did not know the issues on which the demonstrations were organized: they went just because their friends asked them to keep them company.

Most of these women say that they do not feel like participating in political activities because, first, they have to have the permission of the male members of their family and, second, since they are preoccupied with their household and professional duties, they have not time or interest left for political participation.

The women of this generation also dislike the aggressive and bold participation of women in politics. They believe in the inherent moral superiority of the male and feel that women's participation should be within the established order of the society and the family. According to these women, there are inherent differences between the talents and the temperaments of the two sexes and there are no compelling reasons to alter the conventional functions and divisions in the family. They therefore do not want to participate like male members of their families.

Women who are active politicians not only take part in political activities but also organize these activities. They feel that participation should not disrupt the male–female relationship in the family. They even feel that only those women should be active in politics who have fulfilled the responsibility of bringing up their children. These women accept male authority and guidance in their personal lives and political careers.

The younger generation of women feel that an educated woman should always exercise her right to vote, and 60 per cent very proudly pointed out that they exercise their voting right independently. Surprisingly, 10 per cent of these women, who were highly educated, said that they had supported and would continue to support the party supported by their husbands. Casting a vote is not necessarily an indication of political consciousness among women. Even the women of this generation cast their votes without knowing the importance and significance of the vote. They take part in this activity as they take part in any other social activity. Though they say that they cast their votes independently, this is not true. As a matter of fact, they confessed that, like the older generation, they do keep in mind the likes and dislikes of male members of their families in this respect. Once these women cast their votes they forget about politics.

The trends of political participation in the two generations of Indian women suggest that women of the first generation had national objectives and the national movement was an important agent of their political socialization which inspired them to participate politically. They wanted to participate within the traditional norms of society and they considered electoral participation essential. They wanted to attend meetings and participate in the demonstrations against foreign rule, but could not do so because of the authoritarian structure of the family. In the post-Independence Indian society they do not find any high ideals like the ones prevalent in the pre-independent India, yet they exercise their right to vote because they regard it as their duty.

The second generation of women feels that the participation of women in politics is limited. Their only concern is their voting right. They do not take part in demonstrations or strikes because they do not feel like doing so: the transformation process of Indian society has put a considerable burden on their shoulders and so they do not feel like participating actively in politics; they do not want to be members of any political party. When they do become involved in politics they seek the advice and agreement of the male members of their families.

Political Education, Political Socialization and Role Perceptions

The questions that arise from the debate about political education and socialization of two generations of Indian women are numerous: whether education in general and political education in particular have played any role in the socialization of Indian women; whether there is any change in the pattern of their education and socialization; and, if so, how women view this change. Do women think that they have any special role to play in the socioeconomic and political process, or do they adopt and accept the traditionally defined values and roles? How do women view the future of Indian women? Do they want women to be independent from old social norms or do they want to function only by accepting those values and roles?

The First Generation

From the analysis of the responses of these women, it was found that very few (only 5 per cent) think that there is scope for political participation of women in the Indian system. The rest of these women accept the traditional educational pattern which socialized and prepared them to discharge their principal duty of looking after their family and household. They do not want any confrontation with the male members of the family and they think that women should be ready to make sacrifices, including giving up their careers in the interests of their husbands and children; a woman should respect the views of her parents or in-laws when taking part in any political activity.

While talking about the relationship between political participation and family life, a large majority of the women (96 per cent) said that they will give preference to domestic happiness and will sacrifice anything to achieve it. They opined that it is better that husband and wife have the same political opinion and support the same political party. In the case where the wife has different opinions, she must change them to accord with her husband's views. However, a few women (4 per cent) have a different point of view in this respect. They say that husband and wife can have different opinions and that the husband should show tolerance and respect and encourage his wife's opinions.

When these women were asked to state whether there should be greater participation of women in political affairs, the majority of them (85 per cent) felt that there is no need for this. Those who were illiterate (7 per cent) did not know what to say. Only 8 per cent said that greater participation by women in political affairs is very significant because it will generate awareness regarding their rights and it will lead to general progress and improvement in women's status in society; women's participation in political affairs will help to solve their problems and will provide equal opportunities for both the sexes.

Some 85 per cent of these women believed that women should keep away from politics because it will hamper their domestic duties. Even the highly educated women (5 per cent) feel that women should not enter politics because it is a dirty game; politics does not suit the temperament of Indian women because of their commitment to moral values. One women went so far as to say that 'women belonging to respectable families will never come near politics'.

The active women politicians feel that politics is like any other profession for women. However, after Independence the enthusiasm and political activity of women underwent a downward trend. If the pre-Independence tempo had been maintained, women would have assumed greater political responsibilities both at state level and at national level. These women accept that they have to accept male domination in politics because politics still remains predominantly an area of men's activity. Some of the women feel that integration of women in politics is not possible until the traditional role of the woman in the family is changes and redefined. As long as women are assigned primary responsibilities for home making and child rearing, their participation in politics will not be without problems.

With regard to the preference of these women concerning political parties, we find that 60 per cent gave first preference to Congress-I, because they believe it is a secular party and capable of ruling the country. The remaining 40 per cent gave first preference to the Bhartiya Janta Party (BJP) because they feel that it is the only party which can save and promote Hinduism and its values. Whereas the women preferring Congress-I belonged to various castes and religions, the women preferring BJP belonged only to upper-caste Hindus.

When asked whether women voters should vote for women candidates, 85 per cent of women rejected this and said that they would like to vote for the party they liked, rather than voting for women. They felt that, if women take an active part in politics, they will not perform their household duties properly. These women said that they were satisfied not only with the existing women's representation in Parliament (4.8 per cent) but also with their performance in Parliament.

Since this chapter was written a few weeks before the mid-year elections (May 1991), it was interesting to study their commitment to awareness of the elections. All the signs indicated that they would cast their votes in the coming elections. When asked who they were going to vote for, 90 per cent of them named Congress-I. Though they were critical of the performance of all the political parties in India, their answers showed a kind of political apathy. They said that it hardly matters which political party comes to power, because all of them are the same: they utilize women's votes to gain election and hardly bother about improving the condition of women in society.

The Second Generation

Only 15 per cent of women of this generation feel that Indian women have some scope for political participation; the remainder think that household responsibilities, illiteracy, the subordination of women to men and the attitudes of society towards women were the factors responsible for women's limited participation in politics. They themselves feel that women should not ignore their household duties and only when they have spare time should they take up any political activity.

Most of these women do not want to discuss political issues with their husbands, especially when they support different political parties. According to them, women's political participation may lead to unpleasantness in their family life. Some 60 per cent of these women pointed out that the only women who participate actively in politics are those whose family is in no position to support them or to care about their activities, or those who have lost their husbands. Only 5 per cent of these women wanted women to be able to go out of their homes and take part in active politics like men. They thought that there should be equality of opportunities for men and women to participate in politics and that men should share the household duties with women and should encourage them in their active political participation. The remaining 95 per cent said that, because of increased responsibilities both in and outside the home, they do not feel like participating in political activities. They pointed out that, because of increasing violence, character assassination and a decline in moral values, women's participation in politics is becoming increasingly difficult.

On the question of women voting for a woman candidate, these women answered in the same manner as the earlier generation: they feel that they do not want to vote for a candidate just because she is a woman. They just want to be sure about the qualities of a person before voting. Of the second generation, 25 per cent felt that more representation should be given to women in the legislative bodies, but 75 per cent felt that there is no point in having more women representatives because ultimately men, who are in the majority, control the decision making in legislative bodies. Some of these women even raised doubts about the capabilities of women in decision making in representative bodies.

About the coming elections, almost all the women said that they would go and cast their votes. When they were asked to indicate the party they would vote for, 50 per cent of them felt that Congress-I was the party they would support because only this party can bring stable government to the country; 30 per cent of them felt that supporting BJP would ensure a better government; the remaining 20 per cent could not name the party they would vote for. Surprisingly, none of these women had shown a preference for any party of the left. Though 80 per cent of these women wanted to cast their votes in the coming elections, they were not very enthusiastic about the past performance of these parties. They felt that all the political parties are alike; leaders of the parties have no values as in earlier times; they just want to come to power and are not concerned about the way they do so. They can hardly be bothered about the welfare of the people. When asked whether they read the election manifestoes of the different parties, 98 per cent of the women said 'No'; they either had no time or did not feel like reading them. They said that in these manifestoes only false promises are made. None of the parties tries to fulfil the promises made by it in its election manifesto. 60 per cent of these women said that they would vote independently in the coming elections; 20 per cent said that they would consult their husbands or male members of the family before casting their votes; the remaining 20 per cent did not give any answer. Though these women had shown their interest in voting during elections, this does not mean that there is no political apathy among them.

Concluding Observations

Though it is difficult to reach any definite conclusions in the present study, because of the inadequate nature of the data, certain patterns do emerge which help to create a picture of the political education and political socialization of Indian women.

In Indian society, people do not want to socialize women, for a variety of reasons. For example, the family does not want to do so because it believes that women are meant for the home and if they leave the home they will not be in a position to discharge their duties towards home and family properly. Therefore the family does not encourage women to take an interest in politics and so on, and any effort by women to do so are strongly resisted and suppressed.

Similarly, no political party wants to socialize women because it fears that a socialized woman will be a difficult person to control. It cannot just take a socialized woman for granted. A socialized woman will give rise to new challenges which cannot be successfully met with the existing structure, orientation and philosophy of any Indian political party.

Surprisingly, women themselves do not want to change. They just accept the 'inferior' status, limited role and unfair treatment. What is shocking is that most of them are happy with the present state of affairs. There is no urge within them to change the situation. The history of human civilization clearly shows that chains have been broken only by those who realized that they were slaves and that they alone can cut the chains and free themselves. If we really want Indian women to free themselves from their 'chains' and to become equal partners with men in the reconstruction of Indian society, then, first, we have to inculcate in them the realization that they are second-rate citizens and that they alone can change their fate. We do find some sparks here and there, but they have to be fanned, nurtured and strengthened. If we do it then only a fundamental change will come in the thinking of not only the society but also of the women. And when this change comes, we will soon find women and men moving together as equal partners and thereby according to women what has been due to them for so long.

Political education has been regarded as an important agent of political socialization. It has a direct bearing on the formation of political attitudes and values. Educational institutions therefore play an important role in the process of political socialization. Almond and Verba[10] have discussed the important role played by educational institutions in the process of socialization in their five nations study, but the present study does not confirm their findings. According to Almond and Verba, a more educated person is more aware of the impact of government on the individual than is the person with less education. But in the present study it was found that educated women from both generations did not show such awareness. These women attended formal educational institutions and even studied political science, but failed to explain how the government influences the lives of ordinary citizens. Their replies in this respect can be summed up in one phrase borrowed from the *Ramayana*, and actually used by a few respondents: 'Let anybody be the king, it hardly makes any difference to us.'

Almond and Verba further point out that more educated individuals are more likely to follow politics and pay more attention to election campaigns and so on than a less educated person, but in the present study it was found that the educated women from both generations knew little about politics; they appeared apathetic towards politics. They had neither the time nor the inclination even to read the manifestoes of the different political parties. Almond and Verba believe that educated individuals are more likely to consider themselves capable of influencing the government, but in the present study we noticed feeling of helplessness in our sample respondents. They said that they are powerless to influence the government, and even asked why the government should listen to them. On the question of organizing themselves as a pressure group, they said that they had neither the inclination nor the time to plan the activities through which they could influence the government.

Almond and Verba pointed out that the more educated person is more likely to be confident in his social environment and to believe that other people are trustworthy and helpful. But in the present study it was found that most of the educated women did not feel confident in their social environment; rather, they felt uncertain about their position, role and status in Indian society. Thus education plays a very marginal role in making women politically socialized.

Education is no guarantee that a person will become wise and humane or less prone to prejudice. Its indisputable virtue is that it promotes the empowerment of the individual. It gives him or her just a little more ability and self-confidence. It enables people to find out things for themselves and gives them a chance to say 'no' – a basic element of a citizen's power. Literacy thus constitutes the first defence against exploitation.

Thus there is an obvious need to restructure and strengthen the educational system. Education will have to play an active role in socializing women. A strategic interrelationship between education and development has to be evolved so that women become conscious of their present state and get themselves emancipated from traditional, outdated and irrational societal thinking about them. Education has to play a dual role here. It has to desocialize women to be rid of old values and resocialize them by inculcating new values, attitudes, knowledge and information. Education has also to desocialize and resocialize men. Unless society gets rid of old, traditional male-dominated values, no improvement is to be expected in the position of women.

Notes

1. I. Rosav, *Socialization to Old Age* (University of California Press, 1977).
2. F. Elkin and G. Handel, *The Children and Society: The Process of Socialization* (Random House, 1972).
3. B. Stacy, *Political Socialization in Western Society* (Edward Arnold, 1978).
4. F.I. Greenstein, 'Political Socialization', in *International Encyclopedia of the Social Sciences*, Vol. XV (Macmillan, 1968).
5. K.P.L. Langton, *Political Socialization* (Oxford University Press, 1969).
6. D.D. Nimmo and C.M. Bonjean (eds), *Political Attitudes and Public Opinion* (The Kay, 1972).
7. Ayodhya, an ancient city regarded as one of the seven holy places of the Hindus, is revered because of its association, in the great Indian epic poem *Ramayana*, with the birth of Rama and with the rule of his father, Dasharatha.
8. Babari Masjid, the 'Mosque of Babur', was built in the early 16th century by the Mughal emperor Babur on a site traditionally identified as Rama's birthplace and as the location of an ancient Hindu temple, the Ram Janmabhoomi. Because of its significance to both Hindus and Muslims, the site was often a source of contention. In 1990, riots in northern India followed the storming of the mosque by militant Hindus intent

on erecting a temple on the site; the ensuing crisis brought down the Indian government. Two years later, on 6 December 1992, the three-story mosque was demolished in a few hours by a crowd of Hindu fundamentalists. It was estimated that more than 1000 people died in the rioting that swept through India following the mosque's destruction.

9   M.K. Gandhi, *Young India Weekly*, 15 December 1927; *Young India Weekly*, 21 March 1927; *Young India Weekly*, January 1932; *Harijan Weekly*, 4 August 1940.

10   Gabriel Almond and Sidney Verba, *Almond and Verba Five Nation Study* (Dartmouth College, 1970, 1971).

PART III
ENVIRONMENTAL AND HEALTH POLICY

4 Gender Dimensions of the Environment and Development Debate: the Indian Experience

Hem Swarup and Ram Rajput

As a prelude to the 'Earth summit' on 'Environment and Development' held in June 1992, two conclaves of women were held. The Global Assembly of Women, 4–8 November 1991 and the World Women's Congress for a Healthy Planet, 8–12 November 1991, both at Miami, focused attention on the gender dimensions of the environment and development debate. Since the publication of *Limits to Growth* in the 1970s, *Building a Sustainable Society* (1981) and *Our Common Future* (1987), the concern for sustainable development, that is a balanced environment–development interface, has grown. The role of women in the conservation of the environment and the sufferings and marginalization of the masses of women in developing countries due to environmental degradation have still not been sufficiently realized.

Until recently, the environmental crisis was mainly perceived as a scientific–technological problem which when studied properly and analysed could be tackled by scientific–technological modes of problem solving. The vast amount of data collected globally, whether through sophisticated instruments or satellites, within the Man and the Biosphere Programme (MAB) taken up after the Stockholm Conference on 'Environment and Development' (1972), was basically scientific. The world was informed of global warming, depletion of the ozone layer and holes in this protective umbrella for all organic life on the planet, deforestation, floods, droughts, desertification, salination and waterlogging of arable land at unprecedented rates and intolerable levels of pollution of land, air and water – life-sustaining elements. Even today it is not yet sufficiently appreciated that the global environmental crisis has been caused by a mode of development and resource utilization which is extremely exploitative of nature, non-western mankind in general and women in particular. That the sociosphere also creates a powerful impact on the biosphere, and that socioeconomic and political relations in human society are becoming the most potent factors in environmental degradation is only now being realized.

'Development' has been the key word for many decades now. Beginning with UNO's First Development Decade (1961–70) we are today in the Fourth Development Decade (1991–2000). The UN Decade for Women ended with the 'Forward Looking Strategies' (Nairobi, 1985). Equality, development and peace were the three focal points of the decade-long consideration, discussion and action programmes. As strategy, the link between productivity of women and the environment was drawn as follows:

> Deprivation of traditional means of livelihood is most often a result of environmental degradation resulting from such natural and man-made disasters as droughts, floods, hurricanes, erosions, desertification, deforestation and inappropriate land use. Such conditions have already pushed great numbers of poor women into marginal environments, where critically low levels of water supplies, shortages of fuel, over-utilisation of grazing and arable land and population density have deprived them of their livelihood. Most seriously affected are the women in arid and semi-arid areas and in urban slums and in squatter settlements. These women need options for alternative means of livelihood, improvement in home and work environments and enhanced capacity to manage their environment and sustain productive resources.

In trying to analyse the progress made, one could safely say that, in spite of so much talk about development, the majority of women in 1991, just nine years before the year 2000, were worse off than in 1975. We would like to say with Peggy Antrobus, a DAWN (Development Alternatives with Women for a New Era) activist:

> What went wrong was that women accepted an agenda which abandoned both the structural analysis, as well as the attention to women's strategic interests – i.e. those derived from an analysis of the power relations between women and men and women and the state. While focus on meeting practical needs in the areas of employment, education, health and nutrition was important, we failed to recognise that even these practical gains are easily reversed if women lack the power to protect them when resources are scarce, which is exactly what has happened in the context of the structural adjustment policies pursued by most of our governments in their efforts to deal with problems of debt, chronic balance of payment imbalances, and budget deficits. (Antrobus, 1989)

Let us listen to two perceptive voices from India on concepts of development:

> The word 'develop' itself has a wondrous meaning, and is poetic in its implications; for it means to unfold; to unfurl; to unveil, disclose, reveal, discover, to lay open by removal of that which enfolds; to bring what already existed under some other form or condition; to progress; to grow....
>
> In no dictionary will one find the word 'development' explained in economic terms and nowhere will one find the word linked to women in terms of income generation schemes, or food preservation, or family planning, or skill development – EXCEPT, of course, in the jargon of 'Women and Development', which itself is only a derivative of that concept of development that floats around in the corridors of Government, Planning Commissions, in U.N. circles, the World Bank and I.M.F. and in bilateral relations. This is the development that addresses itself to Gross National Product; to market forces; to infrastructural development; and to production.... In other words this development is one that is geared to materiality and not to the development of humanity. When we talk of women and development, we tend only to talk of linking women into this narrow definition of growth and see women's development not as an unfolding of creativity but as the development of women as producers of goods and services (and maybe as owners some day). (Bhasin *et al.*, 1987)

The new feminist vision of development is essentially human, compassionate, a new construction of knowledge and a new relationship with the poor, the oppressed and women. Kamla Bhasin of the FAO pleads it with great musical flair and Vandana Shiva, a physicist, with great passionate vehemence perceives 'development' (as being practised and propagated today) as the death of Mother Nature and a threat to survival:

> Contemporary development activity in the Third World superimposes the scientific and economic paradigms created by western gender-based ideology on communities in other cultures. Ecological destruction and the marginalisation of women, we know now, have been the inevitable results of most development programmes and projects based on such paradigms; they violate the integrity of one and destroy the productivity of the other. Women, as victims of the violence of patriarchal forms of development, have risen against it to protect nature and preserve their survival and sustenance. Indian women have been in the forefront of ecological struggles to conserve forests, land and water. They have challenged the western concept of nature as an object of exploitation and have protected her as 'Prakriti', the living force that supports life. They have challenged the western concept of economics as production of profits and capital accumulation with their own concept of economics as production of sustenance and needs satisfaction. (Shiva, 1989)

Is she not absolutely right? Is it not there for all to see that the responsibility for more and more hungry people lies at the door of inexorable processes of expanding and intensive agriculture, industrialization and internationalization rather than the cruel whims of nature?

When India launched itself on a path of development in the post-Independence era, there were only two models of development available to the whole world. One was that of large-scale collective production and private appropriations of gains and profits, and the other was of an attempt at equitable distribution of gains and profits through sociopolitical and administrative measures. Unfortunately, both these models of rapid industrialization and commodity production, sector-wise, were thoroughly rooted in exploitative uses of natural resources. While the first, through colonial and neocolonial methods had a worldwide grip on natural resources, the other one also, in competition with the first, was unable to tread the road to sustainable development. In its anxiety to become a highly industrialized and self-sufficient economy, which today numbers ninth in global statistics, India also launched itself on the same path of stark exploitation of natural resources. With no colonies and no detested colonialism, India had to fall back on its own resources. Coupled with the neocolonial vestiges, the swoop of multinationals in search of high profitability through ill-paid labour and its own brand of greed and corruption, India today is in a situation where the 'Panch Mahabhut' (the five basic elements which constitute nature: land, water, air, energy and space) are all being transformed from life-giving and sustaining ones to disease and death dealing ones. What we are witnessing today is that this 'Prithvi' (earth), in all its manifestations, from being the 'dharitry' (that which sustains) is transforming herself into the 'Maha Kali' (the goddess of destruction, with a necklace of human skulls around her neck) and through uncontrolled floods, cyclones, hurricanes, drought, erosion and salination of soil, impure water and frequent earthquakes seems to be warning mankind to change the path of development from that of devastation of nature to the alternative path of conservation and regeneration: sustainable development. The age-old wisdom of the ancient sages of all lands, of nature–man equilibrium, has not only to be brought back but implemented in all its multifaceted possibilities and prospects.

It is in the context of the above scenario that we wish to reconsider the continuing global debate between development and environment as not being mutually exclusive. Development and environment have to be envisioned as inclusive and complementary.

Destroyers of the Environment or Victims of Development: the Case of Women at Survival Levels

We would now like to discuss some specific cases of groups of women to illustrate how the gender dimensions in environment policy and planning are totally inconsequential. The masses of Indian women who have been affected by this process of development belong to the tribal, nomadic, fishing folk, hill and marginal peasant communities in both arable and arid zones. These are communities which have lived at survival levels and today find themselves at the extinction level owing to the loss of biomass (both fauna and flora) which sustained them. Since they are now forced to forage for survival in forests nearby, they are being branded as destroyers of the environment. In reality these are victims of the concept and grim reality of development which creates two Indias – one of the 10–15 per cent rich and the other of the 85–90 per cent poor of whom 40 per cent are below the poverty line.

Any time one goes by train from Banda or Jhansi, the southernmost districts of the State of Uttar Pradesh, to Gwalior, a former princely state in the State of Madhya Pradesh, one can see hundreds of women, with a load of fuelwood on their heads and a child on their backs, getting into the train or alighting from it. These women have collected the wood from the forests of Vindhyachal, the mountain range dividing India into north and south. These ticketless women at times travel 110 km by train to sell in Banda the wood collected at Manikpur. Very often the ticket inspector will just throw them out, with the load and the child, to lie sprawling on the platform, but they will get up, as soon as they are able, and begin the endless toil, for the survival of the family, once again. The forest guard of the forest, where they go to collect this wood, which has been their main occupation for centuries, often treats them inhumanly, abusing, beating and even raping them at times.

Women, at this level of survival economics, have always been the ones responsible for the survival of the family. Water, fuel, food and fodder are their prime responsibilities. The continual and increasing degradation of their environment, the loss of forests (their source of food, fuel and fodder) and lack of water resources have not only increased their drudgery but expose them to dangerous levels of pollution in their kitchens. Cooking on the traditional open 'chulha' (hearth), researchers tell us, they breathe smoke equivalent to 120 cigarettes a day and suffer from diseases of the eye. Banda is a classic example of environmental degradation, the major cost of which is paid by women. The drudgery and backbreaking labour is taking its toll. In alliance with social evils such as large-scale foeticide, neglect and under-nourishment of female children have, as evidenced by the 1991 Census, brought down the sex ratio even below the 1971 level: in 1971, for every thousand male children born, there were 930 females. The latter figure rose to 934 in 1981, but fell to 929 in 1991. The shared experience of poverty of these women is so strong that none of the infrastructure is available to them. Through the ages, they had depended on nature for the fulfilment of all their needs. The absolute number of the poor has increased. In spite of women's literacy having gone up, from 29.75 per cent (1981) to 39.92 per cent (1991), the absolute number of illiterates has risen during the same period, from 181.03 million to 197.34 million, an increase of 9 per cent amongst females, as compared to 4.8 per cent for males.

In addition to child rearing, providing health care for the family, running the household, cooking and earning a wage, women also act as resource managers. The latest Economic Census Data (1990) have not yet become available to provide comparative figures of women's work for 1981 and 1991, but the rising rate of migration to urban areas is mainly due to marginalization of women's traditional work in the rural areas. The colossal numbers involved in unorganized labour, as testified by the Ila Bhatt Report 'Shram Shakti' (Labour-Power) (1988), indicate that the path of exploitative development followed: and the consequent degradation of land, water and other resources has made women's lives much more difficult. The rising percentage of women-headed households, ranging from 15 to 30 per cent in different areas, also proves to be a contributory factor in women being bypassed or overlooked by the process of development. However, the fundamental issue is this: is the process cruel only to women or is something seriously wrong with the concept of development itself?

We are not limiting ourselves to 'ecology' or 'development, women' or 'men'. Obviously, there has to be development if there is to be a reasonable quality of life for the people. But development itself can be of many kinds, not all of them necessarily beneficial. There can be bad or lopsided development also. What we are interested in is the preservation of our natural heritage; we desire that the kind of development and the technology to be applied should be carefully selected and that the possible environmental impact of the programme should be most carefully assessed to ensure that immediate, short-term gains are not allowed to permit activities which, in the long run, will be disastrous. We are not against development which we recognize is both necessary and inevitable but we feel, in the words of Evelyn Hutchinson, that there is 'the imperative duty of ensuring that species and the entire biosphere can perpetuate for hundreds of millions of years'.

It is of paramount importance to ensure that the basic needs of people are met so that they can have access, in reasonable measure, to what man requires for a decent existence. Looked at another way, people must not live in dire poverty so that they are forced to be unwitting destroyers of environmental resources. Only then can we pass on to posterity a biosphere in which life support systems are still intact. We should perhaps recall the wise words of an American Indian chief, as quoted in Brown's *Building a Sustainable Society*: 'We have not inherited the earth from our fathers, we are borrowing it from our children' (1981).

The Basis of an Alternative Development Strategy

Achievement of the goal of peace – a more just and humane world – is the objective of women's role in development. Finding our observations and thinking to be in consonance with the DAWN group, of which we have been members, we would like to canvass, with Peggy Antrobus, the following strategy for sustainable development, as outlined in her article on 'Women and Development: An Alternative Analysis'.

1. Development has to be grounded in theories of development and social changes which recognize the difference between those who aim at maintaining the status quo (those located in the dominant/equilibrium, or 'integrative' paradigm) and those who fall within the alternative/conflict, what we would term the liberative paradigm. However, the analysis should also recognize the limitations of an economistic, materialistic, positivist approach to the social sciences.
2. To be realistic, the strategy has to attempt to relate experience at the micro level of the sector, community, project or household, to that of macro/economic analysis: it should attempt to address issues of both human agency and structure. A gender analysis of the structural adjustment policies illustrates the ways in which macroeconomic policies affect women's experience at the level of the poorest household.
3. What is needed is a holistic vision, one which seeks to integrate social, cultural and political dimensions into economic analysis: this to be borne out by an analysis of the current economic policies which show the linkage between these dimensions and the futility of focusing on economic production at the expense of the social sector (reproduction).
4. It is essential to recognize the political nature of the process of development: that the concept and causes of 'development' and 'underdevelopment' reflect the imbalance of power within and between nations rather than the presence or absence of resources: the failure of 30 years of development experience should have convinced us of the limitations of strategies based on 'technical/'rational' approaches which focus on growth and modernization in the areas of production, education, health and so on.

5 Finally, we would say that the strategy has to be feminist in orientation, one which rejects the separation of private and public domains: the household from the economy, personal and political realities, the realm of feeling and intuition and that of rationality, above all one which seeks to validate all of women's work and not only that which lies within the monetized sector of the economy.

India's Eighth Plan Draft Policy and Women

In order to sum up the policy and implementation aspects of the environmental situation vis-à-vis women, we would just take a look at the Draft Approach Paper (AP) of the Planning Commission (1990) on 'Environment and Forests in the Eighth Plan'. The AP correctly diagnoses the malady as non-comprehension, at different levels, of the looming ecological disaster. This, the paper says, is leading to growing marginalization, resulting in social unrest, human brutalization, social and regional sectarianism, the breakdown of democratic social institutions, and poverty. The paper cogently argues that 'governmental responses mostly seek to manage the environment rather than control its exploitation; and to protect wasteful lifestyles, rather than protect nature. It notes the glaring fact that 'Today, a large majority of India's population is being increasingly denied access to the natural resources vital for their survival, while the flow of these resources to urban centres, to support luxury consumption, continues unhindered' and adds the perceptive comment: 'The challenge before the government is to reverse this trend and to provide for the legitimate needs and aspirations of a growing Indian population, without impoverishing, forever, the generations still to come. The challenge is to establish patterns of resource use which meet our moral obligations to nature and posterity, while being socially just.'

In commenting on 'the state of India's environment today', of the 15 points made by the AP, 14 refer to physical and natural phenomena and only the fifteenth and last refers to 'the millions of people in rural India who are finding it difficult to collect water, fodder, firewood and raw materials essential for their survival'. For four decades, planning and development have been conceived in terms of the millions in India in the abstract, but have not focused on women as a target group, except in the Sixth and Seventh Plans. Here, too, planners have forgotten to specify that water, fodder and firewood are women's special responsibilities at survival levels. Moreover, the difficulties of water and fuel are not limited to the rural sector: the urban slum and squatter women's problems of water, fuel and sanitation are even more acute since they do not have the space that rural women have around them.

The paper visualizes the national perspective on the environment and enumerates four priority areas: (a) equitable and continued access to the natural resources; (b) decentralization of government control and decision making, the need for a national dialogue and for evolving a national consensus: (c) changing the prevailing unjust and unsustainable mode of development, and the wasteful pattern of resource use and consumption inherent in it; and (d) ensuring internally integrated and coordinated governmental action to protect and regenerate nature. The paper identifies 10 major tasks as a follow-up to the priority areas. Sadly, neither the tasks nor the list of priorities make any mention of women's specific needs, perspective and role in conservation and survival. However, to be fair, the paper calls attention to the need for much greater effort and investment of time and financial resources if the current trends of environmental degradation are to be reversed. In the delineation of the action plans, as and when these come about, it is hoped that women's perspectives may be included, provided both the environmentalists and the feminists are able to make their presence felt by the implementing agencies.

It is in this context that the recent statements made by India's present Minister of Environment and Forests seem to show an emerging understanding of the general issues. Replying to criticism that his ministry stalls development projects by delaying clearance, he stated categorically, according to newspaper reports, 'This ministry's job is not to promote thermal stations or industries but to protect the environment'. He does not mince words when he says: 'A major task of the ministry will be to bring about the marriage of environment and development to remove the erroneous concept of environment versus development.... This is the department of the future, it saves society for the future. You can have a thermal plant two years later but if you destroy environment today you may not be able to recover it in the years ahead' (*Times of India*, June 1991). The minister has plans to institute compulsory environment audit to force the industry to be environment-friendly, and proposes an amendment to the Company Act. Industries will be asked to have an environment cell, appoint environment offices and make mandatory the inclusion of reports on the environment in the annual reports of the company or industry. Environmental tribunals to take up issues out of differences or quarrels between industries and governmental agencies charged with the task of preservation of the environment are to be set up. He is of the view that legislation alone cannot protect the environment. Creation of awareness, the introduction of environmental studies at all levels of education and involving activist citizens' groups at all levels are some other measures suggested.

The problem in India, however, is that policy and plans are all there, but implementation lacks teeth. To be a real 'department of the future', ensuring sustainable development with equity and social justice in allocation of resources is bound to be a challenging task and will require lots of political influence, synchronization with other ministries and the support of activists. Here, too, it seems that the women's perspective and a realization of their proper roles in the environmental scenario have not been properly impressed upon the minister.

Forest Policies and Grass-roots Women's Movements

Since the time the British arbitrarily declared proprietary rights over the forest and subjected it to commercial exploitation, the forest wealth of India has been dwindling. In post-Independence India, the trend towards intensive commercialization continues. Only 19.47 per cent (64.01 m.ha.) of the total area of India is under forest cover and 11.51 per cent is under adequate forest cover. Satellite imagery reveals that India is losing something like a million and a half hectares of forest a year. Below 2000 metres, there are literally no forests. Even the virgin forest is being cleared for terrace cultivation. To earn revenue, the government is selling forests to the cities and to the international markets and in doing so they do not take into account either the legal rights or the natural rights of the people who live within these forests, thus creating problems of survival for the forest people (Agarwal, 1987).

Government's Response

Responding to the ecological imbalances and the threats posed by the denudation of the forests, the government of India has initiated two major policy measures, the establishment of the National Wasteland Development Board in 1985 (reference to this will be made later) and the pronouncement of National Forest Policy in 1988. Significantly, India has had a forest policy since 1878, when the Forest Act was enacted to serve colonial interests. It was under this Act that the state acquired control and ownership over the forests which were hitherto customarily common 'village property' (Ramachandra Guha, 1990). There was stiff opposition to this move from many quarters, including the government of Madras.

The issue is very much alive today as the legacy of state monopoly continues and so the debate goes on over whether the forests should be returned to the village and tribal communities, there should be a mix of control of individual, community and the state over the forest, or the monopoly rights of the state should continue. The debate today however, emanates from the concern for the environment. In the post-Independence period, the forest policy was first revised in 1952, but there was no basic change. However, it had fixed the target of having one-third of the land covered by forests. It was only in the 1980s that the government initiated policy measures to halt the dangerous trends that followed the depletion of forests. The Forest (Conservation) Act 1980 was enacted to check indiscriminate deforestation and diversion of forest land for non-forest purposes. But the major policy initiative came through the National Forest Policy (NFP) of 1988, with protection, conservation and development of forests as its main planks.

The strategies spelt out in NFP 1988 were for one-third of the total land area to be under forest or tree cover; in the hills it should be two-thirds. The policy also provided for social forestry and farm forestry. A massive need-based time-bound programme of afforestation and tree planting, especially for fodder and fuel, was deemed a national imperative. The NFP also envisaged measures by which village and community land which is not required for other productive uses should be taken up for development of tree crops and fodder resources with technical assistance from the government. The revenue generated through such efforts will belong to the Panchayats, where the lands are vested in them; in other cases revenue is to be shared by the local communities. The policy also suggested the possibility of vesting in individuals, particularly those from the weaker sections (including women), certain ownership rights over trees, in return, they would be responsible for the security and maintenance of the trees.

Emphasizing the symbiotic relationship between the tribal people and the forest, the policy enjoined all agencies responsible for forest management to involve the tribal people in the protection, regeneration and development of forests. To supplement the programme, the policy emphasized the importance of forest extension, forestry education, forestry research, forest surveys and data. Finally, it called for investment on a substantial scale in forests which maintain ecological processes and life support systems, and preserve genetic diversity. The policy made a categorical departure in stating that the forest should not be looked upon as a source of revenue: it is a national asset to be protected and enhanced for the well-being of the people and the nation.

People's Response

The declarations and policy measures pronounced by the government for environmental conservations notwithstanding, the fact is that the target of covering 33 per cent of the areas with forests remains elusive. Commercial interests and lobbying by vested interests dominate. Urbanization and industrialization take their own toll on the forests. Construction of roads, canals, dams and so on have covered a great deal of forest area. The felling of trees for forest-based industries, the manufacture of furniture, the bodies of vehicles, the packing of fruit and so on continues. One estimate is that, for one hectare of apple orchards, 10 hectares of forest need to be cut down every year to supply the wood required for packing. With rampant corruption and the indifference or connivance of the bureaucracy and political pressures the depletion process goes on unabated. Regeneration of forests is also subordinated to commercial gain by the planting of high-yielding varieties of trees. While the greed of man has overtaken survival needs, it is heartening to note the emergence of grassroot movements which manifest themselves both in the form of protest and resistance to the destructive processes and also in a positive participatory action in conserving the environment and creating awareness among the masses. The 'Chipko' and 'Appico' movements have spread their ideology far and wide in the country. These movements reflect the strength of people's power and also their concern for survival.

The famous 'Chipko' movement, which had both an ecological and an economic basis, originated in the Alakhnanda valley, which had witnessed devastating floods, loss of lives and misery for the people with the destruction of sustenance resources as a result of the deforestation of the area. 'Chipko' means 'hugging'. It started in 1973, initially in the hill town of Gopeshwar of the Chamoli district. When the representatives of a sports goods factory came and wanted to cut down the marked ash trees, the villagers, women included, pleaded with them not to do so. As their pleas went unheeded, they hugged the trees, and thus foiled the attempt to cut them down. The same contractor went to another village, Rampur Phata. On hearing of this, the villagers of Gopeshwar marched to the village, banging drums and singing songs, arousing consciousness and gathering more people, and repeated the experiment of hugging the trees and thus saved them.

Women have been the real actors in this movement. In 1974, when the men of the village of Reni were away in the town of Joshimath to protest against the auctioning of a neighbourhood forest, the contractor, taking advantage of their absence, arrived in the village to axe the trees. Undaunted, the women, led by Gaura Devi (Gaura is one of the names of the Goddess Parvati, especially worshipped by women), 50 years of age and illiterate, frustrated the attempt of the contractor, who had no other option but to go away. Women, as would be seen later, have their own perspective, which is clearly reflected in the song they composed and sing: 'Forest is our mother's home, we will protect it with all our might.' The movement has been a great success. An Expert Committee set up by the state government agreed with the women's viewpoint and recommended that, in view of the sensitive nature of the watersheds situated deep in the Himalayas, all felling should be banned. Thereafter, the movement spread from Uttar Pradesh to Himanchal Pradesh and other hill areas of northern India.

'Chipko' was given another name in the south: 'Appico', meaning the same. The 'Appico' movement was launched in 1983 by the people of Western Ghats against the destruction of forests. To be precise, it was in September 1983, in the Silkani forests of the Sirsi district of the state of Karnataka that men, women and children hugged the trees to save them. This soon spread to other areas. In the Kalase forests, 'The First Citizens' Report' (1982) reveals, apart from hugging, the Appico activists appealed to religious sentiments. The activists have since been spreading the message and creating awareness among the people. The three objectives of this movement are conservation, growth and rational use of forest resources (Pandurang Hegde, 1991). In Maharashtra (Bhandara and Chandrapur Districts) people had launched the 'bamboo roko' (stop bamboo) agitation against the diversion of large quantities of bamboo to the paper mills. The basket makers and other craftsmen found the repository of their raw materials denuded, hence this protest.

The Chipko movement has spread far and wide. It signifies people's protest against deforestation but it does not stop there. The Chipko activists are mobilizing people and creating awareness among them to conserve the resources. Dasholi Gram Swarajya Mandal has been organizing ecodevelopment camps and has carried out the largest voluntary afforestation. The survival rate of plants is said to be nearly 90 per cent, which, no doubt, is an indication of the intensity of identification with nature of those who plant and nurture. 'Saving the trees is only the first step in the Chipko movement,' says Bhatt, the leader, 'saving ourselves is the real goal. Our future is tied up with them.' The ideology of this non-violent movement is the conservation and development of the forests in tune with the needs of the people living in and around the forests, and in tune with the needs of the forests (Bhatt, 1991).

The Chipko movement has another dimension, in that it has brought out the critical role of women in sustaining ecodevelopment. As a matter of fact, this movement has been described as a feminist movement. The destruction of the environment poses a threat to marginal cultures and occupations like those of tribal communities, nomads, fisheries and artisans who depend on their immediate environment for survival, but the impact of destruction of biomass sources is greater on women (Agarwal, 1986). Against the backdrop of the impact of destruction of biomass on women, their interest in environmental regeneration is perceptively different from that of their men. As it was aptly put by a member of the Grameen Mahila Shramik Unnayan Samiti of Bankura, where women are engaged in reclaiming forest wasteland, 'For us they are living things. The forests give us food, fodder, fuel and a livelihood. These are like our limbs; each time they are cut, our chances of survival are reduced' (Sharma, 1991). This explains why women prefer fuel and fodder trees, as against the preference of men for cash economy trees. Women have, in some places, risen against their own cash-hungry men. The Citizens' Report' accounts for two such dramatic incidents, in Bhyunder valley (1978) and the village of Dungari-Paitoli (1980), where the women took up cudgels against their own men. In the first case, women were confronted by their relations from a neighbouring village who wanted to cut down trees to meet the fuel needs of 250 000 pilgrims but were not allowed to by the Bhyunder women, who stole the men's axes and refused to return them until they agreed to go away.

In Dungari-Paitoli village, the 'Report' reveals that the battle was more bitter and set wife against husband and mother against son. This happened when the horticulture department negotiated with the male-dominated Panchayat for the acquisition of a community forest to set up a seed potato farm. Induced by the prospect of employment opportunities on the farm and in its construction, the facilities it would bring to the village such as electricity, a health centre, a school and so on, and not realizing the difficulties their womenfolk would face in fetching fodder and fuel, the men agreed to the proposal. Defying their menfolk, women of the village protested and refused to let the forest be destroyed. There are a number of instances where women have taken the lead and acted as pressure groups. Madhu Sarin, in her situational analysis of Himachali women, records that, during 1989, the Mahila Mandals of Devri, Beria and Khadeen villages (of the Dharampur block) and Baddal village (of the Nalagarth block) forced the forest department to plant saplings and at least 50 per cent of fodder species by threatening to uproot the pine saplings. Women's active political engagement in these movements has an added dimension. Women of Chamoli have demanded that the women should be elected to the forest Panchayat.

Wasteland Development

More than 50 per cent of India's total land, to be precise 175 m.ha. is affected by water and wind erosion; a further 25 m.ha. is affected by waterlogging, salination, shifting cultivation, torrents and so on (Jha, 1990). To reclaim and develop this wasteland and increase the pace of afforestation, the government of India set up a National Wasteland Development Board in 1985. With emphasis on people's participation, the board has various schemes for rural fuelwood plantations, soil and moisture conservation in the Himalayan tract, development of decentralized people's nurseries (with the involvement of schoolchildren, women, youth and rural groups), tree growers' cooperatives and so on (India, 1990). The NGOs have a pivotal role to play in the whole programme of afforestation and development of wasteland. About 336 projects have been allocated to about 250

NGOs but an evaluation study of the NGOs in wasteland development does not present a very happy picture (Arora, 1990). Salvation perhaps lies in mobilizing and organizing non-governmental organizations at the grass-roots level, particularly women. Here the example of Sukhomajri village in Punjab is very relevant.

So far, an area of 9 m.ha. has been covered. India, it is estimated, needs an additional 60 m.ha. of land by 2000 (10 m.ha. for crops, 40 m.ha. for fuel and 10 m.ha. for fodder) to meet the pressing needs of its population, both human and animal (Jha, 1990). To invigorate the programme, the National Technology Mission on Wastelands Development was launched by the government on 5 October 1989, with defined objectives of checking land degradation, putting wastelands to sustainable use, regenerating degraded forest, creating green public lands, promoting farm forestry, increasing biomass availability and restoring the ecological balance. During the Eighth Five Year Plan, it is expected that an area of 17 m.ha. will be covered. The target is to cover the entire 175 m.ha. area of wasteland by the year 2010.

An important concomitant of the social forestry is employment generation. It is calculated that one hectare of wasteland gives employment to 5.5 persons for one year. For five million hectares, the annual target, 27.5 million persons receive employment in the first year and 50 per cent more in the second year. A broad calculation is that 60 per cent of the total population can receive employment. Thus, if properly implemented, in addition to saving the environment, the plan can solve one of the biggest problems of India: unemployment.

It is in this sector of social forestry that women's specific roles have to be given due recognition. Women's involvement in the forestry sector is not limited, however, to collecting fuel and fodder for household and subsistence farming needs. Because of their traditional reliance on forestry resources, women are often the chief repositories of knowledge concerning the use and management of trees and forest plants. Women also comprise a large proportion of the labour force in forest industries: nurseries, plantation establishment, logging and wood processing. Nor are women exclusively subsistence-oriented: their agroforestry preferences include commercial fruits and (pole-generating) cash-crop trees as well as fuel and fodder species.

In India, minor forest products (MFP) are a major source of income for the local people. Women are often the main collectors and users of these products, which include plant fibres, medicinal plants and herbs, fruits and nuts, seeds used in condiments, both edible and industrially important oils and resins, and so forth. 'In India, MFP account for two-fifths of the forest revenues and for about three-fourths of net export earnings of forestry products' (Kaur, 1988). Women's roles in forestry are diverse. The importance of other forest products to women and the very active role that they play in forest resource management have remained largely unrecognized and unspecified. Women's critical concerns for food, fuel and fodder shortages cannot be satisfied by their passive inclusion as 'beneficiaries' in male-initiated and male-executed activities. Wherever given a chance to take the initiative, women have demonstrated their capacity as nurturers of nature and conservationists. Some attempts have been made to involve them in forestry on public lands as well as tree cropping within the farming system on private land, but it still needs to be recognized that involving women in forestry can be vital both to rural productivity and the achievement of expected results, and to sound forestry investment. A proper implementation policy can lead not only to a better quality of life but also to better nutrition, health, welfare and equity.

Mega-dams, Rehabilitation and Women

Another major concern of the environmentalists in India has been the big dams which the planners have considered essential for development. When Bhakra Dam was built in the Punjab, it was declared the temple of modern India. This is no longer true today. The negative impact of these projects, as the 'First Citizens' Report' points out, is mostly on the tribal communities, peasants and hill folk whose daily lives are largely dependent on their immediate environment. In thousands these people are displaced and, as a result, face total social, cultural and psychological collapse, quite apart from the economic hardships. The environmental groups have been raising their voices and protesting against the dams. These include Silent Valley and Munnar in Kerala, Bedthi in Karnatka, Tehri and Vishnuprayag in Uttar Pradesh, Keol-karo in Bihar, Lalpur in Gujarat, Bhopalapatnam and Inchampali on the Madhya Pradesh, Maharashtra and Andhra Pradesh borders. While it is possible to go into the details of all the resistance to the dams, discussion of a few, in particular the Narmada Project and the issues involved, may be in order to bring out the complex web of development concepts, government policies and their implementation, and impact on the people.

The Narmada Dam Controversy and Movement

The Narmada Project has caused the fiercest environmental debate in the country and the issue has been internationalized as the Narmada Bachao Andolan activists have gone round Japan, Europe and the USA to build pressure on the donor agencies, in particular the World Bank, which is the major funding agency, to stop providing aid for the implementation of the project. Narmada is the largest west-flowing river in India on which it is proposed to construct 30 massive dams. It is claimed that the Narmada Valley Project would be the largest and, on completion, it would increase by 16 per cent the total land under irrigation in India. The environmentalists, however, are opposing the construction of the two controversial mega-dams: the Sardar Sarovar Project (Gujrat) and the Indira Sagar Project (Madhya Pradesh). The construction of these projects, it is alleged, would submerge about 130 482 ha. of forest. As regards the environmental cost of the loss of these primeval forests, according to the Ministry of Environment and Forest, this will amount to 30 923 crores for the ISP and around 8190 crores for the SSP.

Coming to its impact on people, 300 000 thousand of them, half of them from tribal communities, from Madhya Pradesh will be uprooted. A number of NGOs have been opposing the construction of these dams, but mainly it is the Narmada Bachao Andolan, an organization headed by a Gandhian, Baba Amte, which has been spearheading the resistance movement with non-violent methods of peaceful demonstrations, fasts and so on. There is a large participation of women in the movement and Medha Patkar is the front-runner. The questions that are posed concern first, the costs the people of Madhya Pradesh and Gujrat are being made to pay and, second, whether it is possible to work out an alternative to the Narmada Project.

Population Explosion and the Environment

Demographers tell us that the rate of population increased from perhaps 2 per cent per thousand years in the prehistoric past to 2 per cent per year in the 1950s. Approximately one billion people are added to the human race every 11 years. Every minute, global population grows by 170; every day by 240 000; every year by over 90 million. World population passed the four billion mark in July 1987; by the turn of the century, there are expected to be 6.25 billion people and the population is not expected to stabilize before reaching the 10 billion mark a century from now.

Population growth is concentrated in developing regions of Asia, Africa and Latin-America, which from 1960 to 1985 accounted for 85 per cent of the increase of the global population. In the industrialized world, fertility has declined and the population rate is not growing rapidly. Until a decade or so ago, population gain reduced but did not preclude gains in per capita production of such commodities as forest products, seafood and petroleum. Only as world population moved towards the four billion mark did it begin to outpace the production of the basic commodities on which humanity depends. That is why Brown says: 'Among the forces that are undermining society, population growth ranks at the top. Population growth can not continue indefinitely on a finite planet' (Brown, 1981).

India was one of the first countries to take up population control measures. The 1976 Population Policy of the government of India gave a further fillip to these programmes because it was very well realized that excessive population growth diffuses the fruits of development over increasing numbers instead of improving their standards. A reduction of current growth rates was considered essential by the GOI and, as regards policy, the Ministries of Health and Education responded. Health made more resources available to follow programmes enunciated earlier and Education responded by formulating and trying to implement policy and programme decisions on 'Education for Women's Equality' (1985). The results of the 1991 Census show that, while literacy rates of women are increasing, those of the overall population show a downward trend. The correctness of the policies and the necessity of a more vigorous implementation and a larger budget allocation are obvious if progress is to be made towards the goal of sustainable development and lower fertility rates, because the two are intimately connected and mutually reinforcing, to enable the economy to provide for basic needs, not just for today but for generations to come.

The Brundtland Report (*Our Common Future*, 1987) has, of necessity, discussed the question of interlinkages in great depth:

> Measures to influence population size cannot be effective in isolation from other environment/development issues. The number, density, movement, and growth rate of a population cannot be influenced in the short run if these efforts are being overwhelmed by adverse patterns of development in other areas. Population policies must have a broader focus than controlling numbers: measures to improve the quality of human resources in terms of health, education, and social development are as important.
>
> A first step may be for government to abandon the false division between 'productive' or 'economic' expenditures and 'social' expenditures. Policy makers must realise that spending on population activities and on other efforts to raise human potential is crucial to a nation's economic and productive activities and to achieving sustainable human progress – the end for which a government exists. (p.105)

The Report further comments on management of population growth policies that these should pursue broad national demographic goals in relation to other socioeconomic objectives and correctly regards social and cultural factors as dominant over others in affecting fertility:

> The most important of these is the roles women play in the family, the economy, and the society at large. Fertility rates follow women's employment opportuni-

Gender and the Environment and Development Debate 87

ties outside the home and farm, their access to education, and their age at marriage all rise. Hence policies meant to lower fertility rates rot only must include economic incentives and disincentives, but must aim to improve the position of women in society. Such policies should essentially promote women's rights. (p.106)

Successful programmes concerning either population or environment, therefore, have women at their centre. The question of population is also basically related to the dynamics of growth with equity in a society. In a situation where 40 per cent of the 850 million population live in dire poverty, squalor, illiteracy and undernourishment, that is, a subhuman existence, population control appears to be a superhuman task. Stabilization of population growth rates is essentially dependent on achievement of a real equitable growth, or at least smaller gaps in income levels, and also on political will.

There is, no doubt, an inverse relationship between a growing population and the conservation of natural resources; but, as regards policy, to put the entire blame for environmental degradation on population increase and not on an exploitative, profit- and surplus-oriented development concept, which is proving to be maldevelopment in its essentials, is not only uncharitable to the poor, suffering millions, but also an intellectually dishonest attempt to divert attention from the reality of a development destructive of the balance between man and nature. Whether it is the tribal communities, the nomads, the fishermen, the environmental refugees or the migrants to the urban areas, it is easy for the elite, secure in their comfortable existence, to blame them as destroyers of the environment, but in fact they are victims of the Eurocentric model of indiscriminate industrialization, commercialization, and the export-oriented market economy which takes resources away from the needy and showers them on the altar of greed, whether of individuals, state bureaucracy or corporate multinationals.

The authors applaud the vision of the Brundtland Commission Report in this respect:

Industrial countries seriously concerned with high population growth rates in other parts of the world have obligations beyond simply supplying aid packages of family planning hardware. Economic development, through its indirect impact on social and cultural factors, lowers fertility rates. International policies that interfere with economic development thus interfere with a developing nation's ability to manage its population growth. A concern for population growth must, therefore, be apart of a broader concern for a more rapid rate of economic and social development in the developing countries. (p.97)

The basic question, for a country like India, still remains whether the 'structural adjustment' policy, accepted by a relatively independent government, under duress, to liberalize the economy in order to procure an IMF loan in order to ward off the debt repayment crisis, is really going to restore the economic equilibrium. Will not these manoeuvres increase the international and intranational gaps between the rich and the poor still more and worsen the situation of the masses of women and children?

Urbanization and Women in Slums and Squatter Settlements

Major cities, since ancient times, have been centres of power in national settings. Kautilya, the ancient political theorist of India, in his *Arthashastra* ('Artha' means land populated by people and 'Shastra' is systematic knowledge), lays great stress on how the king should choose his capital and utilize the resources of the hinterland. The word 'hinterland' itself denotes the relationship between the user and the used, in fact a power equation, as between the centre and the periphery, both globally and within a nation. Since the continuum of power relations has remained unbroken, the importance of the city has rather increased.

It has been estimated that, by the turn of the century, almost half the world will live in urban areas, from small towns to mega-cities. The world, demographers tell us, is in the middle of an urban revolution. Since 1950, the urban population has almost trebled, and in 1985 reached nearly two billion. In the developed world, the urban population increased from 477 million in 1950 to 838 million by 1985. The urban population of the developing world quadrupled over the same period, mushrooming from 286 million to 1.14 billion. It has been estimated that, by the end of this century, 75 per cent of Latin America's population, 42 per cent of Africa's and 37 per cent of Asia's will live in urban areas. The number of people living in cities of over a million grew from one in 100 in 1940 to one in 10 by 1980.

India was formerly considered to be a country of villages. However, the 1991 Census calculates the urban population at about 25 per cent, stretching the country's resources still further.

Environmental Refugees

Migrants driven from the land by rural poverty are pulled towards the city by the lure of better access to education, health services and jobs. One of the major causes of poverty, in India or in developing countries generally, apart from other structural factors such as uneven distribution of incomes and services, is an increasingly degraded environment. This forces the already poor off the land, whether they are marginal farmers, agricultural labourers or artisans. The total number of these refugees is impossible to calculate.

Gender and the Environment and Development Debate 89

Most of the survivors end up in urban squatter settlements (without any basic facilities) or on pavements. The Brundtland Report points out:

> In most Third World cities, the enormous pressure for shelter and services has frayed the urban fabric. Much of the housing used by the poor is decrepit. Civic buildings are frequently in a state of disrepair and advanced decay. So too is the essential infrastructure of the city; public transport is overcrowded and overused, as are roads, buses and trains, transport stations, public latrines, and washing points. Water supply systems leak, and the resulting low pressure allows sewage to seep into drinking water. A large proportion of the city's population often has no piped water, storm drainage, or roads. (p.239)

And what are the authorities, national or local, doing about it? The B.R. points out with great clarity:

> Few city governments in the developing world have the power, resources, and trained staff to provide their rapidly growing populations with the land, services, and facilities needed for an adequate human life: clean water, sanitation, schools and transport. The result is mushrooming illegal settlements with primitive facilities, increased overcrowding, and rampant disease linked to an unhealthy environment. (p.238)

In this steady stream of those coming to the big cities the men far outnumber women, but more and more women are beginning to migrate to the cities, sometimes with their families and sometimes even alone. Many of them end up in the red-light areas, the dens of prostitution; a large number become domestic servants to the relatively affluent middle classes living in proper houses. Women, young and old, carrying head-loads up many flights of stairs can be seen any day. Illegal factories and manufactories, not obeying any labour law at all, accommodate a large number of women, who are paid, on average, two-thirds or three-quarters of what men would be paid. The underpayment of this 'underclass' ensures that they will never be able to extract themselves from illegal squatter settlements or slums. They are a prey to many water- and air-borne diseases. The same water supply often serves for both drinking and sanitation. WHO estimates that 1.2 billion people, that is 24 per cent of the world's population lack safe drinking water. Without proper sanitary waste disposal facilities, water-borne diseases – cholera, typhoid and diarrhoea – particularly among children, malaria and intestinal worms claim many lives. Women and girls are the worst sufferers because their undernourished physique and the relative paucity of medical facilities provided to them by their own families, take their toll. Because of this adverse effect of the environment on their health, more women die in childbirth; pregnancy doubles the risks of common illnesses such as pneumonia and influenza.

Kanpur has the distinction of the largest tuberculosis-ridden population because of its textile industry, coal dust and smog in winters. During the summer months, when the water level of the Ganges goes down and the water supply is vastly reduced, the incidence of epidemic jaundice and deaths have become an annual feature. In Lucknow, the capital of Uttar Pradesh, only recently, there was an epidemic of cholera, euphemistically called gastroenteritis, as if the name you give to the cause is going to make any difference to the dead and their families! And who is the greatest sufferer? The undernourished woman and the girl child, who will not even be taken to the hospital, but will be just left there to die or survive! Mulk Raj Anand, a very sensitive and perceptive Anglo-Indian novelist, writing in the early 1930, wrote in his *Coolie*: 'The bigger the city the more cruel it is to the sons of man!' Our action research and observation tell us that these mega-cities are even crueller to the daughters of Eve. They hardly have a chance to escape from this squalor, the back-breaking grind of child bearing and rearing, domestic chores and also earning an income, unless vast investments are made in the cities, as is being done for the rural areas.

The environmental movement, unfortunately, has not yet caught on in the cities as it has in the hills. The people's response is just a hopeless acceptance of things as they are. Just like the 'Green The Hills' slogan, we need 'Clean The Cities' movement and some of the voluntary organizations should take it up. Whatever the goals of population policies, the elimination of poverty and measures to improve the health, education and status of women are essential for their success. These are also essential for sustainable development.

The Right to Development

A fresh approach to environmentalism was articulated at a conference of the Asian Coalition of Human Rights Organisation (ACHRO) in Manila in mid-October 1991. The focus of elaboration was the Declaration of the Right to Development adopted by the UN General Assembly in February 1987. This embodies the third generation of human rights which stress group rights and collective rights which, in turn, include the right to development.

The activist approach, as adopted in the Chipko, Appico and Narmada Dam people's mass movements, is now part of the current phase of the debate on the right to development and this has been linked to environmental concerns. The two-day Manila conference devoted one full session to the 'Impact of Development on Ecology', which discussed development and environmental protection. Two questions were repeatedly asked regarding development: for whom, and at what cost? It was also noted that sustainable development alone can promote intergenerational equity, and that better appreciation of the interrelationship between development and the environment as two sides of the same coin would improve environmentalism immeasurably. A stronger and more determined environmental movement was suggested. What is needed is activism with the fervour of the Earth Week celebrations in the USA. This mass action by environmentalists, scientists, politicians, economists and other concerned citizens is accompanied by an outburst of publicity, preaching and prognostication, generates public recognition of the environmental crisis and produces some positive action on various aspects of environmental protection.

Concluding Remarks

We have dealt in this chapter especially with tribal, hill and marginal peasant women and also with environmental refugees who throng the cities, having been deprived of their forest, land, occupation, culture and social status. It should be noted here that there are also women in fishing and nomadic communities facing similar as well as unique obstacles not described here for lack of space. The fact of the matter is that environmental depredation and destruction in the name of the false god of progress has uprooted, impoverished and rendered homeless millions upon millions of people who today form that section of the population which exists below the poverty line. Even if calculated at 35 per cent of the population, it would come to approximately 300 million (more than the entire population of the USA and a few European countries) of the present population of India. This means that about 130 to 140 million women and female children are faced with a totally bleak future, along with the communities they live in.

Government policies have to keep this vast population in mind, but the number of women involved in policy and decision making at any level is microscopic. Political and bureaucratic elites are dominated by men. Women belonging to these groups are not in their milieu, their feminine sensibilities. Only in places where grass-roots organizations or groups of women have emerged in the course of their struggle for survival, have they succeeded, even if at micro levels only, in participating in decision making and moulding of policy, as in the 'Chipko', 'Appico' or 'Jharkhand Mukti-Morcha', and other movements. Nowhere else have they been able to make much headway. The lesson to learn obviously is: understand the reality, struggle, organize, win positions on representative bodies at all levels and become decision makers.

Bibliography

Agarwal, A. (1986), 'The Fifth World Conservation Lecture: Human Nature Interactions in a Third World Country', *The Environmentalist*, 6, Autumn, 165–83.

Agarwal, A. (1987), 'Gandhi, Ecology and the Last Person', 13th Gandhi Peace Foundation Lecture, New Delhi.

Agarwal, A. and S. Narain (1985), *The State of India's Environment (1984–85)*, The Second Citizens' Report, New Delhi: Centre for Science and Environment.

Agarwal, A. and S. Narain (1991), *Global Warming in an Unequal World: A Case of Environmental Colonialism*, New Delhi: Centre for Science and Environment.

Agarwal, A., K. Sharma and R. Chopra (1982), *The State of India's Environment*, The First Citizens' Report, New Delhi: Centre for Science and Environment.

Agarwal, A., Darry D'Monte and Samarth Ujawala (eds) (1987), *The Fight for Survival: People's Action for Environment*, New Delhi: Centre for Science and Environment.

Antrobus, Peggy (1989), 'Women and Development: An Alternative Analysis', *Development* (1), 26–8.

Arora, Shakuntala (1990), 'Role of Non-Government Organisations in Wasteland Development', *Proceedings of the National Seminar on 'Technology for Afforestation of Wastelands'*, 6–8 November, F.R.I., Dehradun.

Bandyopadhyaya, Jayant and Vandana Shiva (1988), 'Political Economy of Ecology Movements', *Economic and Political Weekly*, 11 June, 1223–32.

Bhasin, K. *et al.* (1987), 'Lecture on Women and Development', at the Third International Interdisciplinary Congress on Women, Dublin.

Bhatia, S.C. (1984), *Operationalising Environmental Education*, New Delhi.

Bhatt, Chandi Prasad (1991), 'Chipko Movement: The Hug That Saves', *The Hindu: Survey of the Environment*, Madras, April.

'Blue Supplement to the Monthly Commentary on Indian Economic Conditions of the Indian Institute of Public Opinion' (1990), *Focus on Environment*, **XXXII**, (1), August, New Delhi.

Bose, Ashish (1991), *Population of India 1991: Census Results and Methodology*, New Delhi: B.R. Publishing Corp.

Brown, I.R. (1981), *Building a Sustainable Society*, New York: Norton.

Chaturvedi, Pradeep (1990), *Sustainable Agriculture in India*, New Delhi: Indian Association for the Advancement of Science, Food and Agriculture Organization.

Club of Rome (1972), *The Limits to Growth*, New York: University Books.

Deshbandhu, D. Bandhu, H. Singh and A.K. Maitra (1989), *Environmental Education and Sustainable Development*, New Delhi: Indian Environmental Organization Society.

Diwan, Paras (ed.) (1987), *Environment Protection*, New Delhi: Deep and Deep Publications.

Fairclough, A.J. (1991), 'Global Environmental and Natural Resource Problems – Their Economic Political and Security Implications', *The Washington Quarterly*, Winter.

Gandhi, Indira (1972), 'Speech delivered at the UN Conference on Environment and Development', Stockholm, New Delhi: GOI.

GOI (1985–9), *Years of Fulfilment, Prime Minister Rajiv Gandhi on Protecting our Environment*, New Delhi.

Guha, Ramchandra (1990), 'An Early Environment Debate: The Making of the 1878 Forest Act', *Wasteland News*, May–July, 3–11.

Hegde, Pandurang (1991), 'People's Movement: Striking Roots in the South', *The Hindu: Survey of the Environment*, Madras, April.

The Hunger Project, Planning in Action: An Innovative Approach to Human Development.

India (1990), *Reference Annual*, New Delhi: Ministry of Information and Broadcasting, Research and Reference Division.

Jha, M.N. (1990), 'Wasteland Afforestation in India: A Perspective for Policy Consideration', *Proceedings of the National Seminar on 'Technology for Afforestation of Wastelands'*, 6–8 November, F.R.I., Dehradun.

Kaur, Ravinder (1988), 'Women's Role in Forestry in India', *Consultant Report for the India Country Women in Development Study*, World Bank, PHRWD, September.

Nanda, A.R. (1991), *Census of India: Provisional Population Totals*, series 1, New Delhi: Samrat Press.

'National Seminar on The State of Environment in the Doon Valley: Pollution, Population and Plan for Citizen Action' (1990), 16–18 March, Dehradun.

'National Seminar on Environmental Pollution – Its Magnitude and Remedies' (1991), 23–4 February, Kanpur.

Pruthi, S. and P.S. Nagpaul (1985), *Science and Technology Indicators for Development*, New Delhi: National Institute of Science and Technology and Development Studies.

Report of the Committee for Review of National Policy on Education, Towards an Enlightened Society (1990), New Delhi: GOI.

Report on Monitoring of Indian National Aquatic Resources: Water Quality Statistics of India (1979–87), no. 60, New Delhi: Central Pollution Control Board.

Report on Monitoring of Indian National Aquatic Resources: Water Quality Status of Indian Aquatic Resources (1990), no. 61, New Delhi: Central Pollution Control Board.

Report on National Ambient Air Quality Statistics of India (1987–9), no. 63, New Delhi.

Sadik, Nafis (1990), *Safeguarding The Future*, New York: UNFPA, p. 15.

Sarin, Madhu (1989), *Himanchali Women – A Situational Analysis*, Jagjit Nagar: SUTRA, 57–74.

Sharma, Kumud (1991), 'Role of Women: The Crucial Connection', *The Hindu: Survey of the Environment*, Madras, April.

Shiva, Vandana (1989), *Staying Alive: Women, Ecology and Survival in India*, New Delhi.

Shiva, Vandana (1990), 'Development: The "New Colonialism"', *Development*, (1), 84–7.

Terwari, D.N. (1984), *Primitive Tribes of Madhya Pradesh*.
Terwari, D.N. (1987), *Victims of Environmental Crisis*, Dehradun, U.P.: Educational Private Ltd.
Tietenberg, T.H. (1990), 'The Poverty Connection', *Challenge*, September–October, 28.
World Commission on Environment and Development (1987), *Our Common Future*, New York: Oxford University Press.

PART IV
SCIENCE AND TECHNOLOGY POLICY

5 Science, Technology and National Goals: a Study of the Role of the Indian Council of Agricultural Research in the Agricultural Development of India

O.P. Sharma

The standard of living is low for the majority of the people in developing countries like India. Improvement of living standards of the poor is, therefore, one of the most important tasks of the Indian government. Agriculture can play an important role in accomplishing this objective. This is so because the agricultural sector provides the basic economic development in the country. Experiences elsewhere show that modern science-based agricultural technology can help in increasing food production. Agricultural research is capable of contributing to the gains of the society in terms of food production, economic growth and improved living standards.

Agricultural research is now playing an ever-increasing role in India. The success of the 'green revolution' suggests that agricultural research and modern technology are extremely powerful tools for expanding food production. Agricultural research influences not only food production but also economic growth, patterns of income distribution and the well-being of the people. This makes the use of agricultural research and technology one of the most important issues in the overall development strategy.

Growth of scientific research and its organizational development have followed a unique pattern in India. From a small, haphazard beginning in the pre-Independence era, the development of scientific research in the post-Independence period has been planned and systematic. Scientific research in India is now carried out in large centralized systems whereby a number of research institutes or laboratories in a particular field spread all over the country are 'controlled' by the agency headquarters which is generally located in the capital city and is interlinked with other departments, agencies and ministries of the government of India. This system is followed because its survival depends heavily for direction and support on various other agencies of the government of India, such as the Planning Commission. More than 90 per cent of all national research, including agricultural research, is organized on this pattern.

Scientific agriculture in India started in the 18th century with the realization by the then British government of the necessity to meet the raw material needs of the industry in Britain and to relieve the country of recurrent famines. J.A. Voelcker, consulting chemist at the Royal Agricultural Society of England, looked at Indian agriculture and submitted a detailed report for its improvement. The report led to the establishment of the Imperial (now Indian) Agricultural Research Institute (IARI) in 1905.

With the constitutional changes brought by the Government of India Act of 1919, the government of India transferred all powers pertaining to supervision, direction and control over administration of agricultural and veterinary subjects to the provincial governments. Provincial governments were thus made responsible for development of agriculture and agricultural research. There was no central body to guide and coordinate their policies. A Royal Commission on Agriculture was appointed in 1926 to inquire into the agricultural set-up and the rural economy of the country resulting from the absence of central organization in the country, with the specific purpose of coordinating work on agriculture and animal husbandry in different provinces and bringing it into line with the policy of the central government, and to make recommendations. Thus, on the recommendation of the Royal Commission, the Imperial (now Indian) Council of Agricultural Research (ICAR) was set up in July 1929 as a society registered under the Societies Registration Act, 1860. Its objectives were to promote, guide and coordinate agricultural research in India. It was also to serve as a link between agricultural institutes in India and foreign countries.

Independence necessitated the strengthening of agricultural research and education. The government of India appointed two joint Indo-American teams, in 1954 and 1959, to look into the problems of agricultural education, research and extension. The Third Review Team (1963) comprising eminent agricultural scientists from the UK, the USA and India was appointed with the specific objective of inquiring into the existing agricultural research set-up in India and suggesting suitable changes. This team, in its report in 1964, suggested fundamental changes in the structure and scope of activities of the ICAR. On the basis of the recommendations of the Third Review Team, the ICAR was reorganized in 1965 as a central agency for coordinating, directing and promoting agricultural research and education in the country. All the research institutes under the Ministry of Food and Agriculture and Commodity Committee were transferred to the ICAR. There was revision of rules and bye-laws to provide more functional autonomy for the ICAR.

In 1973, there was another reorganization of the ICAR which led to further changes in the organizational structure to provide greater autonomy and flexibility in operation of management and recruitment. The status of the ICAR as an office attached to the Department of Agriculture was changed. The Department of Agricultural Research and Education (DARE) was set up in the Ministry of Agriculture to provide government linkage to the ICAR and deal directly with the central and state governments, international organizations and foreign governments. The director general of the ICAR was given the status of secretary to the government of India in the DARE. The governing body and the standing finance committee were also reorganized and the director general was made chairman.

Mandate

The ICAR is the national body in the country responsible for the following:

1   to aid, promote, conduct and coordinate research and education in agriculture, animal husbandry, including fisheries and social sciences related to agriculture;
2   to act as a clearing house of information on these subjects and support transfer of technology programmes;
3   to provide services relating to the production of basic breeders' seeds and planting material of improved agricultural and horticultural crops, production and supply of improved agricultural breeding stocks of animals, stocking material for fish culture and production of immunological cultures, bacterial cultures and so on; and
4   to do such other things as the Council may consider necessary or conducive to the attainment of the above objects.

There had been tremendous expansion in the agricultural research and education systems in the country over the years through the establishment of many ICAR institutes, several agricultural universities, and so on. In the changed circumstances, the original mandate of the ICAR needs to be critically looked into for a more meaningful outcome.

It is to the credit of the ICAR that India has achieved self-sufficiency in food in spite of grave doubts expressed by the international community. This, on the one hand, gives satisfaction and, on the other, keeps the ICAR on its toes. It has continuously to improve its performance. The primary responsibility of the ICAR is to set up long-term goals and to help and service its institutes and personnel. To be effective, it should be more a service organization than a control organization. It has to consider and seize upon technology development which may come from unexpected events. Technology by its very nature tends to branch and diversify. The primary objectives of going in for technology assessment are to identify then analyse the relevant socioeconomic, technical, legal, psychological, institutional, environmental and political consequences and to identify and analyse the uncertainties and risks associated with alternative policy choices.

Technology assessment is expected to prevent negative effects, act as an early warning system, help understand the dynamics of the industry, anticipate and forecast events, help guidance of the regulatory process and provide a range of feasible options and dues for a comparative analysis of these options.

Organization

The agricultural research system in India in terms of its size, with approximately 27 000 scientists, may perhaps be the largest in the world. The ICAR, with its 46 institutions, 20 national research centres, nine project directorates, four bureaus, the National Academy of Agricultural Research Management (NAARM) and 26 agricultural universities constitutes the major organizational set-up for agricultural research in the country. The ICAR is the apex organization which enjoys autonomy, being a registered society, although it follows *mutatis mutandis* rules and regulations of the government of India and is subjected to statutory audit and scrutiny by the Parliament. The major funding is from the government of India grants and from the Agricultural Produce Cess Fund, although foreign assistance, both through bilateral cooperative research programmes and from funding agencies like the World Bank (IDA), USAID, UNDP, IAEA, IDRC, SIDA and so on is also available. The ICAR aims at undertaking, aiding, promoting and coordinating agricultural and animal husbandry (also including fisheries and social sciences) research and education acting as a clearance house of information, establishing a research and reference library and taking up transfer of technology programmes and consultancy. The ICAR carries out its functions through the following bodies:

1 the General Body, which is the chief policy-making body and is chaired by the president of the ICAR, the ICAR Minister of Agriculture, and meets annually. There is also a vice-president of the Society who is generally the Union Minister of State in the Ministry of Agriculture and discharges the responsibilities of the president of the society in his absence;
2 the Governing Body (GB) which is the chief executive body of the council and is chaired by the director general and meets quarterly;
3 the Standing Finance Committee (SFC), a sub-committee of the GB, to look into the financial matters;
4 regional committees for the eight agroecological regions which help in looking into the research and training needs of the region in relation to the development programmes;
5 management committees or boards for each of the 46 institutions;
6 the ICAR headquarters;
7 the Agricultural Scientists Recruitment Board (ASRB) for recruitment of scientists;
8 the Department of Agricultural Research and Education (DARE) which looks after international cooperation and provides government linkage to the ICAR and thus allows the ICAR to have linkage with the state governments, offices and ministries in the Union government and with foreign governments and institutions;
9 the Norms and Accreditation Committee for deciding on matters related to universities;
10 the ARS (agricultural research system) Committee for deciding on matters related to ARS.

The Headquarters

The ICAR headquarters has a major role to play in project planning and evaluation. The ICAR headquarters has a strength of 84 scientists out of 6500 scientists in the system and spent Rs.189.3 million out of Rs.5204.3 million spent on the ICAR during the Seventh Plan. This involves the expenditure not only on the technical department but on all other departments: finance, personnel, international cooperation, and publication and information. The ICAR directly administers research institutes, bureaux, national research centres and project directorates. In addition, it has a large national network of multilocational and multidisciplinary all India Coordinated Research Projects which are funded on a 75:25 and 50:50 basis as far as centres located in agricultural universities and state departments of agriculture or animal husbandary are concerned. The centres located in the

ICAR institutions are generally part of their non-Plan research activity. The ICAR also funds ad hoc research schemes out of the AP Cess Fund and the US-held rupees (PL-480) and administers foreign-aided projects such as UNDP/FAO and bilateral cooperative projects. It also supports research by establishing chairs of Professor of Eminence, national fellowships and Emeritus professorships.

The ICAR is headed by an eminent senior agricultural scientist as research manager designated as the director general, who is also secretary to the government in the Department of Agricultural Research and Education (DARE) in the Union Ministry of Agriculture. He is the chief executive of the Council. He is assisted on the technical side by the seven subject matter divisions: Crop Science; Soils, Agronomy & Engineering; Animal Sciences; Horticulture; Fisheries; Agricultural Education; and Agricultural Extension. Each division is headed by a deputy director general (DDG). The DDGs are not responsible for the national institutions which report directly to the director general. They are assisted by the assistant directors general (ADG) and senior scientists. There exists at the headquarters a Plan Implementation and Monitoring Unit headed by the ADG (PI&M), a Project Implementation Unit primarily related to US-assisted projects, also headed by the ADG (PIU) and the unit related to the centre–state relationship headed by the ADG (Cdn). There is also a Project Implementation Unit to monitor the UNDP-assisted projects under the supervision of the DDG (Edn) who is national project director.

The director general is assisted on administrative and financial matters by the secretary, ICAR, who is also the joint secretary, DARE, and a number of administrative units: International Cooperative Division, Finance Division, Personnel Division and Publication and Information Division headed by directors. A small unit (DARE) provides government linkage to the ICAR.

The administrative and technical wings have reasonably independent responsibilities; the latter is to provide only technical support and has very little to do with the administration and financial matters. The DDGs are staff officers of the DG (to advise him on technical matters) and do not have administrative responsibilities and associated powers. The ADGs, however, are branch officers and look after the coordinated projects and ad hoc schemes from financial angles in addition to the technical angles. They, however, have little role to play in evaluation of the institutions' research programmes. Major administration responsibilities lie with units other than the technical divisions.

To provide administrative and financial support to the ADGs, there exist scheme sections. Similarly, to support the administrative wing, there are external establishment sections which primarily deal with the institutions. There exists a dichotomy of the technical and administrative wings at the

ICAR headquarters which adversely affects the functioning of the ICAR: For the administrative and financial matters of the institutions, the under-secretaries, the deputy secretaries, the secretary and the director general are responsible. The ADGs and the DDGs are responsible only for the technical matters of the institutions.

Though the DDGs have been delegated powers, in actual practice there is very little exercise of such powers because of the dichotomy of operations. Whereas the ADGs who are not responsible for the institutions have financial powers with regard to coordinated projects and AP Cess-Funded projects, the DDGs, who are responsible for the institutions and are the only competent authority to take decisions on technical matters, have no financial powers at all. The dichotomy of functions also results in multi-channel communication from the headquarters to the institutions, which causes confusion and affects the functioning of the institutions. There is a 'cold war' going on between the administrative and technical wings at the headquarters; there is a feeling that the administrative wing, instead of serving the scientists, expects the scientists to serve them.

The ICAR needs to be restructured so as to abolish the dichotomy of operations and make it an efficient agricultural science management organization. The present cumbersome and procedure-oriented administration should be cut out. Powers and functions of various functionaries should be clearly defined. There should be close linkage between the administrative and technical wings and the DDGs should be the persons to whom ultimately the institutions have to report and they, in turn, should service and guide the institutions on all matters.

Autonomy

From time to time the rules and regulations of the ICAR have been revised to make it functionally and technically more sound and an autonomous organization. The ICAR, at present, is a registered society and enjoys an autonomous status. It follows *mutatis mutandis* government of India rules and regulations. It seeks approval of concerned government departments on personal, financial and legal matters. As a chief executive body of the Council, the Governing Body manages all the affairs and funds of the ICAR subject to the bye-laws and orders of the society.

In actual practice the ICAR is a government department. In spite of its society status, it has little administrative and financial autonomy. The government of India gives block grants to the ICAR. The ICAR has no freedom of appropriation and reappropriation to different programmes within the block grant. It has to refer each and every proposal, in detail, to the Finance

Department for approval. Thus the ICAR has little financial autonomy. Though the Governing Body has almost absolute powers with respect to the functions of the ICAR, all its decisions are subject to the concurrence of the Additional Secretary (Finance) who is the Member (Finance) of the Governing Body. He virtually enjoys veto power. All those matters where he disagrees have to be taken up at the level of Ministers for Agricultural and Finance. Even for modifying any plan proposal or for effecting changes in the staffing pattern, the ICAR has to seek concurrence of the Planning Commission and Finance Department, which leads to inordinate delays.

The effective functioning of any scientific organization depends upon the technical and operational autonomy it enjoys. The ICAR, being the premier scientific organization responsible for promotion of agricultural research and education throughout the country, has to be given full autonomy to enable it to carry out its objectives effectively. Existing rules, regulations and operational procedures should be streamlined to restore real autonomy to the ICAR. The Governing Body should have all the financial and executive powers and its decisions should be final.

ICAR and the National Agricultural Research System

The ICAR is responsible for aiding, promoting and coordinating efforts in agricultural research and education in the country. As an aiding and promoting agency, it is expected to make available funds to institutions for undertaking agricultural research and education. As a coordinating agency, it is expected to maintain close relationships with various institutions. Towards optimizing the available resources in the country, it should strive hard to bring in complementarity of research efforts amongst the institutions involved in the National Agricultural Research System.

For obvious reasons, we are selecting state agricultural universities and ICAR research institutions for our discussion here. This is so because it is through them that the ICAR implements its mandate of promotion of agricultural research.

Agricultural Universities

There are 26 agricultural universities in India, the majority of which have Faculties of Agriculture and Veterinary and Animal Science. There is integration of agriculture, education, research and community outreach education. The majority of them participate in the coordinated research projects and also obtain funds for research on specific research problems identified by the teachers/scientists from the AP Cess Fund of the ICAR. The universities receive grants from the ICAR for developing infrastructural facilities for undergraduate and postgraduate education. Universities also receive assistance from the ICAR for transfer of technology programmes. In addition to the support from the ICAR, universities receive grants from the state governments and other scientific agencies.

Almost all the universities are unhappy with the present system of the ICAR providing them with research support. Difficulties encountered pertain to technical programme formulation, implementation, release of funds, sharing of resources and integration of research. This calls for a review of ICAR's funding system for research.

Research Institutions

The ICAR conducts research in the areas of agriculture and related fields in its own institutions and research centres. The number of such research institutions has increased markedly over the years. At present, there are 46 institutions, four bureaux, nine project directorates and 20 national research centres. The ICAR assigns specific responsibilities to the institutions along with a certain amount of autonomy. The institutions function under certain guidelines provided by the ICAR headquarters. The role of the headquarters is mainly that of guidance and servicing, on administrative and technical matters.

To a large extent, the research institutions are autonomous and are provided with separate budget and administrative support. They also have their own management committees to help in gaining consensus on decision making as well as to review the institutions' programmes. One of the senior officers of the ICAR headquarters (DDGs for national institutions and ADGs for other institutions), is on the management board or committee. The Financial Advisor and Director (Finance) are also on the management boards of the national institutions. The three national institutions which comprise more than one-third of the manpower and infrastructure facilities report directly to the DG, whereas the other institutions report to the DDGs with respect to their technical matters. The ADGs have little part in monitoring institution programmes except in assisting the DDG/DG. There is a provision that the Staff Research Council (SRC) proceedings, proceedings of the management committee and annual reports of the research, technical and extension activities of all the institutions be made available to the ICAR headquarters servicing scientists so that they can review them and provide such advice as may be necessary.

The institutions face some serious problems in carrying out their activities. They view the role of the ICAR headquarters as that of supervision and control and not that of guidance and servicing. There is no communication between administrative and technical wings of the headquarters and, therefore, a lot of confusion, delay and contradiction. They complain about showing favours to some in the sanctioning of research grants. Furthermore, personnel policies after the constitutions of the agricultural research service which relate to generalized recruitment by the independent ASRB, and placement of scientists at the various research units by the ICAR headquarters, rotations of heads of divisions, tenurial appointment of the research management personnel and five-yearly assessment of research and technical personnel have created problems for appropriate management of research both by the institutions and by the ICAR headquarters.

Quality results from scientists can be achieved only with their autonomy and freedom and in an atmosphere devoid of controls. The ICAR should play the primary role of identifying national priorities and target areas that it would like to support during the Plan period. This may be done with the help of task forces. These priorities may then be circulated to universities and research institutions who may be encouraged to develop specific research projects in their areas of interest for funding by the ICAR. With this, the ICAR should give more autonomy to institutions in administrative, financial and operational areas. Such a procedure will ensure that local initiative and expertise, along with the necessary autonomy, are utilized in development and implementation of research projects. Steps should also be taken to see that all the research organizations ultimately are independent of the ICAR and can compete on equal terms for the projects, so that the feeling of preferential status and preferential treatment will have gone.

Here we would also like to emphasize that universities should be used more for basic research, training and community outreach and the state agriculture departments should be extensively used for transfer of technology, while research institutions and national institutions should be utilized more for applied research and for training personnel in research methodology and giving them experience in applied research. The major difficulties in such a collaboration seem to be lack of faith in the scientific abilities of others, personality problems and refusal to share equipment and other resources. It is time that universities and research institutions emphasized that research is essentially a team activity: project teams are created for a specific purpose and have to accomplish a specific task within the specified time.

The ICAR should pay special attention to promotion of social science research. Subjects like rural sociology, social and cultural anthropology, regional geography and agricultural economics are assuming greater importance in the field of agricultural research. Socioeconomic factors play not only an important but a decisive role in transfer and adoption of technology. However, the ICAR has not so far paid much attention to this crucial aspect of agricultural research.

The role of the social scientists in the research planning process needs to be more clearly defined and understood. Social scientists should invariably be associated with all major research programmes of the ICAR and their contributions to the development of these programmes should be ensured.

Research Planning

At the time of formulation of the five-yearly Plans, the Planning Commission constitutes a Steering Group on Agriculture and allied sectors under the chairmanship of the Union Minister for Planning and Deputy Chairman, Planning Commission to identify specific working groups or task forces for undertaking in-depth studies of the problems and for working out proposals in different sectors, to develop guidelines on approaches, strategies, objectives and targets of agricultural development under the Plan and finally to consider the reports of each working group and make suitable recommendations to the Planning Commission. The steering group in turn constitutes several working groups, one of which is on agricultural research and education, under the chairmanship of the director general, ICAR and secretary, DARE in the Union Ministry of Agriculture. This working group comprises senior officers of the ICAR headquarters, directors of selected ICAR institutions, vice-chancellors of selected agricultural universities, a few senior scientists outside the ICAR system, representatives of the Planning Commission, Department of Science and Technology and Department of Agriculture and Cooperation, development commissioners associated with agriculture, animal husbandry, fisheries, representative of finance, and so on. The working group in turn constitutes sub-groups on different major activity areas, such as crop sciences, animal sciences, fisheries, education and transfer of technology, with respective DDGs, senior directors or vice-chancellors as chairman and institution directors, and project coordinators and senior staff members from the Union Ministry of Agriculture and from agricultural universities as members.

The sub-groups are to make a critical review of the achievements of the previous Plan and to suggest proposals for implementation of the current Plan. They are to recommend strategy regarding specific target areas and infrastructure development. In addition, they are to suggest measures for ensuring effective coordination, examine further scope of linkages between research and development, and critically examine the existing staff strength and non-Plan expenditure involved. Lastly, they are to make proposals for incremental staff, and in such specific areas of agricultural research and education which may need special consideration.

The sub-groups review the progress of the ICAR institutions, coordinated projects, bureaux, national research centres and so on in their sector with respect to their performance, infrastructural development, staff strength and expenditure both under the Plan and non-Plan, and identify national priorities and new targets in relation to the national development plans. They develop a long-term prospective plan and a comprehensive plan for the current Plan, identify areas where strengthening is required and examine further scope and linkages between research and development. These groups keep in view the recommendations made by the quinquennial review teams (QRTs) of the institutions, mid-term appraisal committee (MTAC) of the coordinated projects and other recommendations made by groups specially constituted by the ICAR. The report of the working group is submitted to the Planning Commission and is considered by the steering group, which approves major target areas, programmes and the Plan allocation.

The subsequent responsibility of implementation of the Plan rests with the ICAR headquarters, where there exist a Plan Implementation and Monitoring Unit and subject-matter divisions, the latter headed by the DDGs.

Financing Agricultural Research

Most of the funding for agricultural research coordinated and supported by the ICAR comes from the grants given by the Union government. Union government also places at the disposal of the ICAR the Agricultural Produce Cess Fund. Foreign-aided projects such as those conducted with assistance from UNDP, IDRC and SIDA, funds provided under bilateral cooperative projects and US-held rupees, provide the ICAR with additional financial resources for funding research projects at its own institutions or at the agricultural and other general universities. In addition to receiving funds from the ICAR specially under the All India Coordinated Research Projects and out of the AP Cess Fund and US-held rupees, the agricultural universities receive funds from the state governments for specific research projects.

The annual plan and non-plan allocations, although always increasing, bearing in mind the escalation in prices, increase in salaries and so on, as well as the need to support new programmes, has been for recent years, millions of rupees under the Plan and non-plan. These funds were allocated by the Union government as a block grant. This money does not include other sources such as the Agricultural Produce Cess Fund, US-held rupees and external assistance. One of the major sources of external assistance is the World Bank/IDA loan for the implementation of the National Agricultural Research Project.

Considering the size of the agricultural research system both under the ICAR, agricultural universities and general universities, it will not be possible to provide figures for institutional infrastructure in scientific research, experimental fields, outreach community services and so on.

Human Resources

The National Agricultural Research System (NARS) in India has a sanctioned strength of around 27 000 scientists, distributed as follows:

1 State agricultural universities (SAUs)   18 500
2 ICAR research institutes   6 500
3 General universities and attached colleges   1 000
4 Agrobased industries   1 000
5 Voluntary organizations and related departments   250

The majority of scientists in the agricultural research system both of the ICAR and of the SAUs have at least a master's degree, except in the case of agricultural engineering, where in the ICAR system the minimum qualification for entrance in the ARS is a graduate degree in agricultural engineering.

No detailed analysis of the manpower requirement in the agricultural research of the country has been worked out, but, in the agricultural universities and the ICAR system, about 25 per cent of the total available posts are vacant. The number of vacant posts is slowly increasing. There is a shortage of trained manpower, especially in the areas of veterinary and animal sciences, and agricultural engineering and technology.

Research Monitoring and Evaluation

The ICAR monitors and evaluates its own research programmes and the programmes supported by it through a variety of mechanisms at various levels. At the micro level, the individual projects are monitored and evaluated by the project leaders, heads of divisions or institutions' directors. At the macro level, the research activities of its institutions, national research centres, bureaux and project directorates are monitored and evaluated by the ICAR headquarters either on its own or in association with outside experts.

The reviews done by the headquarters of current research programmes in the institutions have not been very successful. Whereas some research (like that funded from the AP Cess Fund), which is not critical from the financial point of view, gets more attention, other research, quite significant both from the academic and the financial point of view, does not receive due attention. The institutions do not send their reports in time to the headquarters, which affects monitoring and evaluation of research. Then there is no satisfactory interaction between various technical divisions at the headquarters.

At the institution level, the Staff Research Council (SRC) is responsible for the planning, monitoring and evaluation of institutions' research programme. The SRCs meet twice a year for a couple of days. This makes it difficult for them to discuss critically all the projects. Moreover, the SRCs are headed by the director of the particular institute, with very little external input. Thus the present system of monitoring and evaluation is not satisfactory and needs strengthening, both at the headquarters and the institution level. A strong planning and monitoring division at the headquarters, with adequate powers, should be set up to review the research programmes of the institutions and to implement the recommendations of various bodies through effective follow-up. At the institution level, the SRCs should be made functionally more effective.

Agricultural Community Outreach

One of the major aims of the ICAR is to act as a clearing house of agricultural information and to take up the transfer of technology programmes and consultancy. The ICAR disseminates research findings and scientific information through publication of scientific literature on agricultural and related subjects. The publications and information programme is a means, not only of announcing the results of research on increased production, but also of building up valuable scientific knowledge in the country. However, the efficacy of this programme is very limited. It failed in its objective of providing concerned persons with up-to-date and timely scientific information. It has not been able to cope with the ever-increasing scientific literature, both within and outside the country.

With the development of telecommunication facilities through satellites, computer networks, microwave links and so on, it is now possible to disseminate information widely throughout the country. It is urgently necessary for the ICAR to monitor the latest R&D efforts in agricultural science both within and outside India. International data bases now give instantaneous (on line) information on any aspect of agricultural science. Such comprehensive information gives one a complete picture for decision making. Making available all the international and national information to the researchers on on line terminals should be identified as one of the urgent functions of the ICAR.

The transfer of technology is undertaken by the ICAR through its operational research projects (ORPs) scheme. This scheme is operated by the ICAR through its own institutions and agricultural universities. To impart technical literacy to illiterate farmers and give them improved farming skills, a scheme of Krishi Vigyan Kendras (KVKs) is implemented by the ICAR. Towards bridging the gap between potential and actual yield, an intensive nationwide community outreach drive was launched by the ICAR under the 'Lab to Land' programme. The outreach programmes of the ICAR implemented through its own institutions aim at demonstrating the latest technologies to the farmers and extension workers, testing and verifying the technologies in the actual socioeconomic situations of the farmers and getting first-hand feedback for making changes in its research, education and training systems.

Community outreach work is a specialized job and therefore needs skilled manpower and sophisticated infrastructure. The ICAR institutions however, are not adequately equipped, in terms either of manpower or of other infrastructure facilities to enable them to carry out the work effectively and efficiently. Nor do they have linkages with the state developmental departments and agricultural universities. It would therefore be advantageous if the ICAR transferred this function to the states, agricultural universities and voluntary organizations, especially as, with the passage of time, a wide network of these has developed in the country. This would, on the one hand, enable the ICAR to concentrate on more important matters and utilize its limited resources more gainfully and, on the other, would entrust the specialized task of agricultural community outreach to specialized bodies for efficient implementation.

Concluding Observations

Research in the agricultural field has certain unique features that distinguish it from research in the industrial field. In the industrial world, basic research is translated into technological innovation through engineering, pilot plants and production plants. The fate of technology is determined by market forces: if the product is commercially viable, the technology is said to be successful; if the product fails, the technology itself is discarded. In the agricultural field, the production technology emanating from research has to be tested in field conditions and adopted by the individual farmers, who lack the organization of an industry and who may not be so well informed and educated as those in industries. Moreover, the fact that the farming community is dispersed and thinly spread precludes the technologist from claiming any part of the gains the technology brings about.

The other two characteristics of agricultural research which have to be kept in mind are, first, that it is generally focused on a particular issue, such as physiology, improved quality, productivity, water management or improving the breed yield, so that it may be called problem-oriented research; and second, that it is located, crop, soil, weather and animal-specific and has therefore to be conducted at predetermined sites. The first characteristic helps to facilitate measuring the success of the research project, while the second shows that the project can best be undertaken at a predetermined site and the success thereof can be ascertained from the reaction and response of the site surroundings. In other words, the problem, the research methodology and the evaluation are all tied to the location. Both these characteristics suggest that optimum benefit from agricultural research can be had if it is carried on at locations of concern and if the decisions regarding research methodology and evaluation are decentralized.

In today's rapidly changing world, in order to carry out its objectives, the ICAR has to adopt a multidimensional strategy for research. The components of such a strategy will be adaptive, applied and upstream research. Each type of research has distinct organizational requirements. For example, the adaptive research, which is very practical research in agronomy and allied fields, is best adapted to the work of individual researchers or small groups of researchers. It must be decentralized and developed close to production activities. It does not require a detailed and sophisticated programming mechanism to select research priorities and to organize the allocation of resources. With the focus moving on to applied research, including the development of technologies and products, the organizational requirements become complex. Multidisciplinary teams organized around well-defined projects or programmes are needed to carry out this type of research. Here the selection of competitive research objectives makes it necessary to develop more sophisticated programming mechanisms to allow a rational and orderly allocation of resources.

Upstream research is the research which is not 'directly' related to the productive system and, therefore, it is not possible to relate it to declared objectives. This research, by its very nature, cannot be rigidly planned. It requires a flexible, loose organization that enables the continual redirection of research based on feedback from early results and the intuitions of the researcher. Here research results are more related to the imagination and perception of individual researchers than to the work of interdisciplinary teams. Such research, therefore, does not need a large and solidly structured team or departments but an organization that follows more closely disciplinary lines. It also requires an intellectual environment that provides for permanent and flexible mechanisms for consultation and exchange of ideas.

The ICAR has to adopt an organizational structure which will take into account the distinct requirements of three broad types of research, as outlined above. Any organization chalks out its strategy and policies while keeping in view its objectives. Its objectives have to be continually looked into so as to effect changes in them necessitated by the changing environment. The ICAR is going to play an ever-increasing role in the development of agriculture in India. It has to adopt a more sound direction and strategy, on the lines suggested in this chapter. This also necessitates a change in the objectives of the ICAR. We would suggest that the first objective should be to undertake, promote and coordinate agriculture, animal husbandry and fisheries education, research and its application so that the country attains self-sufficiency and achieves international standards of production and productivity. The second objective should be to set up an on line information system to collect and to provide instant access to research and general information pertaining to agriculture, animal husbandry, production and productivity.

A clear-cut and well-defined objective will ensure clarity at all levels and help in restructuring the ICAR to enable it to help the country in meeting successfully the growing agricultural needs of a rapidly increasing population.

6 The State and Information Technology in India: Emerging Trends

Pradip Thomas

This chapter seeks to elucidate the relationship between the state and information technology in India within the broad parameters of a discourse that is rooted in the political economy tradition. Given the expansive nature of the subject and its complexity, it has merely attempted to consider some of the more salient aspects of this relationship. For instance, there is no attempt to locate the analysis of the state in India within the larger debates on the state – not only because of the time factor but, more importantly, because the constantly shifting terms of coalitional politics in India and the existence of both centrist, authoritarian tendencies and the rhetoric of federalism and autonomy have led to a theoretical vacuum, an inability to understand the nature of the 'transition' affecting the state. The recent onslaught on 'secular' India by right-wing revivalists and the response of Indian intellectuals to this crisis illustrate attempts to redefine the essence of the state in India, its juridical limits and its scope for legitimate action vis-à-vis the peoples of India.

Such concerns are outside the scope of this paper, but it must be noted that the legitimacy crisis affecting the state in India has indirectly affected various sectors of the economy: political wrangling at the centre has led to a situation where the budget has not been passed, the balance of payment situation has worsened and credit ratings have decline alarmingly. The information technology (IT) sector has also been affected adversely; government measures to conserve foreign exchange (*Financial Times*, 28 March 1991, p.4), including moves to restrict the import of raw materials, components and capital goods, affect the IT industry in particular because of the import-dependent nature of its production. However, the present crisis affecting the inability to adapt the large-scale capitalization of the economy to the needs of a highly differentiated transitional state and society.

The State: Continuity and Change

The state of India needs to be analysed on two levels, as a complex whole and as an instance in organic relationship to other instances. The post-colonial state in India, in its constitution, its institutions and practices, reflects an affinity with the colonial state in India. During the colonial period, the state was clearly an ally of capital – in fact, its predominant role was to aid the formation of capital for the sake of both the colonizers and their local counterparts. During the struggle for independence, the structure and functioning of the colonial state came under attack from the nationalists. At Independence, an attempt was made to mould the state into a democratic entity, legitimized primarily through electoral politics. However, given the composition of the Indian National Congress, with a leadership base that overrepresented the industrial and agricultural elite, it was not surprising that the post-colonial state, at its birth, was a compromised entity. It is interesting to note that Indian industrialists were not allies of the Independence movement until quite late in the freedom struggle. It was only when they realized that Britain's intransigent economic policy had no intention of accommodating their interests as well that they joined the struggle.[1] However, their involvement in the struggle helped them immensely in post-colonial India. As Basu (1988:145) has noted, it was 'this amalgam of social classes, of an agrarian oligarchy and industrial monopolists, of traders and businessmen, of bureaucrats and professional groups, which came to dominate state power in post-Colonial India'.

The most important question that faced the Congress-I just after Independence was on the approach that needed to be taken to develop the nation. Given the influence of the Gandhians in the party, a form of Gandhian socialism was adopted. It was decided that a 'planned' process of development based on a mixed economy, but with a primary role for the state, was the optimum approach. The state was given the task of planning and implementing growth and also controlling crisis. Under a planned economy, the state invested vast amounts in building an economic infrastructure. Under the provisions of the Industrial Policy Statement adopted at the Avadi session of the Congress government in January 1955, basic and strategic industries, including heavy industrial plants and machinery, defence and so on, were exclusively reserved for public-sector manufacture. Self-reliance and import substitution were adopted as key economic policies of the state. A series of Five-Year Plans provided the blueprint for the state's development policies. Simultaneously, various protectionist measures were adopted by the state to extend the reach of private enterprise in the country. The private sector needed capital, infrastructure and protection from foreign capital. A series of measures, including price control, progressive taxation policies and the exemptions, made capital accumulation a lot easier. Sanyal's comment (1988:30) on the fiscal implications of this relationship between the state and private capital is worth repeating: 'the Indian State has two major expenses to manage. One, to aid the development of capital by developing physical and financial infrastructure, and the other, to finance the cost of maintaining the coalition – but also the cost of the huge structure of governance.'

On the agricultural front, an attempt was made to follow a growth-cum-distribution policy. However, given the extreme concentration of land in the hands of an agrarian oligarchy, the state's attempts at equitable agricultural development have been fraught with difficulties. In the early years of the post-colonial period, an attempt was made to redistribute land through the evoking of legislations that were to allow for definite land ceilings and ownership for those workers who were under a tenurial arrangement of one form or another. However, given the rural political economy, land reform could not be carried out according to plan. This has been a stumbling block in the development efforts of the state and is a continuing cause of the existence of large-scale rural poverty. This has resulted in immense disparities in rural areas between the rich and the poor, a steady rise in unemployment, pauperization and immiseration. Given that 68 per cent of the total workforce in India are in agriculture or related occupations, out of which 40 per cent are rural labourers (see the 1981 Census), the lack of land reform has hit landless labourers the most. And as Kurien (1987:6) has pointed out, planning has been least beneficial to this class of wage labourers, whose ranks continue to grow: 'For the period from 1901 to 1961, cultivators accounted for about 53 per cent. There was a very drastic change in this composition in the decade of the sixties. The share of cultivators came down from 52.3 per cent in 1961 to 42.9 per cent in 1971, while that of agricultural labourers increased from 17.2 per cent to 26.9 per cent which has continued through the seventies as well.'[2]

The state's espousal of the 'green revolution' in the late 1960s, coupled with an agricultural policy that emphasized selective, intensive growth, led to the reinforcement of rural class divisions. Pressurized both from within by the landlord lobby and from the outside by the World Bank and other financial bodies, the state opened up the agricultural sector to capitalist agricultural development. The 'green revolution' was based on the use of an optimum mix of high-yielding variety seeds, fertilizers and pesticides and was dependent on assured water supplies, large holdings and a regular supply of non-organic inputs. Despite the well-publicized success stories in the Punjab, the after-effects of the 'green revolution' have been quite disastrous, not only in terms of decreasing fertility of the soil and the degradation of the environment but, more importantly, the institutionalizing of a certain attitude to agricultural development that is highly capital-intensive and therefore outside the scope of the ordinary farmer. (See Menscher, 1978; Frankel, 1978.)

The role of exogenous capital in the redirecting of Indian development policy needs to be considered in the context of the study of the post-colonial state in India. Given the increasing strength of the pro-capitalist lobby in the Congress, the foreign exchange crisis of 1956 and the serious drop in agricultural production, the state compromised on its community development-based policies and opted for a settlement with foreign aid. Both agriculture and industry came under the influence of foreign capital, especially from the USA. The extent of foreign fund investment in the Indian five-year plans is an illustration of growing dependency. Between the first and second plans, exogenous funding for the plans increased from 9.5 per cent to 31 per cent of the total financial outlay. The aid factor was used to liberalize the economy and, by 1973, continuing a process that had started earlier, a further 17 key industries, hitherto reserved for public-sector manufacturing, was thrown open to national and international capital. Ilchman (1967), Omvedt (1975:1982) and others have written at length on the political economy of foreign aid and its impact on local development policy. The following statement made by Eugene Black, the ex-president of the World Bank, in a letter addressed to T.T. Krishnamachari, the former finance minister of India, is illustrative of the conditions imposed by the west for funding development in India:

> India's interest lies in giving private enterprise, both Indian and foreign, every encouragement to make its contribution to the development of the economy, particularly in the industrialised field. We would have to consider the pace and scale of our further loan operation in India from time to time in the light of economic conditions and prospects taking into consideration the economic policies pursued by [y]our government. (Quoted in Chenoy, 1985:18)

The State in Crisis

In the early years of the post-colonial period, the influence of the Congress spread from the Centre to local village level, through a tiered form of governance. The Panchayat system and community development were both meant to foster self-help and local government. The Congress party spread its influence through a diffused party organization. Power was to a large extent decentralized and there were powerful local leaders who sustained the Congress through periods of crisis. In fact this diffused power structure acted as a bulwark against any local crisis assuming national importance and affecting the work at the Centre. However, with the induction of Mrs Gandhi as the leader of the nation in the late 1960s, the power of the 'Syndicate' – a group of powerful local leaders – came under attack from the Centre. It was thought that they concentrated power in their hands and that they were a threat to the leadership at the Centre and to the stability of the nation. Soon after her appointment, Mrs Gandhi went on a systematic campaign against the Syndicate. They were stripped of their power, and power became centralized at the Centre. The consequence of this was ultimately self-destructive. For, with the demolition of the tiered power structure, local crises, that would normally, under the previous system, have been contained, began to affect the Centre. There were few people that were trusted or structures that were intact that could defuse conflicts at a local level. This restructuring of political power marked the end of value-based political rule in India. Populist and, increasingly, personalized politics replaced the ordered rule of the early post-colonial state.

This resulted in a situation where the hitherto rule-bound institutional structure consisting of the party system, Parliament, the judiciary and the police became instruments of patronage and profit (Kothari, 1983). Centralization of power vis-à-vis the real need for autonomy for the local state governments has been a source of much conflict. The economic, political and cultural hegemony of the state was resented by the local elite and soon a diverse range of non-Congress political parties appeared on the regional scene. They represented regional interests, at least on paper, and they asserted their right to cultural autonomy. There was a gradual breakdown of both the economic and the political systems and this resulted in economic shortfalls in the early 1970s, followed by serious riots all over India. Centralized government did not allow for a respect of the basically pluralistically diverse secular tradition, based on cultures and ways of life and very local specific needs. While 'national integration' was necessary, the exercise was overdone at the expense of respect for unity in difference, which is at the very heart of the Indian nation.

The party at the Centre was soon caught in a vicious circle. It was unable to defuse conflicts at a local level and, in response to crises in various parts of the country, it arrogated more powers to itself. The infamous Emergency period (1975–7) was a response to a crisis that had got out of hand and that had affected the very legitimacy of institutions like the Parliament and its representatives, who were more often than not well-entrenched criminals with a penchant for power. The mounting crisis was also a reflection of the state's inability to control a real revolution rather than a 'passive revolution'. The state allowed and benefited from legitimizing the coexistence of precapitalist forms of exploitation with capitalist forms. Incremental, gradualist change, populist measures and the legitimization of the cult of the charismatic leader became ways in which the state elicited consensus from its polity. The state had continuously to adapt and accommodate itself to the demands from the precapitalist domain and this affected the nation as a whole, its institutions and values, its growth and development.

The growing dissatisfaction with state policies led to various movements all over India, among tribal communities. Dalits, minority groups and other ethnic and religious communities. Secessionist movements in the north-east, especially Assam, Mizoram and Nagaland, in the Punjab and in Kashmir, may be seen as legitimate responses to the state's communalization of politics and its rule through force. Political oppression was complemented by cultural oppression that was based on the denial of the right to self-determination, the forced integration policies of the state and the inability to deal with the linguistic needs of its people. The saga of the Punjab is a microcosm of the crisis affecting the state in India. The state's response to worsening Centre–state relationships has been to use a maximum amount of force to control the situation. This has not always worked in favour of the state: whole villages have been destroyed, families have disappeared and hundreds of people have been killed in the name of national security. Singh's dossier (1988:19) of the legislative measures adopted by the state specifically to deal with the problem in the Punjab is a telling illustration of the crisis that it faces and its response to it.

> Since 1983, 25 acts have been passed by the Parliament in respect of Punjab alone. They include amongst others – Punjab Disturbed Areas Act, 1983; Chandigarh Disturbed Areas Act, 1983; Armed Forces (Punjab and Chandigarh) Special Powers Act, 1983; Terrorist and Disruptive Activities (Prevention) Act, 1985 (which has already been amended thrice, twice in 1985 itself and once in 1987); the Constitution (48th Amendment) Act, 1984; and the empowering in August 1986 under Article 249 about [sic] a security belt.

Various other factors can be attributed to the crisis affecting the state in India; these include its espousal of a policy of industrialization within a framework of extreme land concentration, widening disparities between the rich and the poor, a steadily increasing external debt, a fiscal crisis that has affected the federal economy, a breakdown of the public distribution system and large-scale criminalization and communalization of the political process.

The state's attempt at forging a political and cultural hegemony has been largely conducted through its centralized media system – both Doordarshan and the All India Radio, and various other state-run media outlets attached to the state's multifarious institutions involved either directly or indirectly with development. These media institutions have functioned as little more than propaganda pieces of the state.[3] They have been used to elicit consensus in periods of crisis and at times of relative harmony. The SITE (Satellite Instructional Television Experiment),[4] the massive expansion of the television infrastructure from the mid-1980s and its strategic support for the making of the television serials, the *Mahabharata* and the *Ramayana*, can all be seen as the state's attempt to extend its cultural and political hegemony. The private media, although less controlled, have nevertheless acted as allies of the state at most times. Given the highly skewed pattern of media ownership in the private sector, extreme concentration and links with big business, the private media taken as a whole have not really questioned the legitimacy of the state. The private media, especially the press, have on occasion been at the vanguard of calls for the restoration of democracy in India, but they have not in any way questioned the terms or the essence of the hegemonic principle.

Hegemonic rule implies legitimization through the play of consensual economics and politics. It allows for a permissible range of disagreement, for the movement of groups within the ruling bloc without affecting the centrality of its core principles. The media in India have played an important role in providing the consensus that has been necessary for supporting state power. Femia's comment (1981:39) on the logic of hegemony and its principle for survival is a pertinent reminder that hegemony is never complete, that it has continuously to renew itself, modify and defend itself through its protection of its core principles:

> Hegemony [embodied] a hypothesis that within a stable social order, there must be a sub-stratum of agreement so powerful that it can counteract the division and disruptive forces arising from conflicting interests. And this agreement must be in relation to specific *objects*, persons, beliefs, values, institutions. (Emphasis in original)

The Monopoly Capitalist State

Over the last decade, the state has steadily moved away from its earlier commitment to the cause of self-reliant development towards a policy based on economic liberalization and a free trade economy. The state has diluted its direct economic interest in the managing of the economy and has given both private and transnational capital various opportunities to shape the Indian economy. In a sense, this stage in the development of the state in India can be seen merely as a culmination of a process of accommodation that had started much earlier. But it is also important to read this era as the triumph of the interests of the ruling bloc, especially of the industrial elite vis-à-vis other factions within the ruling bloc. The following three important dimensions characterize this era of state monopoly capitalism.

The Opening up of the Public Sector to Private Capital

There has been a marked increase in private-sector investments in the public sector. Liberalization has led to big names in the private sector, including the Tatas, the Birlas and Ambani, to extend their economic interests and tighten their hold over large areas of commercial and industrial manufacturing. The coalition of interests between the state and capital has led to a situation where the state has become a spokesperson for the private sector and its interests. Joint ventures, such as the partnership between the Indian Oil Corporation and the Tatas for the Kernal Refinery Project, between the IOC and the Birlas for the Mangalore Refinery, and between the state and the Jindal group for the Kalinga integrated steel plant,[5] are a few examples of emerging trends. The advocates of privatization have maintained that such a policy would lead to greater competition, quality products and a source of foreign exchange. However, given the existence of 'natural' monopolies and the determinations of a debtor economy, it is debatable whether liberalization will lead to a healthy climate of competitive growth and all-round development.

The Opening up of the Economy to Exogenous Capital

As was pointed out earlier in the chapter, foreign capital played an important role in shaping development policy in India from the years of the First Five-Year Plan onwards. However, the large-scale involvement of foreign capital in India started in the early 1980s. Given the fiscal crisis affecting the state and the need to service mounting foreign debts, the state opted for a policy of export-led growth, based on the active collaboration of western and Japanese multinational companies (MNCs) with public and private firms in India. Chenoy (1985:22) notes the quantitative growth of MNC involvement in Indian industrial manufacturing over the last decade: 'From an earlier peak of 359 in 1974, these increased to 526 in 1980 (almost double the 1979 level of 267). Since then this trend has been accentuated, with the number of foreign collaborations agreements moving from 389 in 1981 ... up to 590 in 1982, increasing to 673 in 1983 and jumping to an all-time high of 740 in 1984.' Foreign investment has been actively wooed by the state and various legislative restrictions and loopholes have either been removed or amended. A 100 per cent equity is now allocated for companies that are 100 per cent export-oriented. Various licensing regulations have been withdrawn and there has also been a relaxation of the rules on the importing of capital goods and raw materials. This liberal economic climate has also allowed for the repatriation of profits to the Centre and for higher rates of royalties. It is of course too early to judge the impact of transnational corporations (TNCs) on the health of the Indian economy, but, as we shall see in the following section, the indications are that indigenous manufacturing capacity, local R&D and the economy as a whole are bound to be affected adversely by these new developments. Given that India today is the world's sixth largest borrower, its debt service liability alone was US$1.5 billion in 1984 and US$3.7 billion in 1987. It is estimated that in the 1990s this amount will increase to US$4.3 billion.

The Privatization of Essential Services

As a reflection of the dominant norm of consumerism and consumption-based development, there has been a steady influx of NRI (non-resident Indian) capital and the creation of a number of initiatives that have helped the development of privatized services, especially in the area of health care, education and housing. At the very same time, the state's involvement in the provision of essential services has been cut. This has led to the reinforcement of the situation of unequal access to basic human rights and necessities.

In retrospect, the state in India can be characterized on the basis of the following observations:

1 it has a monopoly on the use of coercive force;
2 it is increasingly becoming an active supporter of TNC capital;
3 it is the major disburser of cultural and economic hegemony;
4 it is the site for the condensation of contradictions and a source that unites the general will of the ruling bloc with that of its policy.

Although the state's political hegemony has been contested from time to time, as the election victory for the National Front has demonstrated, it has not led to significant, far-reaching change in Indian state and society. Under the rubric of monopoly capitalist rule, the state has consistently tried to reinforce its image as a caring institution through presenting a set of collective goals based on a common world-view. The recent moves towards decentralized government, the granting of autonomy for the media under the

Prashar Bharathi Bill, and its commitment to rapid industrial development of the nation, have been interpreted as a new and progressive phase of the state in India. However, this can also be seen as the state's attempt to extend its hegemony in an era of coalitional politics. It is to an analysis of the state's active support and development of the IT industry in India and its impact on local industry and labour that we now turn.

Information Technology and the State in India

General Observations

Although the development of the nation has been the key reason cited by official sources in justification of the massive amounts of public funds deployed in the state's IT programme, it has been shown from past experience that, in very many cases, media deployment on a national scale has not helped the masses as such but has merely aided the spread of consumerism, individualism and the legitimacy of the state. Both television, which started in 1959, and SITE in particular were meant to further the cause of development in India. But a combination of factors, including political expediency, the exigencies of transnational capital and pressure from local, private capital, played a part in changing the course of its deployment and use. Murphy (1983:107), in a study of the third world IT scenario, has commented that SITE did not affect the 'feudal constancy of India. It was not designed so much for India as for the international community interested to have a general case study of educational broadcasting by satellite.' And Mody (1986:91) has speculated on the reason for the deployment of satellites in India (a direct consequence of the SITE experience): 'the direct instantaneous access to every village that the daily satellite news programme gave to the party in power that controls the air waves in India had a major part to play in the timing of the decision in favour of an Indian national satellite system. Direct broadcast television had proven its worth to the political powers that be.' Similarly, the political reasons behind the rapid expansion of television in the mid-1980s has been well documented (Ghorpade, 1986, Thomas, 1988).

The reasons for the large-scale use of IT in India are couched in the language and ideology of modernization. The lack of information has once again been resurrected as the main reason for underdevelopment. Well-worn phrases like the 'take-off' stage of growth, and the 'trickle-down' theory have once again come into fashion. It is widely stated that IT will catapult India into the 21st century. The official reasons for rapid development of the IT programme are based on the following assumptions:

1   that liberalization of the IT industry will boost Indian exports of both hardware and software and thus enable the country to earn foreign exchange;
2   that it will lead to competition in the manufacture of quality goods;
3   that it will lead to the modernization of the telecommunications sectors and higher efficiency in the service sectors;
4   that it will lead to greater employment;
5   that it will lead to the import of state-of-the-art technology that will indirectly help the development of local R&D; and
6   that it will lead to a synergetic effect on the Indian IT industry, that is, the complementary growth of other related industries.

There is no denying the fact that growth has occurred. This is to be seen in the exponential growth experienced in most sectors of the IT industry in India: in domestic manufacturing and exports, in revenues earned, in the mushrooming of private and state-sponsored computer literacy programmes, in the steadily increasing number of software programmes – the largest in the world – and in the bewildering variety of IT-related magazines that are available. Let us have a look at some of the growth statistics.

1985–6	Rs.300 million
1986–7	Rs.450 million
1987–8	Rs.900 million
1988–9	Rs.2.6 billion
1995 (estimate)	Rs.15 billion

In the post-1980 period, the consumer electronics industry in India has witnessed 40 per cent growth, professional electronics 20 per cent growth and the components industry 17 per cent growth. Lakha (1990) gives us overall growth rates of the electronics industry in India:

1985	40.1 per cent
1986	30.1 per cent
1987	36.4 per cent

The total value of production in the electronics sector in 1987–8 was US$4065 million. The sales of the Indian computer industry, according to Singhal and Rogers (1989), were as follows:

1983–4	US$ 96 million
1986–7	US$270 million
1987–8	US$370 million

There was 60 per cent growth in the computer industry between 1984 and 1987 and its value rose from Rs.920 million to Rs.3750 million. To add to these growth statistics, Bhattacharjee (1989) has imputed a 40 per cent growth in data-processing equipment, 30 per cent growth in communications and broadcasting equipment and 30 per cent growth in aerospace and defence-related equipment – all over the past few years. To a large extent, these developments were aided by the state's liberalization of the IT industry. Starting with a Policy on Electronic Components (1981), Colhando (1989:25) notes the rapid attempts at deregulation through policy initiatives:

> After 1981, a series of policies were formulated in a rush towards the development of electronics, including computerisation: February 1983, industrial licensing policy for colour TV receiver sets; August 1983, measures to speed up electronics development; March 1984, manufacture of telecom equipment and relaxation from 100 per cent public sector manufacture; November 1984, new computer policy; March 1985, integrated policy measures in electronics; and November 1986, policy on computer software export, software development and training.

To this can be added a computer software policy, December 1987.

In the following sections, we will look at the fit between IT policy and practice, especially regarding the impact of exogenous capital on the Indian IT industry, and its consequence for labour in India.

The Myth of Self-reliance

Economic liberalization has led to a host of ventures with TNCs, both of western and Japanese origin. Computer hardware and software industries, the telecom industry and the industries involved in the manufacture of components and peripherals are all dependent on TNCs for technology transfer, R&D and expertise. The software industry in particular is saturated with joint projects. Most of the major software manufacturers have subsidiaries or have teamed up with local counterparts. Texas Instruments, Motorola, Ashton-Tate Inc., Cullinet Inc. and Lotus Development, amongst others, have established subsidiaries or joint partnerships in India. Joint ventures include Microsoft Corp. with Tata Unisys; Lotus Development Corp. with Computer Point India Ltd.; Oracle Corp. with Tata Consultancy Services; Digital Equipment Corp., Hinditron Computers and Wang Laboratories with Datamatics. Monopoly houses in India have been quick to cash in on the boom and a number of them, including the Tatas. Birlas, the TVS Group, Reliance, DCM, the JK Group, the Motwanis and other top private companies have got into joint ventures with TNCs for the manufacture of telecommunications equipment, computer peripherals, hardware and software.

As was pointed out in an earlier study (Thomas, 1988), conglomerates such as the Tatas and the Birlas have diversified into a number of media sectors. The Tatas, for example, have substantial interests in the press, computer and telecommunications hardware manufacturing, advertising and public relations, and the disc industry. And the Tatas have a virtual monopoly on software exports. In fact, out of the 150 firms involved in software manufacturing, Tata Unisys and Tata Consultancy Services account for 80 per cent of the software exports. In a situation characterized by natural monopolies and the politics of big business and the nexus with the state, this has resulted in a further concentration of ownership. Murdock (1990:2) has pointed out the nature of the relationship between ownership and the use of power:

> The potential control it bestows over production does not arise solely for specific exercises of power within the corporations directly owned or influenced. It is also a function of pre-existing and enduring asymmetries in the structure of particular markets or sectors, which deliver cumulative advantages to the leading corporations, and enables them to set the terms on which competitors or suppliers relate to them.

The state has provided a number of incentives to firms involved in IT manufacture, including the setting up of free trade zones, software parks, the dilution of MRTP and FERA[6] regulations and various other tax cuts. However, the state has not exactly given its support to local industry when it mattered. In fact, there have been cases where the state has actively discriminated against local industry in favour of an MNC. Vyasulu (1986) has reported the case of the state's bypassing of Bharat Electronics Ltd's proven capability for producing liquid display technology for Japanese technology. At other times, the state has used loans, such as the World Bank loan given in August 1987, for the importing of cables and other equipment that could have been manufactured locally (EPW, 1989). In some cases the wrong technology has been imported, as was the case of imported teletext kits from France costing Rs.31.1 million and including decoders, key-pads and interfacing cards (Telematics, 1989). It is in fact highly debatable whether the present IT scenario in India has led to any benefits for local R&D. In fact, there is a good case for the opposite opinion: that liberalization has led to increased dependence and the replication of the kit culture, minus substantial spinoffs, that have been the case in the Philippines, Malaysia, Thailand and other countries in South and South East Asia involved in IT production.

The import density of electronics and IT production is extremely high. It includes an import bias, not only for components, but also for raw materials used for the manufacture of products including silicon, germanium, electronic grade material, ferric oxides and ceramics, to the extent of 35 per cent of the produce. Tulpule (1986) and Mahalingam (1989) have both commented on the excessive import dependency of the Indian IT industries. The Ministry of Industry's 'BICP Report on the Computer Industry' (1987) quoted in Mahalingam (1989:2377), uncovers the extent of this dependency specifically in the computer industry:

> The BICP analysis reveals that the import-intensity in the bill of materials (including the indirect import components of the indigenously manufactured components) account for 83 per cent in the case of PCs, 84.6 per cent in PC-ATS, and 90.2 per cent in PC-XTS, exclusive of duties. In the case of peripherals, it is lowest in the case of switch mode power supply at 57.6 per cent of the bill of materials, but is as high as 93.6 per cent in a monochrome monitor.

The case of Tata Unisys's software is particularly illustrative of the nature of dependency. In this case, it is clear that the US-based parent company is in total control of the operations of its Indian subsidiary, so that Indian input has been merely in terms of skilled labour and very little else. The parent company, Unisys Ltd, provides the specifications for the development of software at TUL, supplies the skilled technical manpower, draws up planning sheets and project proposals and manages and oversees its Indian operations. As a result, there is very little domestic fallout and local industry does not benefit in any substantial manner. There is therefore a strong case for arguing that IT manufacture in India, under the aegis of the state and private capital, has become dependent on the international IT industry and its major players.

A Captive Labour Pool

The globalization of production and the emergent international divisions of labour have allowed for a repeat of colonial forms of relationships between the centre and the periphery, the main difference being that, unlike the situation in colonial times, when the centres provided finished goods and the peripheries provided raw materials, today the Centre provides both capital and knowledge and the peripheries provide a captive labour pool. IT production and manufacturing has allowed for a number of flexible work patterns that have had their impact on work, power and wage relationships. These include the employment of casual labour on an ever-increasing scale the world over, the segmentation of the IT labour market through the search for the cheapest markets with a steady supply of cheap labour (the US IT industry was the first to move their operations to more cost-effective regions – to Mexico in the early 1960s, to Southeast Asia in the 1970s and to South Asia in the 1980s), the de-unionization of labour, the exploitation of (particularly) female labour and maintaining a monopoly on vital knowledge on product design and plant layout, management and coordination.

Automation and the computerization of production have, in particular, affected labour in India. Mechanization and the computerization of heavy industries like mining (see Tulpule, 1986) have proved to be damaging to the interests of workers in these traditionally labour-intensive operations. An article by Singh (1990:115) on the mechanization of the Bhilai iron ore mines reveals that nearly 7000 workers and their families had been adversely affected by the process of large-scale mechanization. But he points out that this is merely a reflection of a trend: 'When the Rajhara section of the mines was earlier mechanised, the workforce came down from 3,500 to 500. And in the nearby Bailadilla iron-ore mines in Basta, 10,000 workers got the sack after machines took over.' The point that needs to be made is that, in a country like India, redeployment of labour, especially the unskilled and those in manual work, is just not possible in the event of large-scale deskilling through the deployment of mechanized, computerized forms of work activity. In fact, the logic of IT use is such that, although it does allow for the retraining and redeployment of skilled labour, it is just not cost-effective to retrain and redeploy the average worker.

New technologies, IT in particular, when adapted in a haphazard manner, without a careful assessment of the future implications of their use for both individuals and communities, may lead to social and familial disruption on a large scale, especially in labour-rich countries like India. It is a fact that, in India, the use of personal computers (PCs) has led to the replacement of people in white-collar menial work – clerks, for example, who are involved with payrolls, accounts and inventory control (see Patel, 1987). Indiscriminate introduction of automation, especially in traditionally labour-intensive industries, was a major concern and the need to control its use was a key recommendation of the Committee on Automation's report submitted to the Indian government in 1972. The Committee's recommendations are still valid today. They include the following:

> a) computerisation and automation should not be adopted just because the technology and hardware are available but only if and when specific needs and justifications for them exist, b) the justification should be subject to check by an agency independent of the enterprise seeking to automate, c) the impact of automation on the employees of the enterprise should be given the most serious attention, and introduction of automation should be subject to agreement with the union of the employees.

Studies on the sociology of labour in the IT industries (Ernst, 1986; Gothoskar, 1986; Tulpule, 1986; Lim, 1981; Mitter, 1984; Yue, 1986, amongst others) have shown that, increasingly, NICs go in for joint deals with TNCs based on an agreement that guarantees exports in return for the provision of a de-unionized labour supply. The pawning of indigenous industrial capacity to the MNCs has been complemented by the pawning of Indian labour to the dictates of the MNCs. Unlike labour employed in traditional industrial sectors, who have both job security and the protection of unions, part-time labour used in IT assembly does not belong to unions or have any kind of job security. TNCs employ labour, especially women, with infinite restrictions on their unionizing. In a study done at the Santa Cruz Electronic Export Processing Zone (SEEPZ),[7] Bombay (Gothoskar, 1986), it was shown that 91 per cent of the workforce at SEEPZ were women, of whom 70 per cent were unmarried and between the ages of 19 and 27. Their average monthly salary was Rs.500 – a paltry sum considering the expenses involved in living in a big city in India. It has also been reported that attempts at unionization at SEEPZ have been crushed and there have been cases of the 'disappearances' of trouble-makers. Lim (1981:183), reporting on the situation of female labour in IT industries in South East Asia, points out some of the features of the state's compromise with transnational capital:

> to guarantee low wages and labour stability, restrictive labour legislation has been introduced, in many cases prohibiting labour organisation, unionisation, strikes and other actions in multinational subsidiaries. To permit the employment of women on night shifts, 'protective' labour legislation has been removed. The 'political stability and labour docility' required of multinational investors has been provided by a variety of politically repressive measures.

Subcontracting, deskilling and the de-unionization of labour are characteristic elements affecting the political economy of IT production in India. Its cultural and social consequences, including the disruption of normal family life, frequent health problems due to the handling of hazardous substances, the lack of employment tenure, little scope for internal mobility and sexual exploitation at work have been high prices to pay for the insecurity of barely sustainable wages.

The IT industry does impose certain definite patterns of work and relationships. It provides an ideology of life and work. And, taken in its entirety, it is related to the larger dynamics of power and control in society. Although IT promises choice, access and control, in reality, deregulation and privatization help consolidate the power of those who are already economically and politically dominant. The products of the IT industry have more than economic value – they shape the general consciousness of society. Unless the IT industry is adapted to local needs and unless it is integrated with the sociocultural environment and based on cultural coherence, there is no doubt that the gap between the information-rich and poor will continue to grow.

Conclusion

In the preceding pages, we have tried to study the relationship between the state and the IT industry specifically within the determinants of monopoly capitalism. In its economic as well as political manifestation, the state in India has moved away from its earlier commitment to growth and distribution and the pursuance of equitable development, based on justice and freedom for minorities and the dispossessed in Indian society. Instead, through its use of both coercion and consensus, it has tried to impose a structure and ideology of development that is fundamentally unable to include the mass of people within its purview.[8] In fact, one may conjecture that the moves by the State to develop and expand the IT industry are yet another cynical attempt to consolidate the power of state monopoly capital and its allies at the expense of the Indian people.

There is no reason to believe that IT will solve the country's myriad problems. IT does of course have its benefits, but the question that needs to be asked and answered by policy makers is: How can the use of IT lead to the equitable development of the nation? At present, the benefits of the IT revolution accrue to a small percentage of the overall population. Needless to say, the beneficiaries are those who are already information-rich. The Indian state has deep-rooted structural problems. These have to be dealt with and changes need to be made, either simultaneously with changes in the IT environment or prior to its large-scale induction. Land distribution, a reassertion of state involvement in the production and distribution of essential services and the participatory approach to development are essential concomitants to the success of the IT revolution. Today, more than ever before, the unity of the nation is in danger of being eroded through the cynical manipulation of the masses by politicians and unscrupulous power brokers. The growth of the Baratiya Janata Party (BJP) and its alliance with right-wing Hindu groups and causes, the resurgence of militant Hindu nationalism supported by sections of the media, and the very fragility of the ruling coalition are symptoms of a struggle, a 'war of position' within the ruling bloc.

However, despite the reality of the crisis affecting the Indian state, a number of groups in India, based in rural and urban areas, working with women, the landless and other oppressed sections of the Indian population, have attempted to counter the dominant cultural and economic hegemony of the state and to replace it with counter-hegemonies that are based on the aspirations, local–specific needs and the strength of underlying consciousness. The media have been used by these groups in their struggles. These include traditional media like the popular theatre and folk theatre, and interactive media like video. IT has not been used to any great extent by these groups, partly because of the costs involved, but PCs have been used by a number of groups in the NGO sector as a basis for documentation of people's struggles, underlying history and culture and vital political, legal and economic information pertaining to people's struggles. It has also been used for networking, although on a smaller scale.

There have not been, as yet, any concerted moves by the general public to influence the state's communication or information policies. Although there have been commissions in the past that have specifically addressed issues related to the structure and functioning of the public media – for example, the Chanda Commission (1965), the Verghese Commission (1978) and the Joshi Commission (1981) – their recommendations have not generally been heeded by the state, nor have they been made the bases for informed policy making. There is as yet no indication that the Prashar Bharathi Bill on media autonomy will actually lead to the freeing of public media structures from the control of the state as a step towards a form of community control of public services. There is a need for an informed IT policy, a policy that allows for people's access, education and use of IT. Such a policy must, however, be based on the understanding that information is but an input to development, that its success is dependent upon basic structural changes in the political economy of the country.

Notes

1 Both Chenoy (1985) and Ghosh (1983) have commented on the initial vacillations of local industrialists vis-à-vis the Swadeshi movement and their later accommodations. The Bombay Plan, also called 'A Plan for Economic Development of India' (1944), drawn up by J.R.D. Tata and G.D. Birla, supported private enterprise and state support for protectionist policies to stave off exogenous competition.
2 Bhalla (1989), in a study on employment in Indian agriculture, has noted the cumulative growth rate of casual wage labour and the decreasing land–man ratio over the last few years.
3 See Thomas (1987) for an analysis of the use of the media by the state, especially in the aftermath of Mrs Gandhi's assassination.
4 SITE was conducted between August 1975 and July 1976 and its footprint covered 2330 villages in six Indian states. One of its more interesting by-products was the Kheda Experiment, which arguably is the most progressive communication for development project organized to date by the state in India. Unfortunately, the project has been

discontinued and the transmitter has been shifted to Madras to strengthen reception of the second television channel.

5 See Samal (1988) and a report in the *Financial Times* by K.K. Sharma (25 July 1990, p.3) for information on joint ventures between the state and private capital.

6 The Monopolies and Restrictive Trade Practices Act and the Foreign Exchange Regulations Act (MRTP and FERA) were meant to control concentration in industry and conserve foreign exchange.

7 As written in the *World Communication Report* (Unesco, 1989, p.96), SEEPZ 'offers export manufacturers a five-year tax exemption, guaranteed power supplies, compulsory conciliation of trade disputes and duty-free import of equipment and materials. Forty per cent of the zone's exports go to Asia, 38 per cent to North America, 13 per cent to Eastern Europe and 7 per cent to Western Europe. SEEPZ has around 60 firms, half of them collaborating with foreign companies, mainly American.'

8 Gramsci (1975, quoted in Mouffe, 1981:232) has commented on the ideological significance of state policies like national integration and nationalism: 'the particular form in which the hegemonic ethico-political element presents itself in the life of the state and the country is "patriotism" and "nationalism" which is "popular religion", that is to say, it is the link by means of which the unity of leaders and led is effected.'

Bibliography

Arnold, D. (1984), 'Gramsci and Peasant Subalternity in India', *The Journal of Peasant Studies*, **11**, (4), July, 155–77.

Bardhan, P. (1984), *The Political Economy of Development in India*, London: Basil Blackwell.

Basu, S. (1988), 'State and Industrialisation in a Post-Colonial Capitalist Economy – The Experience of India', *Economic and Political Weekly*, 23 January, 143–50.

Bhalla, S. (1989), 'Employment in Indian Agriculture: Retrospect and Prospect', *Social Scientist*, **17**, (5–6), May–June, 3–21.

Bhattacharjee, A. (1989), 'After the Boom, the Budget Blues', *Telematics India*, April, 46–8.

Bhattacharjee, A. and K. Colhando (1989), 'Telecom Boom – India's Humming Lines', *Telematics India*, October, 66–70.

Buci-Glucksmann, C. (1980), *Gramsci and the State*, trans. D. Fernback, London: Lawrence & Wishart.

Carnoy, M. (1984), *The State and Political Theory*, Princeton, NJ: Princeton University Press.

Chenoy, K.M. (1985), 'Industrial Policy and Multinationals in India', *Social Scientist*, **13**, (3), March, 15–31.

Colhando, K. (1989), 'The Helpful Hand of Government Policies', *Telematics India*, April, 25.

Ernst, D. (1986), 'New Information Technologies and Developing Countries – Implications for Human Resources Development', *Economic and Political Weekly*, **XXI**, (35), 30 August, pp. M-103–M-108.

Femia, J.V. (1981), *Gramsci's Political Thought: Hegemony, Consciousness and Revolutionary Process*, Oxford: Clarendon Press.

Frankel, F.R. (1971), *India's Green Revolution – Economic Gains and Political Costs*, Princeton, NJ: Princeton University Press.
Frankel, F.R. (1978), *India's Political-Economy – 1947–77*, Princeton, NJ: Princeton University Press.
Gaur, K.D. (1988), *Law of International Telecommunications in India*, Baden-Baden: Nomos Verlagsgesellschaft.
Ghorpade, S. (1986), 'Retrospect and Prospect: The Information Environment and Policy in India', *Gazette*, **38**, 5–28.
Ghosh, S.K. (1983), 'The Indian Bourgeoisie and Imperialism', *Bulletin of Concerned Asian Scholars*, **15**, (3), 2–16.
Gothoskar, S. (1986), 'Free Trade Zones: Pitting Women Against Women', *Economic and Political Weekly*, **XXI**, (34), 23 August, 1489–92.
Gramsci, A. (1958), *Studi Gramscini*, ed. A. Riuniti, Rome: Instituto Gramsci.
Gramsci, A. (1975), *Quadernidal Carcere*, ed. V. Gerratana, Turin: Einaudi.
Guha, R. (ed.) (1982), *Subaltern Studies I*, Delhi: Oxford University Press.
Hall, S. (1985), 'Signification, Representation, Ideology: Althusser and Post-Structuralist Debates', *Critical Studies in Mass Communication*, **2**, 91–114.
Hardgrave, R.L. (1970), *India: Government and Politics in a Developing Nation*, New York: Harcourt.
Held, D., J. Anderson, B. Gieben, S. Hall, L. Harris, P. Lewis, N. Parker and B. Turok (eds) (1983), *States and Societies*, Oxford: Basil Blackwell/Oxford University Press.
Ilchman, W.F. (1967), 'A Political Economy of Foreign Aid: The Case of India', *Asian Survey*, **7**, (10).
Jha, S. (1980), *India – A Political Economy of Starvation*, Bombay: Oxford University Press.
Kaviraj, S. (1984), 'On the Crisis of Political Institutions in India', *Contributions to Indian Sociology*, **18**, (2).
Kaviraj, S. (1986), 'Indira Gandhi and Indian Politics', *Economic and Political Weekly*, **XXI**, (38, 39), 20–27 September, 1697–1708.
Kaviraj, S. (1988), 'A Critique of the Passive Revolution', *Economic and Political Weekly*, **XXIII**, (45, 46, 47), Special Number, November, 2429–44.
Kothari, R. (1970), *Politics in India*, Delhi: Orient Longman.
Kothari, R. (1983), 'The Crisis of the Moderate State and the Decline of Democracy', in P. Lyons and J. Manor (eds), *Transfer and Transformation – Political Institutions in the New Commonwealth*, Leicester: Leicester University Press.
Kurien, C.T. (1987), 'Planning and the Institutional Transformation of the Indian Economy', *Social Scientist*, **15**, (7), July, 3–29.
Kurien, K.M. (ed.) (1975), *India – State and Society*, Madras: Orient Longman.
Lakha, S. (1990), 'Growth of Computer Software Industry in India', *Economic and Political Weekly*, **XXV**, (1), 6 January, 49–56.
Lim, L.Y.C. (1981), 'Women's Work in Multinational Electronics Factories', in R. Dauber and M.L. Cain (eds), *Women and Technological Change in Developing Societies*, Boulder, Colo: Westview Press.
Mahalingam, S. (1989), 'Computer Industry in India – Strategies for Late Comer Entry', *Economic and Political Weekly*, **XXIV**, (42), 21 October, 2375–84.

Menon, V. (1989), 'The Case of India', in M. Jussawalla, T. Okuma and T. Araki *et al.* (eds), *Information, Technology and Global Interdependence*, New York: Greenwood Press.

Menscher, J.P. (1978), *Agriculture and Social Structure in Tamil Nadu*, New Delhi: Allied Publishers Ltd.

Mitter, S. (1984), 'On the Global Assembly Line – Women and Multinationals', *Development*, 31–3.

Mody, B. (1986), 'How Third World Countries Make Satellite Adoption Decisions', *Telecommunications for Development: Exploring New Strategies*, international forum, 28 October, sponsored by INTELSAT, New York University.

Morris-Jones, W.H. (1971), *The Government and Politics of India*, Bombay: BI Publishers.

Mouffe, C. (1981), 'Hegemony and Ideology in Gramsci', in Bennett *et al.* (eds), *Culture, Ideology and Social Process*, Milton Keynes: Open University Press.

Murdock, G. (1990), 'Redrawing the Map of the Communications Industries: Concentration and Ownership in the Era of Privatisation', in M. Ferguson (ed.), *Public Communication: The New Imperatives – Future Directions for Media Research*, London/Newbury Park/Delhi: Sage Publications.

Murdock, G. and P. Golding (1989), 'Information Poverty and Political Inequality: Citizenship in the Age of Privatised Communications', *Journal of Communications*, **39**, (3), Summer, 180–95.

Murphy, B. (1983), *The World Wired Up: Unscrambling the New Communications Puzzle*, London: Comedia Publishing Group.

Omvedt, B. (1975), 'The Political Economy of Starvation', *Race and Class*, **17**, (2).

Omvedt, B. (1982), 'India, the IMF and Imperialism Today', *Journal of Contemporary Asia*, **12**, (2).

Pantham, T. (1980), 'Political Culture, Political Structure and Underdevelopment in India', *Indian Journal of Political Science*, **41**, (3).

Patel, S.B. (1987), 'Software Policy: Westward Ho', *Economic and Political Weekly*, **XXII**, (24), June, 956–8.

Patnaik, A.K. (1988), 'Gramsci's Concept of Common Sense – Towards a Theory of Subaltern Consciousness in Hegemony Processes', *Economic and Political Weekly*, Special Issue on Gramsci, 30 January, pp.PE-2–PE-10.

Poulantzas, N. (1978), *Political Power and Social Classes*, London: Verso.

Saberwal, S. (1986), *India: The Roots of Crisis*, Delhi: Oxford University Press.

Samal, K. (1988), 'Case Against Privatisation', *Mainstream*, **XXVI**, (40), 16 July, 25–8.

Sanyal, K.K. (1988), 'Accumulation, Poverty and State in Third World – Capital/Pre-Capital Complex', *Economic and Political Weekly*, 30 January, pp.PE-27–PE-30.

Singh, J. (1988), 'Beleaguered State', *Seminar*, **345**, May, 14–19.

Singh, N.K. (1990), 'Short on Ore – Crisis over Mechanisation', *India Today*, 15 May, p.115.

Singhal, A. and E. Rogers (1989), *India's Information Revolution*, New Delhi: Sage Publications.

Thomas, P.N. (1987), 'The State in India and Its Media: The Dialectics of an Unholy Alliance', *Communication Socialis*, VI, 1010–14.

Thomas, P.N. (1988), 'State Monopoly Capitalism and the Media in India: The Unfolding Scenario', *ICCTR Journal*, 1, (1), 22–37.

Tilley, L. (1990), 'A Passage to India', *Financial Times*, 17 May, p.36.

Tulpule, B. (1986), 'Computers, Industrial Development and Workers', *Economic and Political Weekly*, XXI, (48), 29 November, pp.M-110–M-114.

Vyasulu, V. in collaboration with A. Jauhari, S. Rangarajan, S. Pant and S. Bagga (1986), 'Destruction of Indian Research and Development: Case of Liquid Crystal Display of Technology', *Economic and Political Weekly*, XXI, (44 & 45), 1–8 November, 1935–6.

World Communication Report (1989), Unesco.

Yadav, Y. (1990), 'Theories of the Indian State', *Seminar*, 367, March, 16–20.

Yue, L.W. (1986), 'The Dark Side of Industrialisation', *Multinational Monitor*, October, 22–3.

7 Administering Electronics: the Experience of India and Brazil

Jørgen Dige Pedersen

Introduction

The revolutionary changes implied by the 'electronic revolution' pose major challenges to countries in the third world. On the one hand, the spread of new production methods in all fields of industry puts increasing pressure on already established industrial strongholds of the more advanced developing countries. The rapid changes and high rate of obsolescence that characterize the new industrial technologies further intensify this pressure. On the other hand, the new technoeconomic paradigm underlying the new economic dynamism has shifted the strategic centre of industry towards the electronic industries in particular, but also towards other R&D-intensive industries like involving new materials and biotechnology.

While these economic changes pose problems for all countries, developing countries face particularly severe problems, for a number of reasons. The general lack of capital and of technological capabilities makes it extremely difficult for these countries to keep up in the technological race, and most developing countries will never attempt to get into the race precisely for that reason. For others, who until now have been able to advance industrially and who aspire to continue in the race, additional problems have emerged, in particular problems of state management of economic development. One problem concerns the management of the relations with those external actors – transnational corporations (TNCs) based in the most advanced developed countries – that increasingly monopolize the new core technologies. Another problem concerns the domestic introduction of the new technologies in societies so different from the ones in which the technologies emerged. Both types of problem point towards the crucial role of the state in developing countries as the key manager of economic change. Can states that in part were successful in transforming their countries industrially under the 'old model' repeat this performance under new circumstances? Is the traditional structure and functioning of the state compatible with new demands of intensive management on the external front as well as on the domestic front? If not, what then are the required changes in the functioning and organization of the state for successful management of the new challenges? These are the questions which this chapter tries to address.

We start by considering some theoretical issues of a more general nature which are then expanded and made specific in order to relate them to the problems faced by developing countries. The main section of the chapter then analyses and compares two third world states struggling to manage the new challenges within the electronics/computer sector – India and Brazil. On the basis of these two case studies, an attempt is made, finally, to specify some preliminary conclusions with regard to the role of public administration in the management of technological development.

Some Theoretical Considerations

Three main theoretical sources of inspiration provide the framework for the discussion in this chapter. A main source of inspiration comes from what has been called the 'French Regulation School' and its theoretical work on the changes in the advanced capitalist economies from 'Fordism' to 'Post-Fordism'. A second, and closely related source is the recent debate on the implications of the new and emerging technologies grouped under the heading of 'flexible specialization'. And, finally, these theoretical strands are combined with and extended by Weberian theories on the role of public administration in capitalist development and considerations on the specific economic role played by the state in the economic development of countries in the Third World.

The French Regulation School has been concerned with the structural changes in the economies of the western world during the 20th century and the accompanying systems of social and economic regulation (Aglietta, 1979; Lipietz, 1987). Basically, these theories argue that there exist various distinct modes of capitalist growth termed 'regimes of accumulation', each accompanied by a specific 'mode of regulation' that provides a certain degree of stability to the otherwise contradictory and inherently unstable national economic systems. The prime example is the transformation to 'Fordism': a regime of accumulation characterized by industrial mass-production and a mode of regulation comprising the central institutions of the Keynesian interventionist welfare state that ensure a mass-consumption market. This Fordist mode of development has, from the 1970s onwards, been in crisis, the way out of which is seen in the transformation to a not yet fully defined 'Post-Fordist' regime of accumulation (for an overview, see Jessop, 1990b). While acknowledging the unique role played by the state in social and economic regulation, most work done by the regulation theorists has concentrated on economic issues neglecting the closer analysis of the state (Jessop, 1990a;315ff; 1990b:196–200). There is, however, nothing inherent in the regulation approach that excludes considerations on the state, on the importance of different forms of the state for the mode of regulation and eventually for the regime of accumulation.[1] It would therefore seem fruitful to extend further the analysis of the connections between the economic structures and the regulatory mechanisms to include also an investigation of the administrative and political institutions involved in these regulatory practices.[2] Before this is considered further, another supplement to the regulationist approach should be considered.

This theoretical addition mainly concerns the specification of the continuing changes in the economic sphere. According to some theorists, the development and diffusion of new production technologies based on the use of microelectronics can be interpreted as marking a significant transformation away from the old 'technoeconomic paradigm' (Perez, 1985) of mass-production based on electromechanical techniques towards a new paradigm of what has been termed 'flexible specialization' (Piore and Sabel, 1984) or 'systemofacture' (Kaplinsky, 1989). These theories are clearly inspired by and conveniently fit into the concern of the regulationist school theories with the development of a new 'Post-Fordist' regime of accumulation (Kaplinsky, 1989; Perez, 1985; for a polemic/critical review, see Hirst and Zeitlin, 1991). In some of these theories, a claim comparable to that of the regulation theorists on the important implications of the economic and technological changes for the 'socioinstitutional' framework including the regulation of markets, the separation between public and private responsibilities and their interrelations, the structure of the educational system and broad features of international economic relations has also been made (Perez, 1985:445–6). The electronics industry (especially when combined with the telecommunication infrastructure – the 'informatics industry') has in this perspective been regarded as the future economic core sector of this new era. Flexibility, information intensity, creativity, decentralization and the absence of hierarchy are some of the most important organizational consequences accompanying this change in production structure that are visualized in these theories (Perez, 1985).

While the theories outlined above have their main focus on the changes in the nature of the production processes and only pay limited attention to the broader social consequences, it would be useful to extend the argument to include also the political and administrative arrangements that reflect upon and are affected by the economic changes. A starting point for such considerations can be found in the classical work of Max Weber on the proper administrative form for capitalist societies and its extension in more recent theories. For Max Weber, the optimal form of administration in a capitalist society was 'bureaucracy', a legal–rational 'administrative machine' that, organized in a hierarchical structure, worked in a calculable, predictable, impartial and dispassionate manner, staffed by technically competent and carefully selected personnel (Weber, 1978:956–1005). Furthermore, for the optimal working of this kind of administration, the existence of some external controls was considered essential in order to avoid unguided bureaucratic actions. These controls, according to Weber, could best be provided by an effectively working Parliament, consisting of 'able politicians', and the existence of such controls would be particularly important should the bureaucracy engage itself in the direct management of economic enterprises (Weber, 1978:1456). The parliamentary committees in which the working of the administration could come under close scrutiny would thus be a crucial feature of a democratically organized state and, together with the budgetary prerogatives, they would constitute the most important means of parliamentary control over the executive (Weber, 1978:1381–1469). It is interesting to note that, contrary to much recent theorizing on the prerequisites for the strong developmental states (see *IDS Bulletin*, 1984), Weber does not visualize an 'insulated' or 'autonomous' state as being the optimal regulatory structure for a capitalist economy. On the contrary, he repeatedly stresses the negative features of an insulated bureaucracy, free and unhindered by outside forces.

In a periodization of capitalist development in specific phases in the style of the French regulationists, it is possible to regard Weber's ideal model of bureaucracy as reflecting the structure of an early capitalist epoch characterized by a non-interventionist state and a free (competitive) market economy. Following Göran Therborn, it can then be argued that, in addition to the legal–rational mode of administrative functioning, at a later stage there has emerged within the state what he terms a 'managerial–technocratic' mode of functioning required by the expansion of public interventions in an increasingly complex and thoroughly regulated (Fordist) economy (Therborn, 1978:49–63, 87–97). (The archetypical example of this would probably be the socioeconomic planners.) From this perspective, it becomes important to inquire whether a full transition to a new phase of Post-Fordism, or flexible specialization, in the wake of the microelectronic innovations will in the same manner require changes in the administrative and political arrangements needed for the regulation of this transition and for the stabilization of its working.

The considerations on the political and administrative requirements of the new technoeconomic paradigm, furthermore, become of special importance in the case of developing countries where the role of the state is of substantial importance in the overall regulation of the economy. As an initiator, protector and regulator of economic change, the state in developing countries will not only act as an 'outsider' intervening in the economic processes, but will usually also be a key participant in these changes. This crucial role that is forced upon the state because the new 'technoeconomic paradigm' in these countries not only has to be regulated, but also has to be introduced, makes it plausible to argue that the political and administrative structures will be of extreme importance for a successful regulation.

To sum up, the new opportunities for renewed economic growth promised by the microelectronic innovations and the vision of a new, emerging 'technoeconomic' paradigm pose the question whether the existing socioinstitutional arrangements have to be transformed in order for these potentials to be fully realized and a new stable 'mode of development' established. According to the theories outlined above, this is precisely what should be expected, but until now very little empirical research has been done in this area. This may be due to the fact that most discussions on the subject of the implications of the economic changes have been concerned with the consequences in the advanced capitalist countries, but it would appear fruitful from both a theoretical and an empirical perspective to inquire more closely into the political and administrative repercussions in those developing countries that have tried to take advantage of the opportunities offered by the microelectronic revolution.

Managing 'the Electronics Revolution': the Experience of India and Brazil

The microelectronic revolution has placed developing countries in a fundamental dilemma. On the one hand, as with any other branch of industry, developing countries face the problem of overcoming dependency; that is, the problem of creating a domestically controlled electronics-producing industry and obtaining the ability to master and subsequently develop appropriate related technologies. On the other hand, and to some extent in contradiction with the first objective, developing countries face the problem of optimal utilization of the new technologies in all productive spheres. Choosing to tackle the problem of dependency will often involve a delay in the introduction of the new technologies, while deciding to import and disseminate new technologies may preclude the emergence of an indigenous, self-reliant electronics industry. Furthermore, this fundamental dilemma can be expected to surface in the domestic struggle of diverse economic interests over the course of actual policies regulating the industry. The issue then becomes one of performing a balancing act between the pursuance of self-reliance, on the one hand, and the unrestricted import and dissemination of new technologies and new electronic products, on the other.

Achievements

India and Brazil have made remarkable progress in electronics. In the early 1970s, both countries took their first steps towards the creation of an indigenous computer industry, and by the end of the 1980s both were in possession of a thriving national computer industry producing various types of hardware and, in addition, both had growing software industries. In the late 1980s, there were around 40 companies in India producing some 60 000 personal computers annually (Bowonder and Mani, 1991:M7). In 1989, Brazil had more than 300 national companies operating in the computer and peripherals market, and probably more than 50 in computers alone (Schwartzman, 1988:71), generating sales of over US$3.6 billion, up from US$1.5 billion three years earlier (*IHT*, 10 July 1990; Schmitz and Hewitt, 1989:3). While the Brazilian market for electronics in general and computers in particular has been much larger than the Indian market, during the 1980s the rate of growth of the Indian market and of the production of the Indian computer industry has been somewhat higher.[3] In addition, Brazil has obtained a significant, though of late somewhat stagnating, volume of exports of computers, while India still only has a marginal, though rapidly increasing, export market (Report, 1990:319; Evans and Tigre, 1989a:14).[4] In software, India seems to be ahead of Brazil, at least with regard to exports. Indian exports of software expanded dramatically from the late 1980s onwards, while Brazil so far has not made any significant impact in the export markets.

While these achievements in broad terms seem quite impressive, a closer inspection reveals some more disturbing features, especially with regard to the continuing dependence on foreign suppliers of technology, the inability to produce more advanced computers, the dependence on the importing of components and key raw materials and the dependence on the marketing channels of foreign companies when exporting. Despite successful efforts in developing a domestic software industry, there still exists a considerable dependence in this area as well, especially with regard to standard application software (see notes 6 and 8). A recent threat to the Indian industry comes from the growing practice of foreign companies recruiting software engineers from India, thus depriving the country of much of its best manpower (Lakha, 1990). And in Brazil the precarious financial situation makes it difficult to expand public computer education and increase funds for research and development.

Despite the persistence of various forms of dependency, it must be acknowledged that both countries have achieved a degree of self-reliance and a level of capabilities within the electronics/computer sector that only very few other developing countries can match.[5] These achievements may not protect the national electronics industry from sliding backwards into higher degrees of dependency in the future, but they have provided both countries with a much better bargaining position and a capacity to choose between a range of alternatives in negotiations with technology suppliers (Schmitz and Hewitt, 1990:21). An example of this is the remarkable willingness of large international computer companies to enter into collaboration agreements with local firms in both countries from the mid-1980s onwards (Schmitz and Hewitt, 1989:22; *India Today*, 31 March 1988; Bowonder and Mani, 1991:M10).

Explanations

Explanations of these in many ways impressive achievements in a crucial high-tech industry have generally focused on two sets of important factors: (1) the institutional arrangements within which key groups of social actors have promoted their vision of an appropriate public policy for encouraging the industry, and (2) the particular external circumstances conducive to the successful implementation of the strategy – internationally as well as in the domestic arena (see references in notes 6 and 8). As regards the first set of explanatory factors, it has been pointed out that in both countries a dedicated and highly motivated group of technically competent persons with a strong nationalistic orientation succeeded in penetrating the state apparatus, creating new, strong institutions and through these initiating a process of support for the establishment of a domestic computer industry. Through an intricate process of 'bureaucratic politics', contesting strategies were fought over, modulated and subsequently implemented, leading to the creation of a vigorous domestic industry.

With regard to the second set of factors, it has been pointed out that international opportunities presented themselves through the rapid technological developments in the field and the presence (initially) of a large number of companies willing to share their technological know-how, at a manageable price, with emerging companies in developing countries (Grieco, 1984:ch.3). Domestically, it has been pointed out that the strength, capabilities and orientation of local companies vis-à-vis foreign companies within the sector influenced the strategies and instruments used by the two states and shaped the final outcome.

Strategies, Instruments and Phasing

A closer look at the strategies, the instruments and the phasing of policies reveals some interesting parallels as well as important differences between the two countries. In India, the idea of establishing a domestic computer industry emerged in the 1960s, following the war with China, but it was only in the early 1970s that serious actions were initiated. A separate Department of Electronics was set up in December 1970 under the supervision of a high-level Electronics Commission established shortly after (in February 1971), both with direct reference to the prime minister.[6] The department and the commission were largely staffed by nationalistic, technically educated officials from the research community (the 'network') centred upon the influential Atomic Energy Commission. These specialized scientists, eager to develop an indigenous capability in electronics, thus emerged as winners in the dispute with the military establishment located in the Ministry of Defence, which was more inclined to establish international links in order to get access to the most advanced technologies and, besides, favoured the expansion of their own state-run electronics company. In the staffing procedures the department, because of the perceived technical nature of its tasks, was to some extent exempted from normal regulations, a fact that must have caused some annoyance within the established bureaucracy (Grieco, 1984:119).

The strategy mapped out by the new institutions was largely one of challenging the then dominant position of foreign producers of computers (IBM and ICL) by promoting a 'national champion' in the form of the state-owned Electronics Corporation of India Limited (ECIL). During the 1970s, ECIL succeeded in manufacturing its own computers, based on access to foreign technology and, assisted by import restrictions in combination with restrictions on the activities of, primarily, IBM, the company also managed to sell some of them. In addition, a separate state-owned Computer Maintenance Corporation (CMC) was established to service the plethora of different (imported or locally produced) non-ECIL computers, primarily IBMs. When, in 1978, IBM withdrew from the Indian market in protest against the enforcement of the general rules on foreign ownership of companies, it seemed that the strategy had succeeded, in the sense that ECIL (with CMC) now had a good chance of securing complete dominance over the Indian market.

The forces that prevented this from materializing came from sections of local private capital eager to enter the computer industry, as well as from customers (private and public) dissatisfied with ECIL's services and products. As a result of these pressures, policies were changed, allowing selected private companies to enter the market for microcomputers. At the same time the administration of the electronics/computer policy was re-evaluated by an official commission, the 'network' was broken up and the bureaucracy obtained a much firmer grip on the affairs of the Department of Electronics through the establishment of an interdepartmental committee to coordinate policies and through the replacement of former key officials in the department.[7] Following upon this reorganization, the computer policy in the first half of the 1980s underwent a significant liberalization (BICP, 1988:21ff). Licensing conditions were relaxed, as were import restrictions, and as a result the private companies that had entered the industry in the late 1970s were joined by several newcomers. All new entrants based their products on imported technology obtained through extensive collaboration agreements with different foreign companies (not including IBM), imported components and only modest attempts at local technological development (BICP, 1988; Bowonder and Mani, 1991). By the end of the 1980s, the computer market was bifurcated, with the market for smaller computers crowded with a substantial number of local private companies assembling computers from imported components, technically assisted by foreign collaboration agreements. The much smaller market for larger mainframe computers was shared by the state-owned ECIL plus a private company affiliated to the (then) British company, ICL.

In software, gains were considerable. Using the huge pool of educated, cheap and English-speaking manpower available in India, a number of software producers emerged, assisted by an increasingly liberal policy that from 1986 allowed free import of necessary hardware to exporters and liberal access for foreign investors. In partial contrast to the hardware industry, the software industry became dominated by companies belonging to large industrial houses (in particular Tata) and the industry has been strongly export-oriented, establishing close links with US companies and with the US market (Lakha, 1990). While large private companies dominate the export of software tailored to customer requirements, larger independent consultancy tasks in the nature of system construction have lately been taken up quite successfully by the state-owned companies, primarily by CMC, but also by ECIL (Evans, 1990). Finally, in the field of more advanced computer research, India has maintained its aspiration to stay in the absolute front line with state-funded research projects in supercomputers and other fields of advanced technology (DoE, 1989).

From the initial strategy of promoting a 'national champion' in hardware (and some software applications), the new strategy that has emerged as a result of incremental policy changes during the 1980s appears to be one of adapting to conditions on the world market by de facto giving up ambitions to develop a wholly indigenous industry capable of operating internationally in the highly competitive sector of small computers and in standard software, relying instead on extensive foreign collaborations in order to satisfy domestic demands. By contrast, efforts have been concentrated in more advanced software applications, to some extent in larger computer systems and in basic research – all areas where competition is based to a lesser degree on manufacturing capabilities and more on technological expertise and human intellectual skills. The export strategy has centred on software exports through collaboration with international companies: witness the collaboration of the largest software exporter, Tata, with the American company Unisys (Lakha, 1990). The activities of the state became confined to the production of research-intensive products, pursuance of costly basic research and the provision of skilled personnel through the educational system. As a new ingredient in the overall computer policy, the Indian state has recently attempted, through the marketing of a range of low-cost personal computers by the state-owned Electronics Trade & Technology Development Corporation, to stimulate demand while at the same time ensuring a certain level of competition in the market for personal computers (*India Today*, 31 December 1989; Bowonder and Mani, 1991:M10).

More generally, the strategy worked out by the Indian state can be interpreted as a particular solution to the fundamental dilemma of developing countries outlined above: in order to ensure the spread of computer technologies, the markets for smaller computers have been entrusted to private companies, complemented recently by selective state interventions aimed at ensuring a competitive environment and low prices. This has effectively meant the abandonment of the goal of total self-reliance. Some measure of self-reliance is, however, still being pursued through state activities in the less competitive and technologically more advanced sectors mentioned above and through various fiscal arrangements aimed at promoting local supply of peripherals and components.

Comparing this development with the evolution of the electronics/computer industry in Brazil, one is struck by the apparent similarities in policies and instruments, as well as in the timing of the strategies. Important differences, however, remain. As in India, the first serious initiatives in Brazil to develop an indigenous computer industry were undertaken in the early 1970s. At that time, Brazil was in the middle of an economic boom, making the country an extremely attractive market for foreign companies. The computer requirements of the country were largely served by imports and by local production of subsidiaries of foreign companies, primarily IBM.[8] A fusion of a group of 'frustrated nationalist technicians' (Evans, 1986), all experienced in electronics, with some 'developmental nationalist' segments of the state apparatus, especially the National Economic Development Bank (BNDE), provided the nucleus of what were later called the 'ideological guerrillas' (Adler, 1986; 1987), a group of highly committed individuals who, because of crucial support from within the military establishment (the Navy in particular) in the early 1970s, were able to create and staff new public institutions with the ambition of providing Brazil with an independent local computer industry. In 1972, a special commission for coordinating efforts in data processing (CAPRE) was created under the Planning Ministry and two years later a state-owned company (COBRA) was set up to undertake the development and manufacturing of smaller computers.[9] In 1975, CAPRE was given the authority to regulate all imports of computers and computer-related items, which de facto meant complete control over the development of the local computer industry. In 1976, a dual computer policy was devised: in the market for larger computers, considerations of efficiency and optimal utilization of resources were to prevail, which in reality meant leaving this segment to the multinational corporations (IBM and others). In the market for smaller computers and peripherals, presumably with technologies easier to master, a policy of fostering national productive capabilities was given high priority. At the same time, CAPRE was authorized to control all purchases (and rentals and so on) of data-processing hardware and software by public authorities. In 1977, CAPRE decided, after a round of bidding, to reserve the market for smaller computers for COBRA plus three (later four) local private companies, all with foreign technological tie-ups, but none under foreign control. This 'market reserve' policy aimed at creating a local, predominantly privately owned, computer industry thus replaced the earlier policy of creating a single state-owned 'national champion' (that is, COBRA).

Shortly after this apparent victory for the 'ideological guerrillas', their main institutional base of operation, CAPRE, was abolished following a critical report ordered by the National Information Service (the 'Brazilian CIA', SNI) on its activities. It was replaced by a new Special Secretariat of Informatics (SEI) attached to the National Security Council and staffed by almost entirely new personnel – the former employees in many cases establishing their own private computer companies. Somewhat unexpectedly, SEI continued the policies pursued by CAPRE, and even broadened the policy by including in the market reserve policy some new sub-sectors, and strengthened it by promoting a law on informatics in 1984. While IBM in 1980 managed to penetrate a section of the reserved market by obtaining permission for local production of a medium-sized computer that effectively competed with the minicomputers reserved for the national producers, restrictions on the activities of the company prevented extensive damage to local companies (Adler, 1986:697). In October 1984, the Brazilian Congress voted through the National Informatics Law that, for a period of eight years, restricted the access of foreign companies to the manufacturing of small computers, extended the market reserve policy further to include the requirements of the telecommunications sector, some more peripherals and components, and provided various support mechanisms for strictly nationally controlled companies. In addition, the law established a new institution, the National Council for Informatics and Automatization (CONIN) to supervise the activities of SEI, thus freeing the organization from the grip of the National Security Council. The military grip was further loosened after a civilian government took office in 1985 and created a separate Ministry of Science and Technology to coordinate the activities of CONIN. Finally, in 1988, the administrative structure was changed once more, making CONIN directly responsible to the president, while SEI came under the authority of the Ministry of Industry and Trade (the Ministry of Science and Technology being abolished) (Meyer-Stamer, 1989:33).

The similarities between the strategies and instruments chosen by the Indian and Brazilian states are many. Both countries tried initially to promote a 'national champion' in the form of a state-owned company protected by import regulations, and both had to bow to pressures from local private companies wishing as manufacturers to enter the profitable (lower-end) segment of the computer market or as customers to obtain access to imported up-to-date technologies. In both countries, dedicated groups 'pioneering' the activities had to give way to more established/ traditional groups within the state apparatus, but notably without significant reversal in the overall strategy in Brazil. Likewise, the state in both countries came to be responsible for most research efforts, either through the state-owned computer companies that in both countries were significantly more research-oriented than the private companies, or in public research centres and universities. And finally, the public sector in both countries provided a large and relatively secure market for the local producers, mostly so in Brazil.

Differences in strategy and outcomes are as numerous as the similarities, however, reflecting the different social and economic circumstances prevailing in the two countries. India's strategy has all along been more ambitious in the technological field, while Brazil has emphasized commercial considerations much more. This in part reflected the relative position of international companies versus private and state-owned national companies in the two countries. The strong presence of IBM and other foreign companies in the large and dynamic Brazilian market made it virtually impossible for the Brazilian state to challenge their leadership in the manufacturing of large computers without running the risk of incurring very high costs. The Indian state, in an environment of slow growth, and one which was restrictive for foreign companies in general, found it much easier to challenge IBM, even if the eventual exit of the company from the country was probably not intended. Combine this with a strong Indian tradition for self-reliance and serious engagement in science and technology, and the chosen strategy was almost preordained.

While India ended up leaving the market for small computers to private companies doing little more than assembling imported components, Brazil through the market reserve strategy continued its bid for private national dominance, including technological mastery within this sector. The Brazilian strategy proved initially to be a commercial success, probably helped by the entry of the large private financial conglomerates that, by combining the role of producer with the role of a large customer, greatly facilitated the process of marketing. In the longer run, it seemed difficult, however, for the Brazilian producers to keep up with the rapid international development in the sector that meant a continuous stream of new technologies and a constant lowering of prices on the international markets. By the end of the 1980s, opposition to the market reserve policy had grown considerably: not only international opposition (from the USA in particular), but also domestic opposition from customers increasingly dissatisfied with being compelled to use expensive and old-fashioned equipment (Meyer-Stamer, 1989:24ff). It is still uncertain whether the Brazilian companies can withstand international competition, especially after the termination of the market reserve policy in 1992.[10] As for India, it still has to be seen whether local private companies will be able to indigenize and commercialize the technologies involved in the manufacturing of small computers.

Both countries still have to reap the full benefits of a dissemination of the new technologies throughout the economy, but in this respect Brazil seems to be better off. The presence of IBM in particular has secured for Brazilian customers continued access to large, up-to-date computers, while India's break with IBM, despite the possible attraction to other companies of not having to compete with the 'Big Blue' in the Indian market, has cut the country off somewhat from the mainstream of developments in computer technologies.[11]

The Role of Political and Administrative Structures

Returning to the theoretical questions raised earlier in this chapter, it can be asked whether the evolution of policies and their eventual outcomes were influenced by the political and administrative structures of the two countries, and whether lessons can be learned on the proper management of high-technology industries from the two cases. More precisely, it can be asked whether a new paradigm for political and administrative regulation can be extracted from the history of computer policies in India and Brazil. Obviously, a full answer to these questions cannot be given here – much more research will be needed for that – but it will be argued that at least a tentative outline can be provided on the basis of the cases presented.

Starting with the importance of *the political regimes* under which the two countries pursued their strategies for developing the computer industry, the key question, according to Weber, concerns the role of the Parliament in influencing, controlling and correcting the actions of the administration. The differences between the two countries in this respect have caused differences in the weight and influence of various institutional interests, most importantly those of the military, in the shaping of the computer policy. They have also influenced the way in which important social forces have channelled their demands into the state apparatus and, finally, differences over time in the type of regime may have exerted some influence on the policies.

For a start, it can be noted that Brazil's bureaucratic–authoritarian regime until the New Republic of 1985 – and possibly even after that – effectively excluded any significant interference in the affairs of the state through parliamentary channels. Always dominant, the political system established after the military coup in 1964 nevertheless provided the executive with an exceptional autonomy in economic policy making by excluding the Congress from all decisions on and control over the implementation of economic policies (Packenham, 1971; Skidmore, 1973).[12] Furthermore, the political structure not only gave the military a dominant role in politics, it probably also shaped their interests. While the Indian military establishment failed to ensure a decisive influence on the formulation and implementation of computer policies,[13] the Brazilian military was instrumental in initiating the process of development in the computer sector, and from 1979 onwards it even for a while strengthened its control over events in the sector. Contrary to the Indian military, the Brazilian military pursued a strongly nationalist policy – ideologically expressed in the doctrine of 'National Security and Development' (Alves, 1988:13ff) – which was probably reinforced by the fact that the responsibility for overall economic development resided firmly with the military institution, not, as in India, with the civilian authorities. The Brazilian military, unlike their Indian counterparts, therefore found it more difficult to make economic demands on public finances without considering the overall resource constraints of the national economy.[14]

The only instance when the Brazilian Congress was called to take part in the deliberations over the computer policy was in 1984, when the Informatics Law replaced the previous practice of policy making by presidential decrees. The decision of the military government to involve the Congress, however, seems to have been motivated by a desire to protect the nationalistic policies from attacks from an anticipated future democratic government rather than being a case of truly parliamentary influence on the policy of the administration (Meyer-Stamer, 1989:11). The 'insulation' of the administration from the Parliament has not, however, been accompanied by the same degree of insulation from the interests of powerful social classes. Domestic and international business interests have in general succeeded in influencing the formulation and implementation of economic policies through a large number of formal and informal corporatist channels (Boschi, 1979). In computers, it appears that these interests, especially those of the domestic producers created as a result of the policies, first began to exercise some influence through their representation in the advisory Informatics Council after a reconstruction of SEI in 1981 (Adler, 1986:697), but even then the close links with the military ensured for the administration a relatively large degree of autonomy. The links between the SEI and private industry have accordingly been characterized as being more like patron–client relations than those of private masters and public servants (Meyer-Stamer, 1989:34–5).

In contrast to the situation in Brazil, the Indian Parliament has always had a number of instruments for controlling the government and administration at its disposal (Bhambri, 1971:78–112; Dwivedi and Jain, 1985:137–98). Basically, it is the minister, as political head of the administration, who is accountable to the Parliament, not only through questions and debates, but more importantly through a number of permanent committees and through the general audit of public expenditure. While one may doubt the efficacy of these instruments of control over the overall activities of the administration, it seems that the parliamentary controls have been exercised to a significant degree with regard to the electronics and computer policy. Indian politicians have demonstrated a continuous interest in the developments of the electronics policy through a stream of questions in Parliament.[15] It is doubtful whether Indian politicians would be considered as 'able parliamentarians' in Weber's understanding of the concept, and it has been convincingly argued that the Indian Parliament has only had a little impact on the actual formulation of the electronics policies. There are stronger indications, though, that Parliament through the Estimates Committee, the Public Accounts Committee and the Committee on Public Undertakings has quite closely monitored the policy actions of the administration and the functioning of the state-owned electronics companies, and many of the corrective actions proposed in the reports of these committees have in fact been implemented (Jain, 1985).

The capacity for self-correction this has provided to the Indian state may have contributed to the gradual changes in policies during the 1980s. Moreover, the democratic regime in India has meant that in addition to corporatist channels of influence Parliament and also the press have been used as channels of influence for domestic industrialists seeking to effect changes in policies.[16] Another aspect of the Indian condition that may be seen as at least a partial reflection of the democratic regime has been the existence of pockets of strong labour unions. In contrast to the situation in Brazil, labour unions in the Indian banking sector have been quite powerful and, out of fear of job losses, strongly opposed the computerization of banking services, thus delaying the emergence of what could have been a major market for computers and computer-related products.

A final observation on the importance of the democratic regime in India for the shaping of the computer policy refers back to the period of the Emergency of 1975–7, when essential features of the Indian democracy were suspended. It was precisely during this short period that a number of crucial 'nationalistic' decisions were taken with regard to the computer policy.[17] The decision to promote ECIL as a national champion, the crucial democratic stages in the negotiations with IBM that made the company decide to leave India altogether and the setting up of CMC all took place during the Emergency, that is, in a period when the administration was more 'insulated' from interests in civil society and more free from interference from the Parliament (and the press) than ever before. It is interesting to note that this brief spell of 'strong rule' in India resembled the Brazilian regime in the strategy pursued and the methods involved in the computer industry. It was only after the restoration of democratic order that important policy changes were brought about, amongst other things through pressures from interest groups through the democratic channels – Parliament and the press. That it was not just a change of government, but a change of regime that was significant in this case is indicated by the fact that, when Mrs Gandhi and the Congress Party, who had imposed the Emergency, were returned to power in the elections of 1980, the computer policy was not reversed. On the contrary, the changes in strategy initiated under the previous government were continued and accelerated by letting more independent private Indian companies enter the industry and by gradually liberalizing imports.[18]

It may be concluded, then, that the democratic regime in India provided a broader range of channels of access for interests in civil society to influence government policies in the computer sector than seems to have been the case in authoritarian Brazil. Whether this has been beneficial for the overall development of the industry, or for the dissemination of microelectronic or computer technologies more generally, will be discussed shortly. Before that, the importance of the different administrative structures in the two countries should be considered.

The general *administrative structures* in the two countries have differed considerably, and these differences have also affected the administrative arrangements related to the electronics/computer policies and influenced the outcomes of those policies. India has been famous for the administrative system she inherited from the British, a system built around the unique elite civil service, the Indian Administrative Service (IAS). The IAS has effectively monopolized the top layers of the Indian administration, thereby giving it a strong resemblance to Weber's ideal type legal–rational bureaucracy, but in some areas the IAS has had to give way to more specialized services – a sort of Indian parallel to the Brazilian technocrats. The overall bureaucratic 'Steel Frame' has, furthermore, largely been preserved despite the changes and expansion in the size and range of activities of the Indian state. Even the proliferating state-owned corporations operating in a large number of industries have to a large extent been managed by IAS men.[19] 'Bureaucracy', in the Weberian sense, has thus very much been a characteristic of the Indian state, giving it a substantial measure of cohesion, but the dominance of the bureaucratic tradition over the technomanagerial mode of functioning has also made the Indian state less flexible and less oriented than the Brazilian state towards entrepreneurial activities. In addition, it can be argued that the organization of many Indian technocrats in a 'service tradition', that is organized in a parallel fashion to the IAS, has made them more 'bureaucratically' oriented than their Brazilian counterparts.

Brazil has never had the same bureaucratic tradition as India. The few attempts to create an elite civil service have all failed (Graham, 1968) and, despite US support for various administrative reform measures, the Brazilian administration cannot be said to be fully 'bureaucratized'. The only important institution organized along bureaucratic principles has apparently been the military which, however, by virtue of being in power, lost some of its 'professionalism' and never succeeded in installing bureaucratic features in the civilian administration.[20] Instead, the Brazilian administration has preserved strong patrimonial features with appointments based on patronage or clientist relations rather than on individual merit.[21] This lack of a unified bureaucracy has resulted in a segmented or 'feudalized' state, with many of the new 'developmentalist' institutions acquiring an exceptionally independent position, most visible in the case of the large state-owned corporations like the oil company, Petrobrás, but also institutions like the National Economic Development Bank, BNDE (Assis, 1984). In the wake of the military coup of 1964, there were extensive purges in the public administration (Alves, 1988:41ff). This probably to some extent weakened the traditional 'patronage system', to the benefit of the 'tecnicos' – the technically educated experts whom the military regime promoted as the managers of its drive for modernization and whose influence increased as a result of the establishment and growth of new institutions under the military rule (Mendes, 1980).

With specific reference to the administrative arrangements pertaining to the electronics/computer policy, it has been claimed that 'policy-makers must combine ... comprehensiveness with selectivity and flexibility, in the same way as the electronics industry' (Erber, 1985:306). Expanding this line of thought somewhat, the claim is that the politico-administrative set-up ideally has to possess the following attributes:[22]

1 *flexibility*, the ability to *adapt* to changing external circumstances, technological as well as social and political;
2 *selectivity*, the ability to *choose* appropriate strategies, including the choice between different technologies, between industrial sub-sectors and between public, private national or private foreign ownership;
3 *comprehensiveness*, the ability to *coordinate* activities in different sectors. This is especially important in electronics, because developments in this sector affect (and are affected by) the performance of a broad spectrum of social and economic activities.

It can be argued that these different attributes will be important for the proper management of the electronics/computer industry in general. They must however, be complemented by one more ability, particularly important in developing countries where state-owned companies form an integral part of government interventions in the economy:

4 *entrepreneurship*, the ability to *commercialize* – to operate efficiently in a market-like economic environment.

If we use these preliminary characteristics to discuss the administration of the computer policies in India and Brazil, it can be argued that variations between countries and over time in the possession of these abilities have affected the policies pursued and the outcomes achieved.

The evolution of computer policies in India and Brazil illustrates one additional point, namely the importance of the administrative structures being *permeable* to new emerging actors – in Brazil, the 'ideological guerrillas'; in India, the 'network' around the Atomic Energy Commission. In both cases the introduction of an institutionalized electronics/computer policy catapulted new actors into policy making – the scientists. In Brazil, the scientists worked in close alliance with nationalist economists (in the BNDE and the Ministry of Planning), while in India the scientists reigned almost supreme in the Department of Electronics. This permeability to new forces was only a temporary phenomenon, however. As the electronics sector grew in importance, the traditional administrative structures reasserted themselves. In Brazil, this happened through the military establishment strengthening its controls; in India, through the creation of bureaucratic structures (interministerial coordination committees and so on) that ensured some sort of coordination within the larger administrative framework of the Indian state. ECIL, the state-owned electronics company, was for a longer time kept in the hands of the scientists owing to its strong research orientation and privileged administrative position, being placed under the Department of Atomic Energy. Eventually, even this company had to adopt a more commercial orientation in its activities.[23]

The relatively successful performance of ECIL and CMC in the late 1980s is evidence of both flexibility and selectivity. Their success probably reflects a choice of activities (away from production of small computers, more emphasis on larger system-constructing operations involving software design and application, continued research and development) that demonstrate an ability to adapt to the prevailing economic and social environment, primarily a change to activities complementing the capabilities and interests of the local private Indian companies, but also an adjustment to the technological changes and competitive situation prevailing in the international markets. Furthermore, and in contrast to many other state-owned enterprises, it seems that a stronger entrepreneurial attitude has been installed in the working of both companies. This has been accompanied by organizational changes. There is evidence of changes in both ECIL and CMC, and even in the Department of Electronics, making these organizations more flexible and their structure less hierarchical; and more examples of similar changes in some newly established organizations within the broader 'informatics' sector can be found (Evans, 1990).[24]

Despite the efforts made to coordinate the electronics/computer policy with other policy areas through bureaucratic structures since the early 1980s, it is officially recognized that technological developments like the integration of microelectronics with telecommunications require further administrative adjustments and that they have to be accompanied by changes in other policy areas. The proposals advanced – a creation of a (super-) Ministry of Informatics – however, demonstrate the prevalence in India of a traditional bureaucratic orientation when it comes to suggestions for new administrative arrangements (BICP, 1988).[25]

Compared to India, the lack of a strong bureaucratic tradition in Brazil seems to have facilitated the creation of new, relatively autonomous, institutions and the fusion of technological prowess with an entrepreneurial spirit providing for a high degree of flexibility (Erber, 1985:307). The key institutional structure managing the electronics policy – CAPRE, later SEI – has been working quite efficiently and the organization is reputed to be one of the few Brazilian public institutions free of extensive corruption (Meyer-Stamer, 1989:33; Schmitz and Hewitt, 1989:19). The basic problem in Brazil seems, according to informed sources, to have been the lack of coherence and comprehensiveness in the policies pursued. The computer policy has not been coordinated within the framework of a general industrial policy, and only partially with an educational policy that could secure a steady supply of well-educated manpower (Erber, 1985:307; Evans and Tigre, 1989b:1756; Meyer-Stamer, 1989:30, 91). This lack of comprehensiveness can be interpreted as a result of the segmented and non-bureaucratic nature of the Brazilian administration, and it has apparently not been possible for the military to compensate fully for this situation. Furthermore, the segmented character of the Brazilian state may have made interinstitutional conflicts more frequent. SEI has thus been engaged in a number of conflicts with other public institutions on specific policy issues (Meyer-Stamer, 1988:42–5).

The lack of bureaucratic resistance and the backing of the military probably constituted the key factors allowing for the emergence of the scientists and the economic nationalists as a strong unified group capable of exploiting a situation of enhanced autonomy for the state institutions. On the other hand, it can be argued that the resulting strategy of national self-reliance lacked some of the correcting mechanisms that bureaucratic structures linked to interests in civil society through corporatist or parliamentary channels might have provided. While the private companies have thrived in Brazil, the state-owned COBRA seems of late to have had difficulties in defining its proper role. Since 1988, the company has been earmarked for privatization, and its possible role in promoting the more costly and less market-oriented research in both hardware and software seems not to have been exploited (Evans, 1990:25). The 1991 abandonment of the company's project of introducing a standard software programme equivalent to the Unix programme may signal the end to its striving for technological excellence, and leave the company with no apparent reason for continuing as a state-owned corporation (*Gazeta Mercantil*, 22 April 1991).

In conclusion, it seems that in India the strong bureaucratic tradition made policy coordination and interest mediation easier, but the lack of technomanagerial attitudes made it difficult for the state to fulfil the objectives of producing and disseminating computer technologies. Some measure of flexibility, however, was demonstrated through selective administrative intervention in sectors that were more research-oriented, less commercially oriented, and better adapted to the Indian resource endowments.

In Brazil, the state administration, by virtue of its segmented character, did provide for substantial flexibility and a commercial orientation as a result of the promotion of the technomanagerial ('tecnicos') mode of functioning under the military regime. The comprehensiveness and coherence that a unified bureaucratic structure might have provided was to some extent achieved through the intervention of the military (through the SNI) in the management of the computer policy, though this was not sufficient to change the basic character of the civilian administration. The gradual change to a civilian rule in the 1980s further eroded this particular form of policy-coordinating mechanism without yet replacing it with another.

Conclusion

The development of the computer industry in India and Brazil has taken place within certain structural constraints related to the character of the industry, the international context and the domestic socioeconomic situation. In combination with the different political and administrative arrangements, this has decisively shaped the policies and their outcomes in the industry. The general conclusion regarding the determinants of developments in the computer industry may be summarized as follows. with special emphasis on the role of political and administrative structures.

First, structural constraints of a socioeconomic and technoeconomic nature have shaped the computer policy and its outcome in both countries. Differences in the degree of economic dependence, that is in the interrelationship and relative positions of economic and political power between local and foreign companies, have, in combination with the fundamental dilemma with regard to the electronics industry in general, made for different limitations in the available policy options. Similar strategies may at times have been pursued, but outcomes have differed. India succeeded in obtaining some degree of self-reliance in the capacity to produce larger computers and in the provision of larger software-based systems engineering, primarily because of the retreat of IBM, but at the cost of a lagging behind in the dissemination of such computers and computer-based systems. Brazil's policy of leaving this sector to the multinationals ensured a much larger availability of computer services. The change in the Indian policy towards wholesale imports of technologies for the manufacturing of smaller computers led to a rapid proliferation in the use of these machines. The Brazilian policy of self-reliance, while ensuring a similar outcome, also implied a continuous lagging behind in technology and a constant threat to the established positions of local companies. Despite structural constraints, both countries experienced some very real advances in the capacity to produce various types of computers and in the spreading of the use of computers and electronics in general in different spheres of the economy.

Second, the experience of both countries demonstrates their ability to cope with rapidly changing technologies. This ability has been conditioned by the prevailing political and administrative structures in the two countries, and some of the administrative structures have been transformed in the process of regulating the electronics/computer industry. The authoritarian political system in Brazil, coupled with a segmented administrative set-up, made an initially flexible response to new opportunities and ambitions of new political actors possible, while ensuring through the considerable autonomy of the state apparatus a powerful and persistent support for the chosen policy. A subsequent adaptation to changing circumstances in the form of new social and economic interests and new technological developments seems, however, to have been hampered by the authoritarian structure, and the lack of a coherent bureaucratic framework has restricted the coordination of overall policies. The Indian democratic system, on the other hand, has ensured a degree of adaptation of policies to changing economic interests in society, while the bureaucratic administrative structures have facilitated more coordinated efforts in the pursuance of policies. On the other hand, the administrative structures of the state, including those of the state-owned enterprises within the sector, underwent significant changes that eventually led to a new balance between the bureaucrats keen on regulating and coordinating policies, the economic planners and managers eager to achieve commercial successes and ambitious scientists who wanted to achieve as high a degree of technological self-reliance as possible. In Brazil, some changes in policies and administrative structures implying an adaption to the strengths of the various interests present in Brazilian society were discernible parallel to the gradual democratization, but as yet conclusive changes have not been effected.

Third, on the basis of the experiences of the two countries it would be tempting to seek a generalized model of the 'best policy' for developing countries in their management of the electronics/computer industry. For a number of reasons, this would be premature, however. The two countries are far from typical developing countries, the international circumstances under which they pursued their initial policies are not likely to be repeated again, and the domestic socioeconomic configurations through which the policies take effect are likely to vary to a degree that eludes easy generalization. The only conclusion of a general nature that can be reached on policy matters is probably that the 'best policy' in this as in other policy areas is one that is adapted to the given socioeconomic and technological circumstances, while at the same time exploiting to the maximum the possibilities for desirable changes inherent in the situation.

While this conclusion opens up a whole spectrum of different 'best policies' it can nevertheless be claimed that some general principles for a possible 'best model' of the political and administrative structures through which the development of the electronics/computer industry is regulated can be identified. The evidence presented here is far from sufficient for claiming that a new 'Post-Fordist' model of politics and administration has emerged, but still it is possible to sketch a tentative 'ideal-type' model for successful public administration of electronics/computer policies (see Figure 7.1, below).

The administrative organization should, according to the model, be flexible and selective in its approach, and it should be able to coordinate policies. At the same time, the policies should be continuously adapted (1) to the prevailing political and social environment, as expressed through the political system proper or through interest representation via the bureaucratic structures ('corporatism') and (2) to the technological and economic environment as expressed through changes in the structures and dynamics of the market. The ability to accomplish these tasks will require, as illustrated in the model, a personnel structure that combines and balances different types of 'administrators': the bureaucrats (regulators), the economists (managers) and the scientists (innovators). It may also imply changes in the organizational set-up conducive to the exercise of the tasks outlined above: a more decentralized,

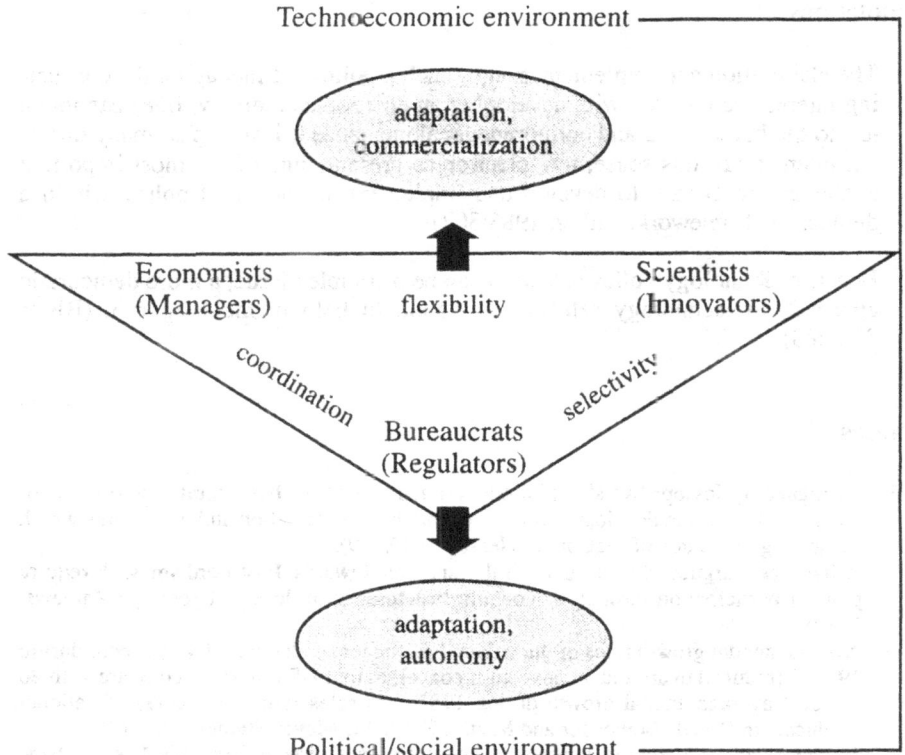

Figure 7.1 **A tentative model of a new administrative paradigm**

but still coordinated structure; an openness towards outside influence, while retaining a considerable degree of autonomy and so on.

From the experience of India and Brazil it can be hypothesized that, before this model is able to function properly, a certain level of development of the industry has to be achieved: the computer industry has to be installed first, so to speak. In both countries this was achieved through a phase of authoritarian rule that provided an enhanced degree of autonomy for the state. While this may not be the only way to reach a viable initial level of development for the industry, the experience of India in particular, but of late also of Brazil, may lead to an expectation that a democratic regime – all things equal – should have better opportunities for managing the complexities of the electronics/computer industry than an authoritarian system, provided appropriate administrative changes are effected. Democracy may thus be a necessary, but not sufficient, condition for the full utilization of the potentials promised by the 'electronics revolution'. That I am not alone in ending with this hopeful conclusion can be illustrated by the following quotations:

> The elaboration and implementation of such a policy [of managing the conflicting interests associated with developing an electronics industry, JDP] cannot be left to the bureaucrats and entrepreneurs alone, since it involves so many different interests. In this sense, too, electronics presents one of the most important challenges to Brazil: to develop and implement an industrial policy within a democratic framework. (Erber, 1985:307)

> Because technology policy/selection can be a complex issue, a more democratic approach to technology selection is bound to help in the long run. (BICP, 1988:83)

Notes

1. As argued by Jessop: 'we should not ignore the role of the bureaucrats and other non-party intellectuals in developing the norms, modes of calculation and procedures which sustain a given mode of regulation' (Jessop 1990:319).
2. It has been argued that a successful transition towards Post-Fordism will require popular participation through democratic structures at all levels of society (Mathews, 1989).
3. Average annual growth rates of the value of computer production of 44 per cent during 1983–9 (reduced to around 34 per cent if converted into US$) in India compare with 26 per cent average annual growth during 1981–8 in sales figures (in US$) of national producers in Brazil (Bowonder and Mani, 1991:M11; Meyer-Stamer, 1989:12).
4. To the extent that Indian exports of computers are directed towards Eastern Bloc countries, optimism regarding future expansion may be overstated. I have no firm information on the direction of exports, however.

5   The only other developing countries with similar levels of capabilities would probably be Taiwan and South Korea.
6   The description of Indian electronics/computer policies is based on Grieco (1982; 1984); Agarwal (1985); BICP (1988); Mahalingam (1989); Evans (1990).
7   ECIL, however, continued to be under the authority of the Department of Atomic Energy.
8   For general descriptions, see Tigre (1983); UN/CTC (1983); Erber (1985); Evans (1986); Adler (1986; 1987); Ramamurti (1987); Meyer-Stamer (1988; 1989).
9   Initially, the company was a joint venture between the Brazilian state (or rather various state-owned institutions), a private Brazilian company and a foreign company. In reality and, later, also formally, COBRA was entirely controlled through the state-owned national development bank, BNDE.
10 Optimists point to the abilities of Brazilian companies in 'creative imitation', while pessimists point to the exceptional circumstances that led to the initial success and to the increasing costs of research in the development of new models (Schmitz and Hewitt, 1989; Schwartzman, 1988).
11 According to some, IBM should not so much be regarded as a major competitor in the computer market, but more as an 'environment' that everybody in the industry has to adapt to (Meyer-Stamer, 1989:49).
12 'the Congress is expendable. It functions when the interests of the state requires the "normal" functioning of the federal, democratic state. When it does not, the Congress is closed, and the state, of course, continues to function' (Roett, 1978:55).
13 It should be recalled that the Indian military through its own production facilities, in particular *Bharat Electronics Ltd* (BEL) had its vital interests served and that it all along managed to obtain abundant economic resources for defence-related research, including research and services conducted by otherwise civilian public enterprises and institutions.
14 This argument seems to be supported by evidence of declining military budgets under the military regime, followed by increases under the civilian regime from 1985 (Stepan, 1988:72–80).
15 Grieco (1984) is to a large extent based on transcripts of the debates in parliament and the reports from various Parliamentary committees; compare his references cited on pp.210–11. Jain (1985: 271–3) also contains references to a large number of parliamentary debates, and an annual report of the Department of Electronics mentions that, in 1988 alone, more than 300 questions pertaining to electronics were asked in Parliament (DoE, 1989:53).
16 For examples of press campaigns in the late 1970s, see Grieco (1984:131ff). Jain (1985:256), argues that domestic producers tried to protect their interests through influencing members of Parliament. In the 1980s, domestic producers on several occasions, with some success, influenced the policy making in the administration, mostly with an eye to avoiding competition from imports.
17 This information is collected from Grieco (1982:625–8; 1984:30–31, 73–81 and *passim*). Grieco does not mention the Emergency, but he does distinguish between a period of 'strong state' (1973–7) and a period of weak and penetrable state (1978–80). Knowing the situation prevailing during the Emergency, it is ironic to note that Grieco ascribes the tough stand towards IBM at the time to 'domestic political limitations' (1984:50) – at no time during Indian independence had 'political limitations' been of so little importance!
18 In an official report it has been noted that the liberalizations in the 1980s were a direct consequence of reappraisals of policies undertaken in the late 1970s by various official commissions (BICP, 1988:17).

19 General descriptions of the Indian administration and the IAS can be found in Potter (1986) and Misra (1986).
20 The creation of the National Information Service (SNI), can be seen as an unsuccessful attempt to create a bureaucratic framework for the civilian administration (Stepan, 1988:13-20).
21 For general descriptions of the Brazilian 'bureaucracy', see Daland (1967, esp. 210ff); Roett (1978:126-30 and *passim*); Daland (1981); Geddes (1990).
22 See also Evans and Tigre (1989a:1761): 'support for the policies must have both breadth and coherence within the state apparatus. ... this implies a diversified but coordinated organizational base.'
23 Witness the following extract from a report by the Comptroller and Auditor General quoting a statement by the company: 'The Company stated (September 1980) that historically they had given secondary considerations to business aspects and the growth was primarily based on the vision of R&D personalities who set out to conquer unchartered markets, not fully mindful of the business risks involved. The Company feel that "it is essential now to de-link projects from personalities and try to institutionalize the organization" and that "a systematic integration and rationalization of activities so as to form efficient systems to satisfactorily cater to the market needs, is unavoidable"' (Report, 1983:104).
24 The Centre for the Development of Telematics (C-DOT), established in 1984, is often seen as a model for future organizational structures in high-tech industries. The Centre combines a high degree of autonomy with flexibility, a 'flat' structure and a highly motivated, highly educated staff. In part because of its high-profile director, Sam Pitroda, it has been involved in a number of political controversies in recent years.
25 The BICP report suggests the creation of a Ministry of Informatics to coordinate electronics policies with developments in telecommunications (BICP, 1988:62-3). It may be doubted whether such a traditional (bureaucratic) solution alone will be able to satisfy the report's own demands on policy making: 'the Government's role will have to be self-correcting, flexible, and able to promote and accommodate creative forces' (60). As the BICP belongs to the Ministry of Industry, this suggestion may also be interpreted as forming part of a struggle within the bureaucracy over the future control of the industry.

References

Adler, Emanuel (1986), 'Ideological "guerrillas" and the quest for technological autonomy: Brazil's domestic computer industry', *International Organization*, **40**, (3), Summer, 673-705.

Adler, Emanuel (1987), *The Power of Ideology. The Quest for Technological Autonomy in Argentina and Brazil*, Berkeley: University of California Press.

Agarwal, Suraj Mal (1985), 'Electronics in India: Past Strategies and Future Possibilities', *World Development*, **13**, (3), March, 273-92.

Aglietta, Michel (1979), *A Theory of Capitalist Regulation. The US Experience*, London: New Left Books.

Alves, Maria Helena Moreira (1988), *State and Opposition in Military Brazil*, Austin: University of Texas Press.

Assis, J. Carlos de (1984), *Os Mandarins da República*, Rio de Janeiro: Paz e Terra.

Bhambri, C.P. (1971), *Bureaucracy and Politics in India*, Delhi: Vikas Publications.
Boschi, Renato Raul (1979), *Elites Industriais e Democracia*, Rio de Janeiro: Edicoes Graal.
Bowonder, B. and Sunil Mani (1991), 'Government Policy and Industrial Development. Case of Indian Computer Manufacturing Industry', *Economic and Political Weekly*, 23 February, pp. M7–M11.
Bureau of Industrial Costs and Prices (BICP) (1988), *Report on Electronics*, New Delhi: Government of India.
Daland, Robert T. (1967), *Brazilian Planning. Development Politics and Administration*, Chapel Hill: University of North Carolina Press.
Daland, Robert T. (1981), *Exploring Brazilian Bureaucracy: Performance and Pathology*, Washington, DC: University Press of America.
Department of Electronics (DoE) (1989), *Annual Report 1988–89*, New Delhi: Government of India.
Dwivedi, O.P. and R.B. Jain (1985), *India's Administrative State*, New Delhi: Gitanjali.
Erber, Fabio Stefano (1985), 'The Development of the "Electronics Complex" and Government Policies in Brazil', *World Development*, **13**, (3), March, 293–309.
Evans, Peter B. (1986), 'State, Capital and the Transformation of Dependence: The Brazilian Computer Case', *World Development*, **14**, (7), July, 791–808.
Evans, Peter B. (1990), 'Indian Informatics in the Eighties: The Changing Character of State Involvement' (manuscript), Berkeley: University of California.
Evans, Peter B. and Paulo Bastos Tigre (1989a), 'Paths to Participation in "Hi-Tech" Industry: A Comparative Analysis of Computers in Brazil and Korea', *Asian Perspectives*, **13**, (1), Spring–Summer, 5–35.
Evans, Peter B. and Paulo Bastos Tigre (1989b), 'Going Beyond Clones in Brazil and Korea: A Comparative Analysis of NIC Strategies in the Computer Industry', *World Development*, **17**, (11), November, 1751–68.
Gazeta Mercantil (1991), 'Cobra Strategy Switch Brings 1990 Profit of US$1.15M', 22 April (obtained through Reuters 'Textline' database).
Geddes, Barbara (1990), 'Building "State" Autonomy in Brazil, 1930–1964', *Comparative Politics*, **22**, (2), January, 217–35.
Graham, Lawrence A. (1968), *Civil Service Reform in Brazil*, Austin and London: University of Texas Press.
Grieco, Joseph M. (1982), 'Between dependency and autonomy: India's experience with the international computer industry', *International Organization*, **36**, (3), Summer, 609–32.
Grieco, Joseph M. (1984), *Between Dependency and Autonomy. India's Experience with the International Computer Industry*, Berkeley: University of California Press.
Hirst, Paul and Jonathan Zeitlin (1991), 'Flexible specialization versus post-Fordism: theory, evidence and policy implications', *Economy and Society*, **20**, (1), February, 1–56.
IDS Bulletin (1984), 'Developmental States in East Asia: capitalist and socialist', **15**, (2), April.
India Today (1988), 'Computers: Thinking Big', 31 March, p.77.

India Today (1989), 'Computers: Price Friendly. Cheaper PCs Storm the Market', 31 December, p.63.
International Herald Tribune (IHT) (1990), 'Brazil Takes Aim at Computer Police', 10 July.
Jain, R.B. (1985), 'Electronics Policy and Indian Parliament', *Indian Journal of Public Administration*, XXXI, (2), April–June, 239–74.
Jessop, Bob (1990a), *State Theory. Putting the Capitalist State in its Place*, Cambridge: Polity Press.
Jessop, Bob (1990b), 'Regulation theories in retrospect and prospect', *Economy and Society*, 19, (2), May, 153–216.
Kaplinsky, Raphael (1989), '"Technological Revolution" and the International Division of Labour in manufacturing: A Place for the Third World?', *The European Journal of Development Research*, 1, (1), June, 5–37.
Lakha, Salim (1990), 'Growth of Computer Software Industry in India', *Economic and Political Weekly*, 6 January, 49–56.
Lipietz, Alain (1987), *Mirages and Miracles. The Crisis of Global Fordism*, London: Verso.
Mahalingam, Sudha (1989), 'Computer Industry in India. Strategies for Late-Comer Entry', *Economic and Political Weekly*, 21 October, 2375–84.
Mathews, John (1989), *Age of Democracy. The Politics of Post-Fordism*, Melbourne: Oxford University Press.
Mendes, Candido (1980), 'The Post-1964 Brazilian Regime: Outward Redemocratization and Inner Institutionalization', *Government and Opposition*, 15, (1), Winter, 49–74.
Meyer-Stamer, Jörg (1988), *Informatik in Brasilien*, Hamburg: Institut für Iberoamerika-Kunde.
Meyer-Stamer, Jörg (1989), 'Technologipolitischen Optionen für die brasilianische Informatikpolitik', (manuscript), Berlin: Deutsches Institut für Entwicklungspolitik.
Misra, B.B. (1986), *Government and Bureaucracy in India, 1947–1976*, Delhi: Oxford University Press.
Packenham, Robert (1971), 'The Functions of the Brazilian National Congress', in Weston H. Agor (ed.), *Latin American Legislatures: Their Role and Influence*, New York: Praeger.
Perez, Carlota (1985), 'Microelectronics, Long Waves and World Structural Change: New Perspectives for Developing Countries', *World Development*, 13, (3), 441–63.
Piore, Michael J. and Charles F. Sabel (1984), *The Second Industrial Divide. Possibilities for Prosperity*, New York: Basic Books.
Potter, David C. (1986), *India's Political Administrators, 1919–1983*, Oxford: Clarendon Press.
Ramamurti, Ravi (1987), *State Owned Enterprises in High Technology Industries*, New York: Praeger.
Report (1983), 'Report of the Comptroller and Auditor General of India Union Government (Commercial), 1982, Part V: Electronics Corporation of India Limited', New Delhi.
Report (1990), 'Report of the Study Team on Electronic Components for Eighth

Five Year Plan for Electronics Industry', *Electronics – Information and Planning*, May–June, 307–31.

Roett, Riordan (1978), *Brazil: Politics in a Patrimonial Society*, New York: Praeger.

Schmitz, Hubert and Tom Hewitt (1989), 'Learning to Raise Infants – A Case Study in Industrial Policy' (manuscript), University of Sussex, Institute of Development Study.

Schwartzman, Simon (1988), 'High Technology Versus Self-reliance: Brazil Enters the Computer Age', in Julian M. Chacel, Pamela S. Falk and David V. Fleischer (eds), *Brazil's Economic and Political Future*, Boulder, Col./ London: Westview Press.

Skidmore, Thomas (1973), 'Politics and Economic Policy Making in Authoritarian Brazil, 1937–71', in A. Stepan (ed.), *Authoritarian Brazil. Origins, Policies, and Future*, New Haven/London: Yale University Press.

Stepan, Alfred (1988), *Rethinking Military Politics*, Princeton, NJ: Princeton University Press.

Therborn, Göran (1978), *What Does the Ruling Class Do When it Rules?*, London: New Left Books.

Tigre, Paulo Bastos (1983), *Technology and Competition in the Brazilian Computer Industry*, London: Frances Pinter.

UN/CTC (1983), *Transborder Data Flows and Brazil*, New York.

Weber, Max (1978), *Economy and Society*, ed. Guenther Roth and Claus Wittich, Berkeley: University of California Press.

PART V
POLITICAL REFORM

PARTY

8 Panchayati Raj: the Indian Model of Local Self-government

Madan Sankhdher

Until recently, it was generally held by western Indologists that India's contribution to the world of letters lay in the fields of metaphysics, philosophy and religion, with none in the realm of political ideas and practices of government. To western eyes, India was a land of tribal oligarchies. It was thought that India's past was barren and her people were ruled in primitive ways by absolute monarchs or theocratic despots. However, the translation of Kautilya's *Arthasatra* and Buddha's *Digh Nikaya* into European languages, as well as well-organized researches by K.P. Jayaswal, R.P. Kangle, J.W. Rhys Davids and H. Oldenberg have gone a long way to removing the long-standing and persistent misconceptions about India's ancient political lifestyle. India had experienced and enjoyed grass-roots republicanism for nearly a thousand years between the 4th century BC and the 4th century AD, possibly long before the Greeks or Romans could develop a liberal democratic set-up or a form of governance touching the interests of the common man at the local level.

A search through the modest library of India's antiquity reveals a profuse literature that illuminates the genesis and evolution of some of the fundamental problems of organized life – the problems that in different forms persist even today. The *Vedas, Dharmashastras, Upanishads, Arthasastras, Nitis* and *Smritis* and the epics, like the *Mahabharata* and *Ramayana*, form the main body of texts and scriptures as classics that apparently speak the language of mythology generally, but when they are examined and analysed more closely, political ideas and beliefs and institutions and also a well-knit theory of the state and the foundations of local self-governance begin to emerge.

The attempt in this chapter is to limit the discussion of the ancient Sanskrit sources to the republican concept of the state in ancient India, with special reference to the specifics of the Panchayati Raj as the original form of political structure. The substance of ancient Hindu thinking is to indicate that the Rajya, that is, the state, like the Greek Polis, was a partnership, having a corporate life in the sense that the Sangh or Gan was a community organized by law, the term 'law' implying Dharma, a way of life based on a value system. One of the most significant formulations, flowing from Sanskrit sources, is the concept of republican polity. According to the acceptable modern definitions, a 'republic' is a form of government which is non-monarchical in spirit, with an elective or consensual rulership, men united for common ends, a moderate and constitutional spirit of governance, delegation and devolution of authority and participation or popular sanction behind power and decision making. These qualifications are all germane to the ancient Indian republican typology.

While it is true that in ancient Indian polity there were neither written nor formal provisions for a universal adult franchise, nor was there a developed consciousness and expression of individual rights or a sophisticated concept of individual liberty, there was a sense of involvement at the common man's level in the business of government. The doctrine of an unarticulated rule of law was validated by the existence of inbuilt mechanisms to counter tyranny and arbitrariness. Dharma was the supreme constitution, which bound the citizen and the ruler alike. Vigilance and conventions worked together to make political life civilized and humane. In the worst cases of mis-governance, the law prescribed even regicide. Limited government had a unique legitimacy and no ruler who ignored the welfare of the people had the moral or legal right to rule. The republican spirit pervaded both hereditary and elective monarchies. Dharma, as a code of conduct, implying a body of norms and institutions, exercised formidable checks on the abuse of power. Republicanism signified a form of government where, according to Altekar, 'power was vested not in one person but in a Gan or a group of people' – a group that enjoyed the trust and confidence of the people at large.

Local governments in ancient India, however, differed widely from one another, though they did signify a common meaning and a form of government. The Janpad, a widely prevalent form, literally meaning a territorial society, was a settled self-governing community. The Sangh was a polity based on plural sovereignty – the rule of many. The Buddhist literature is full of examples of republican states and precepts corresponding to them. The phrase 'Gana-Rajya', inspired by both Vedic and Buddhist scriptures, was institutionalized in Sabhas, Samitis and Panchayats, equivalents of councils, assemblies and local self-government.

The *Mahabharata* gives a scientific and precise definition of the word 'republic' by referring to the 'whole body-politic, the entire political community, and in the alternative, the parliament, not the governing body only'. Jayaswal has cited appropriate shlokas (verses), which prescribe the apparatus of those numerous entities that held and exercised authority. The unique feature of Hindu republics was their adoption of benevolent rule and their subscribing to the creed of reaching out to the last person. While in many cases a particular caste, varna, was entitled to rule, as with the kshatriyas, the power was shared by the whole community. All the kshatriyas were styled kings as a ruling class. The Licchavis, for instance, was a republic of 7707 kings, where a large number of the people were directly involved in rulership. Collective rulership was widely prevalent for, in this form of government, the question of legitimacy would not arise.

In fact, in Hindu thought, the republican sentiment – the sense of belonging – penetrated all walks of life: religion, economics, trade, agriculture, services and politics. Industrial and professional guilds were woven into a pattern of self-governance. The Buddhists practised in their Sanghas a democratic-cum-republican system of religious organization based on election and the brotherhood of Bhikhus, without any discrimination of caste or class. On Megasthenes' testimony, in most towns and villages, by the end of the 4th century BC, local autonomy was a practical ideal exercising tremendous influence on the functioning of governments.

Rhys Davids observes that republicanism had permeated the grass roots of society. The village provided collective ownership of land, pastures and cattle. There was no recognition of proprietary rights. Women had the right to their own personal property. The village was administered by a representative council, the Panchayati, a model of direct democracy.

The concept of grass-roots democracy can perhaps be traced back to either ancient Indian rural Panchayats or to the old Greek city states. In both cases, however, the polities, at best, were elitist rather than grass-roots democracies, since the majority of the populations were denied participation in economic or political privileges. Curiously, the modern liberal democracies have evolved a universal adult franchise and have developed economically through centralization and industrialization in the form of welfare states of one variety or another. The developing countries, on the other hand, have remained poor because of some of their cultural weaknesses or because of colonial exploitation. The level of economic prosperity and social security achieved by the technologically advanced societies is one that the developing societies cannot achieve within a reasonably short time. Secondly, even if economic prosperity is a laudable ideal, how would India maintain its cultural identity in the face of the same problems that the affluent societies are facing in terms of family disintegration, social fragmentation and loss of values? The dilemma of economic progress versus negativities of materialistic lifestyle haunts the Indian psyche.

The welfare states in the west are facing multiple crises and the philosophy of the welfare state is under severe attack from several quarters. In view of this phenomenon, it is relevant to ask whether the path of liberal capitalist economies is worth following in the Indian case although, in the present state of the Indian economy, it would be simply chimerical to visualize such a goal. Should India follow the road of centralized planning and industrialization, or shift her sights to a decentralized economy and policy suited to her genius, tradition and long experience of the past?

In this context, this chapter seeks to examine and evaluate the philosophy and performance of the Panchayati Raj as the model of Indian self-government at the local level. This study is reinforced by my work on the Scandinavian welfare states, where a modicum of economic and political decentralization has been successfully achieved. While these comparisons are tenuous, the focus of the chapter is on the problems of planning a decentralized welfare state at the village level in India. It is assumed that, if the vast agricultural income of India is brought within a tax net and the resources so accumulated are used to satisfy the minimum needs of the most needy, with a view to making the poor and needy self-reliant, it is possible to use the modern techniques of economic development by passing on the decision-making power to the Panchayats. The questionable success of Panchayati Raj institutions in the states where they have been tried is due, among other things, to lack of perception, will and resources. One could argue that, if Panchayats are left to themselves to create resources and use them freely to satisfy their requirements, there can be some reasonable hope in the near future of at least preventing further escalation of poverty.

The tremendous attraction in India, at both the intellectual and the popular levels, to the idea of Panchayati Raj stems from the long-standing belief in the myth of 'panch parmeswar', meaning the voice of the representatives is the voice of God. Also involved is the pride in India's glorious past when the highest civilization had been achieved and the wealth of the country made foreign visitors describe it as a 'golden bird'. Ancient Sanskrit scriptures have paid glowing tributes to self-governing villages and communities spread all over the sub-continent. India was, so to speak, 'a republic of republics'. Kautilya talks of the republican spirit of ancient kingships. K.P. Jayaswal, a prominent Indologist, has discovered a variety of institutions, practices, organizations, procedures and structures to support the theory that, between the 4th century BC and the 4th century AD, India had a full-fledged system of republicanism and democracy. The Buddhist period is exemplary in producing kingless politics and republics functioning on the basis of consensus, consent and collective leadership. Rhys Davids and historian R.C. Majumdar have produced irrefutable evidence in support of the fact that local self-government was a living reality. The role of the Panchayats at the village level is a matter of commonly accepted heritage. No wonder that, after Independence, and even during the national movement, many great leaders, such as, Gandhi, Jaya Prakash Narayan and Deendayal Upadhyaya, gave a clarion call to achieve the goal of establishing Panchayati Raj in India, an ideal eclipsed by Muslim invasions and British rule.

Mahatma Gandhi was never tired of singing the praises of Panchayati Raj. He was so enamoured of this concept that he identified it with Ram Raj – a divine state. For him, revival of the Panchayats was a national aspiration and an unavoidable necessity. He termed it 'Gram Swaraj', implying true freedom for the villages which comprised over 70 per cent of the country's population. Gandhi's love of rural life emerged from two sources: he romanticized India as a big village, and that was his vision of the future; and he reacted against some negative features of western civilization, finding correctives to them in the simplicity, austerity and self-reliance of village life. Real India lives in villages, he said, and he added that it is here that the reconstruction of India will take place. In his view, the restoration of village self-governance would ensure the best and the greatest in human values in personal, family, social and political life.

Jaya Prakash Narayan, the crusader for regeneration of rural life and a leader of the Sarvodaya movement, wrote profusely about the reconstruction of the Indian polity. And in the proper handling of village life, he sought the consummation of his dream of a partyless democracy. His works inspired a whole generation to become motivated for the realization of the Gandhian prescription of Gram Rajya. He advocated the modernization of the Indian tradition and shared with Gandhi his concern over India's imitating the west. J.P., as he was called, carried forward the Gandhian critique of the western way of life, the soulless dreary life in giant urban settlements, the product of consumerist mechanical civilization, unworthy of human existence. Both of them found salvation in imbuing human existence with the naturalness of village culture. It was in life in a rural environment that they found integration of nature and man in the mother–child relationship, free from pollution and suffused with values of simplicity, humility and compassion that would provide durable peace, exalted happiness and bliss.

Another equally important political philosopher and national leader, Deendayal Upadhyaya, echoed the same sentiment. Aware of the hazards of following the western path and desirous of following the rich Indian tradition, he also visualized a blueprint of 'Integral Humanism', whereby all-round development of human life was possible through the regenerating of villages as hubs of vitality and energy. The village life, according to him, should be the foundation of the future reconstruction of India:

> How compassionate, civilized and large-hearted are the village folks even though they are illiterate. They are sustaining the uniqueness and human values of India with great sincerity despite their poverty ... We will have to direct this flow of right conduct present in our villages to the cities.

In the preservation and strengthening of village independence lay the solution of most of India's socioeconomic and political ills. This has been a matter of faith of many leading intellectuals in India. Schumacher's *Small is Beautiful* is the new Utopia.

Briefly, then, this is the Gandhian conceptual framework which seeks to blend traditional experience and wisdom with the modern outlook. To quote Gandhi: 'My idea of village swaraj is that it is a complete Republic, independent of neighbours for its vital wants, and yet interdependent for many others in which dependence is a necessity.'

Decentralization is the battle cry of modern democracies and Gandhi was perfectly convinced of the need and practicality of decentralization. The conception of every village as a small republic was for him a workable ideal in the Indian situation. He was in favour of a broad-based pyramidal structure of decentralized power, with numerous village Panchayats at the bottom as the vibrant sources of power, economic and political, and the National Panchayat at the apex. He envisaged intermediary levels of district and state Panchayats, with the ultimate power vested in the village Panchayats. While the village Panchayats would be elected directly by the people, the Panchayats would elect the intermediary bodies who, in turn, would elect the National Panchayat. Thus he subscribed to village-based government with a self-sufficient, autonomous, village economy. The Panchayat would comprise five people – men and women – annually elected by the village people possessing decision-making powers on their own authority and not by delegation or transfer. The Panchayat of Gandhi's model would be sovereign, legally and politically, and would be subordinate to none. It would hold legislative, executive and judicial powers – a perfect village government where perfect grass-roots democracy would function to ensure individual freedom, social security and common welfare.

The purpose of referring to Gandhian sources on this subject is only to underline the fact that no-one else contributed to the theme of Panchayati Raj as much as he did. And he was able to present a coherent view. He never claimed to be original or innovative, but he was representing Indian ingenuity in terms of an ideology and a way of life inherited from India's antiquity. That is why he had an infallible appeal to both the elites and the masses in the country as a whole. He was only interpreting the Indian model of thought and practice in the light of modern challenges facing India, in particular, and other human societies on the globe, in general. Now that decentralization is the watchword of modern statecraft, Gandhi's thought has acquired greater relevance.

The history of village community or Panchayat as a corporate unit of civic life goes back to ancient Vedic times. The old village administration used to carry out not only judicial functions but also functions related to internal defence, security, public works, collecting of taxes and land revenue. The other sources of income were common property and voluntary labour. The village functioned as the centre of community life, independent of the state, which followed a policy of non-interference so long as it received its share of land revenue, which was its main source of income. In an important sense, the state was dependent on the village, rather than the other way round. The whole situation has reversed over the centuries.

Villages had been the pivot of Indian life through the ages from the Vedic to Buddhist and Gupta periods of history. They functioned as Panchayats because of adequate financial resources at their command, maximum power and autonomy. The concept of self-government facilitated decentralization of political and economic power and the people as a whole shared responsibility and took an interest in the running of their Panchayats, which were not only the vital instruments of governance, but also inculcated a strong sense of fellow-feeling, making the village a self-realized unit. People shared joys and sorrows and basic necessities of life; food and shelter were available to all. No wonder that A.L. Basham, the historian, described it as 'India, the Wonder that it was'.

The Gramani or the Sarpanch was an elective officer who held civil and military powers and was helped in the discharge of his duties by popular Sabhas and Samitis, the latter being the assembly of the whole people and the former a smaller body to settle different kinds of disputes. Both these bodies enjoyed high prestige and were equated with twin daughters of Prajapati, the creator. Reinforced by the ancient, glorious tradition and the Gandhian approach, the importance of Panchayati Raj has been realized, especially, in the making of the constitution for India after Independence. It was obvious to those designing the country's charter that four of every five citizens lived in rural areas, and that the incidence of poverty at village level was much higher than in the towns. Thoughts on rural development or Panchayati Raj should be an integral part of our understanding of social and economic freedom of the village folk.

With a view to achieving the goal of social revolution and economic uplift, the constitution of India resolved to constitute the nation as a sovereign, democratic republic. The constitution pledged to secure, for all the citizens, justice, social, economic and political; liberty of thought, expression, belief, faith and worship; equality of status and opportunity; also to ensure the dignity of the individual and the unity of the nation. The

Constituent Assembly, in the light of its commitments, sought to find indigenous institutions capable of meeting those needs, which would be satisfied by structuring the constitution on the village and its Panchayat – a decentralized polity inspired by the Gandhian model. The incorporation of article 40 in the constitution was less a gesture of romantic sentimentalism than a bowing to the needs of perceived reality. The aim of this article was that of reawakening village life, if India was to progress. The article required the state to take steps to organize village Panchayats and to confer on them necessary powers and authority to enable them to function as units of self-government. The idea underlying this constitutional provision was to introduce democracy at the grass roots. However, it made no detailed prescription about the structure or organization of the Panchayats, leaving it to the state to work out its own specific plans in this respect. The purport of this provision was to provide the masses with a right to participate in the otherwise abstract sovereignty.

The Panchayat system, as envisaged in the constitution, has three main objectives: (1) greater involvement of the people in the process of democratic governance, (2) villages as participants in national development, and (3) self-reliance through decentralization. By placing article 40 in the Directive Principles of State Policy, the constitution has not really lessened the importance of the provision of Panchayati Raj. Indeed, the decision to keep it among the non-justiciable rights is based on the pragmatic consideration of allowing flexibility in terms of launching this important experiment in different states. The Directive Principles are considered 'fundamental' in the governance of the country and could be ignored only at the cost of Indian democracy, which aims at socioeconomic justice for all citizens, irrespective of caste, creed or religion. These Directives not only seek to harmonize individual liberty with social justice, they also introduce direct democracy through the provision of local self-government via Panchayati Raj. They contain an active obligation on the state to secure a social order in which social, economic and political justice shall inform all the institutions of national life, thus bringing about a decentralized welfare state from the village level upwards. Article 40 thus falls into a pattern of political organization conducive to the development of local autonomy within the framework of the goals listed in the preamble of the constitution.

As a passing reference, it would be useful to recall briefly the controversy over the provision of Panchayati Raj in the draft constitution. One of the chief architects and chairman of the Drafting Committee, B.R. Ambedkar, was opposed to the move for incorporating village Panchayats among the provisions of the constitution. Characterizing the village as 'a sink of localism' and a 'den of narrow-mindedness', he had recommended that the draft constitution should discard 'the village and adopt the individual as the unit'.

However, K. Santhanam's amendment to the effect that a new article referring to village Panchayats should be added to the constitution was accepted by the Constituent Assembly.

In the present constitutional framework, however, the Panchayati Raj institutions are not independent of the state and central authorities. The local government is listed as the fifth item in State List of subjects in the seventh schedule of the constitution. The law governing Panchayati Raj at district, village or town levels are passed by the state legislatures, and their execution or adjudication also falls within the purview of the state government. The economic and social planning is put in the Concurrent List and is subjected to the overall control of the Planning Commission instituted by the Central government. Planning for village development and the allocation of resources are vested in the central and state governments. Article 40 of the constitution, as stated earlier, falls in the category of Directive Principles of State Policy and it authorizes the state to organize village Panchayats and delegate power and authority so as to enable them to function as units of self-government.

Subsequently, to constitutional provisions, the Balwant Rai Mehta Committee, set up by the Centre, recommended a three-tier Panchayati Raj system as an instrument for grass-roots planning for development, the three-tier structure comprising Panchayats at the village level, Panchayat Samiti at the region level and a Zila Parishad at the district level. The whole system was supposed to work under the Ministry of Community Development based in the state capital. These recommendations were accepted by several States and, accordingly, they enacted laws to establish the Panchayati Raj institutions. Andhra Pradesh, Rajasthan, Maharashtra, Gujarat, Kerala and Assam set up Gram Panchayats of varying patterns. A nationwide network of Panchayats were in function for about five years in the initial stage. The whole effort was intended to strengthen grass-roots democracy under the guidance and support of central and state governments.

Other states also followed the model, though the patterns were quite different. Karnataka, Jammu and Kashmir, Himachal Pradesh, West Bengal and Orissa too initiated the programme of village development. In due course, Madhya Pradesh, Bihar, Uttar Pradesh and Tamil Nadu also joined the race and even the Union Territories did not lag behind.

One of the primary aims of the Panchayati Raj experiment was to 'to generate and direct a process of integrated social, economic and cultural change with the ultimate aim of transforming social and economic life of the village'. Consequently, the Community Development Programmes were designed to achieve this end through people's participation in the planning and execution of these programmes. The start was both hopeful and bold. However, disillusionment soon set in. A number of committees and evaluative bodies of the Planning Commission came out with mixed reports. The experience with the total output of Panchayati Raj institutions has not been positive. Instead of going into the details of the performance or non-performance of the Panchayats and the bodies associated with the promised revolution at the grass-roots level, we will briefly highlight here the major deficiencies in the structure-function of local governments with a view to seeking remedial measures.

It is most unfortunate that the whole national investment in the business of instituting a Panchayati Raj has gone to waste: the hopes generated by policy framers and planners over 40 years ago have been shattered; nothing worth noting seems to have been achieved; instead of decentralization of political or economic power, we find that the local bodies are either counter-productive or defunct. What has gone wrong and where?

While the Panchayati Raj system has aroused a lot of political awareness in rural areas, that awareness has not been properly channelled. In fact, the lack of responsible leadership at the village level has not allowed the system to grow. It has led to corruption, increased factional conflicts and misuse of resources. The Panchayats have become political tools for manipulating districts and interests by unscrupulous politicians, not necessarily belonging to the village in question. This politicization of the local bodies is the bane of rural development.

If the Panchayats have not come up to expectations, the reasons are not far to seek. They are embedded in their functioning. The very spirit of Panchayati Raj, the spirit of arriving at consensus, is missing. There is a whole contradiction in the precept and the practice. Instead of being self-governing, the Panchayats are totally dependent on external forces. They do not have adequate resources of their own and subsist on pitances from the Centre or the state governments. Their autonomy is simply meaningless and empty. There is a great deal of confusion and overlapping of their obligations, responsibilities and powers. The multiplicity of authority at the local level creates anarchic situations. They bear too heavy a burden without power or money.

The village folk have turned apathetic towards the Panchayat, for there is no effort to really involve the people in the task of making progress. The common villager has developed a feeling that vested interests have developed which exploit him and his simplicity for petty gains. Corruption at the top has seeped in. The Gram Sabha – the real institution of direct democracy – remains dormant because no one is interested in arousing it from slumber. The Panchayat is neither responsible nor responsive to the Gram Sabha. The most vital element of the grass-roots democracy – participation – is missing.

Election to the Panchayats is manipulated by clever feudal or caste elites. The villager has no power to recall or re-elect a Panchayat. There is no process of referendum on any important issue. The village body as a whole cannot take any decision freely. Thus the very institutions of direct democracy are missing. The illiteracy and poverty of the people prevents their coming out boldly against foul practices.

The solution to these problems is not easy. Despite a rich tradition of local self-government and despite the inspiration flowing from great leaders and well-meaning intellectuals, there is first and foremost the problem of ignorance at the village level. The task is one of educating the people in self-governance before embarking on ambitious projects of restructuring or transforming village life.

In the final analysis, therefore, if the Panchayati Raj problem is to work in the spirit that it worked in ancient India to conform to the Gandhian idea of Gram Swaraj, some decisions on the policy front have to be taken.

First, the Constitution has to be suitably amended in order to give the Panchayats an independent status. Their dependence on the state and the Centre has to go. Second, like the Norwegian Communes, the Panchayati Raj should be left free to plan for themselves. The system of planning from above should be replaced by one from below. The panchay should be empowered to take decisions and implement them. Except for limited coordination of activities of the Panchayats, the whole area of socioeconomic development should be left to them, unfettered.

Third, the Panchayati Raj should be allowed to raise their own resources. This should include taxation of income, property and so on, as well as levying of duties on goods and merchandise. Without economic independence and ample revenues the Panchayats remain hampered in their functions. Fourth, the Centre or the state should also extend financial support to the Panchayats. This support should not result in their dependence on the Centre or the state, but should be aimed at creating self-reliance. Any financial support or grant from outside, say in the form of expertise, technology or personnel, should be unconditional and without strings.

Finally, and this is most important, the Gram Sabha, as the legislative and deliberative body, should be made functional. The Panchayat should be both responsible and responsive to the Gram Sabha. But, for that, it is imperative that an institute for the training of villagers in the task of socioeconomic development in its various dimensions should be set up to cater to the needs of a cluster of villages. This institute should provide training in administrative, financial, legislative, planning, execution and other matters related to democratic functioning and problems arising out of decentralization.

Perhaps, if these steps are taken by the state or the central governments, the Indian model of Panchayati Raj may be realized.

9 General Elections in India, 1989

M.V. Pylee

Free elections at regular intervals have been an integral part of parliamentary democracy in India. The first general elections, four years after Independence in 1947, took three months to be completed and involved an electorate of 173 million. The electorate at successive general elections, generally at a five-year interval, steadily increased and in 1989 it stood at 498.9 million. From the point of view of an election, this is a mind-boggling number. The world had never seen an electoral exercise which involved such a gigantic number of people eligible to exercise their franchise. The 1989 elections were completed within a week, in three instalments, each at intervals of two days (22, 24 and 26 November 1989), a remarkably efficient exercise indeed.

In the 1989 elections, 117 political parties participated. Of these, eight were national parties, 20 were state parties and 89 were unrecognized registered parties. The leading national parties were Indian National Congress, Janata Dal, Bharatiya Janata Party (BJP), Communist Party of India (CPI) and Communist Party Marxist (CPM). There were in all 6084 candidates, a large number of them independent candidates with no party affiliation. Under the electoral law of India, any person who has reached the age of 25 years can contest elections for the popular lower House of Parliament, the House of the People. Every citizen who has reached the age of 18 years is eligible to vote, and at the 1989 elections over 300 million people did so (61.95 per cent turnout). Of these votes, 2.68 per cent of votes were declared invalid. There were 579 810 polling booths, each serving roughly a thousand voters. Voting was by secret ballot.

Political parties have to be formally registered with the Election Commission of India, which allots a symbol to each party (also to every independent candidate), so that illiterate voters can identify them in the secrecy of the booth. There are as many as 71 symbols recognized by the Election

Commission. Of these, eight are for national parties, nine are for state parties and the rest are free symbols available for others to choose from.

In 1982, for the first time, an experiment was conducted with electronic voting machines in one constituency (Parur-Kerala State). Later, in an election petition by the defeated candidate, the Supreme Court of India declared the practice invalid as the then existing electoral law (Procedure) did not permit the use of electronic voting machines. There was much talk later about amending the law and introducing the electronic voting machine on a large scale, especially in urban areas, but so far this has not materialized.

The conduct of elections in India (to Parliament and to state assemblies) is entrusted to an independent constitutional body, the Election Commission of India. It is headed by a Chief Election Commissioner. The Commission is a permanent body. All matters connected with elections, including the preparation of electoral rolls, revision of the electoral rolls and the determination of all details connected with the actual conduct of elections, are under the jurisdiction of the Election Commission. The Commission has the authority to countermand the election in any constituency or even a whole state if it is satisfied that there were electoral offences such as rigging, 'booth capturing', violence and so on, and order another poll.

The general election of 1989 was an extremely expensive exercise. It was roughly estimated that the total cost of the election was over 1000 crores of rupees (over 500 million dollars). The official estimate of government spending on the elections was Rs.166 crores (about 90 million dollars). The Election Commission sources, however, said that the actual figure must have been upwards of Rs.180 crores (around 100 million dollars). If we add to this figure the 100 crores spent on revising the electoral rolls and the estimated 50 crores spent on the state assembly elections, the total becomes Rs.330 crores. But that does not give a total picture of the electoral expenses. Political parties, on their own, spent a huge sum. No-one knows even approximately the figure, but it amounted to several hundred crores of rupees. The publicity budget alone of the Congress Party ran to more than 75 crores, including a Rs.20 crore advertising campaign and expenditure of Rs.10 crores on videos. Over 200 crores was possibly spent on 'volunteers', the men who man the polling booths and paste posters on walls. The 6084 candidates must have spent roughly Rs.6 crore on petrol bills alone.

At the government level, the first general elections in 1952 cost the exchequer about Rs.104 crore. In 1957, the corresponding figure was only 5.9 crore, but since then, expenditure has mounted exponentially at successive elections. It is impossible to determine the overall expenditure by political parties, but an intelligent estimate places it at Rs.2000 crores. Legally, each candidate can spend the maximum sum of Rs.150 000 only, but what is actually spent by many candidates is several times that figure. The logistics of electioneering are truly staggering. Hoardings, leaflets, badges, pandals (sheds) and public address systems in tens of thousands cost an enormous amount. At least 100 million posters, costing about Rs.10 crores and consuming over 2000 tonnes of paper, were used. At least 20 000 video cassettes were in circulation. One has to add to these the cost of paint, postage, telephone calls, hotel bills and of course travel. When added up, these would give a figure well over Rs.1000 crores. That will give us an approximate idea of the cost of the ninth general elections.

To the extent that election manifestoes by their very nature are an exercise in hyperbole, their authors would be doing them less than justice if they did not exaggerate. But when the limits of legitimate exaggeration are jumped, it amounts to straining the credulity of the voter and that precisely was the feeling one that while analysing the manifestoes of the leading political parties. Except for the two left parties (the Communists) they had let go all restraint and crammed their manifestoes with promises which anyone with a sense of realism would find it difficult to buy. So similar were the promises that at times it was difficult to distinguish among the parties making them. Thus the ruling Congress Party, the Janata Dal and the BJP vied with one another as they went about promising a new deal to the different categories of people: farmers, factory workers, teachers, agricultural labourers and so on.

Exaggeration to the point of evoking visions of a utopian future marked the approach of most of the parties to the problems of the backward classes, women and youth. Providing employment for every unemployed person was a promise which was most attractive to large sections of the electorate. The parties knew that it was a trump card to attract the youth. Similarly, providing good drinking water and electricity in every village and increasing access to institutional finance or otherwise for housing was a familiar theme for everyone.

While the political parties made such exaggerated promises, a group of eminent citizens gathered together in New Delhi drew up a Citizens' Manifesto for the 1989 elections. It was a remarkable document. Among other things, it said that it was not intended to be an alternative to the manifestoes of various political parties. It was intended to promote awareness amongst the citizens, and also their participation, not merely in the electoral process, but in influencing public policies. Furthermore, citizens had important responsibilities in a democracy, alongside their rights. Citizenship education and development were important prerequisites for their participation in democratic governance. With the average voting turnout in elections in the range of 50 to 70 per cent, there was a great need to promote greater participation; every citizen should vote and encourage others to vote. If necessary, compulsory voting would have to be considered. Enrolment of voters and publication of voters' lists should be on the basis of each polling station.

Finally, arousing expectations by making false promises, and violence during elections, needed to be curbed. Political parties should eschew the practice of divisive politics by pitting groups against groups. Candidates should include a declaration of their assets along with their nomination papers. The high level of expenditure incurred by candidates and political parties should be curbed and regulated by public funding. Even then, the expenses were borne by the community in one form or the other.

The electronic media are now reaching nearly all of the population. They should be used to promote citizens' education and participation rather than to promote the interests of one party or group. The educational function of the electronic media is critical in view of the widespread illiteracy which impedes access to the print media.

There is need to revitalize the vision and skills of political leadership that have tended to fade with the leadership of the freedom movement. The nation devotes a large amount of resources for training and developing the leadership in the realm of armed forces, industry and administration. It needs to make similar efforts to develop the knowledge, skills and values of political leadership.

Voluntary citizens' groups and independent institutions should identify specific and important public issues and facilitate the political parties taking a specific stand on such issues, simultaneously enlightening the public on the same. Citizens should form observers' groups at the constituency level to promote healthy electoral process. Independent organizations should undertake an objective appraisal of the performance of the political parties in power, against the background of their manifestoes, and report to society periodically; a national social audit of the performance of political parties should be done. Ultimately, citizens have a responsible role, along with the politicians and political parties in bringing about change in the political culture of the country.

The past decades have witnessed the enfeeblement of national and constitutional institutions in India as a result of concerted attacks upon them whenever those in power saw them as stumbling blocks in their pursuit of power and personal gain. Institutions constitute the backbone of the nation. Their strength and effective functioning are prerequisites for the sustenance of democratic development. The process and procedures for establishing democracy are as important as the reasons for wanting it and, once gained, for sustaining and nurturing it. The judiciary also has suffered loss of credibility.

One of the most serious problems facing the country is the lack of credibility of political parties and their governments, characterized by corruption and the impeding of the process of democratic developments, leading to social turbulence and violence which are attributed to Naxalism, terrorism, caste and ethnic factors, and the like. The gradual deterioration of the nation's public image during the past decades is a matter of grave concern. The increase of violence in the political process should be contained and the politics of confrontation should be given up. Consensus and reconciliation are important components of the democratic ethic.

The working of Parliament and state legislatures could be made more effective. At present important legislation is enacted in a rush, without adequate consideration, and often without a quorum. Laws enacted are not acted upon. A committee system is an important method of improving the functioning of legislatures. Decorum in legislatures should be restored.

Ensuring free and fair elections is the first prerequisite for the success of democratic development. To this end, the Election Commission should be made more autonomous, so as to enable it to cleanse the electoral process, minimize violence, reduce money power and promote healthy electioneering without bringing in religion, caste or language. Internal elections within the political parties should be made a prerequisite for their participation in the elections to various legislative bodies. People with criminal records should not be adopted as candidates by the political parties.

That government is best which governs the least and confines itself to those areas of the national policy that are uniquely appropriate to governments. The government should be a catalyst, not an obstacle. Areas of activities covered by the government are too wide and can easily be significantly reduced. The government should systematically withdraw from areas where the people can best manage themselves.

There should be openness in the process of governance. In the place of a high degree of secretiveness, citizens' rights to information should be protected. Administrative reform has to promote autonomy, on the one hand, and accountability, on the other. Interministerial coordination is a sine qua non of efficiency. What must be avoided at all costs is assigning various related aspects of a problem to different ministries.

It has been the nation's fundamental error to have crippled the rural structure and to have attempted to replace it with a bureaucratic one. We must systematically undo this trend and restore responsibility to the rural people, not only through meaningful decentralization but also through revitalization of the cooperative structure and voluntary action.

The results of the 1989 general election were astounding. The ruling Congress Party of Rajiv Gandhi was removed from its high pedestal to the position of a minority in the Parliament of India. In 1984, in the eighth general election, the Congress Party had won 415 seats in a House whose total membership was 543. Never since Independence, in 1947, had the party been able to achieve such an overwhelming success. In five years, however, the party's popularity slumped to such an extent that in 1989 it could win only 193 seats.

The party which gained spectacular success was the Janata Dal, a party which came into being a little more than a year before the elections. Led by V.P. Singh, a former finance minister (later defence minister) in the Rajiv Gandhi government, an ex-Congress Party functionary, who had held several important official positions in the past, the Janata Dal scored near total success in almost all the northern States of India, such as Uttar Pradesh, Bihar, Orissa, Gujarat and Haryana. The total tally of the party was 141 seats.

The Party which came third in the race was BJP (Bharatiya Janata Party) with 88 seats. The BJP had only two seats in the outgoing Parliament. Next to the BJP was the Communist Party Marxist (CPM) with 32 seats and the Communist Party of India (CPI) with 12. Independents and others got the rest. The final party position was as follows:

Total seats contested 525

Congress-I	193	Forward Block	3
Janata Dal	141	JMM	3
BJP	88	N.C.	3
CPM	32	IUML	2
CPI	12	TDP	2
AIADMK	11	Congress (S)	1
Akali Dal (M)	6	Indian People's Front	1
RSP	4	Independents & others	20
BSP	3		

Of all the candidates who contested the elections, only 150 were women. Of these only 28 were elected. (In the previous House there were 43 women members.) Of the 28 women members, half were new faces.

Taking into consideration the enormous size of the country, the large number of candidates, the sharply focused issues and the consequent rivalry and intensity of the campaign, the elections could be seen as comparatively peaceful, yet, there were many distortions, Peaceful, free and fair elections were marred by violence and serious malpractices in several states. The most notable among these were Andhra Pradesh, Bihar, Haryana, Uttar Pradesh and Rajasthan. Perhaps the most serious electoral offence for which India has become notorious is 'booth capturing' which is often indulged with the knowledge and approval of the candidate for whose benefit it is done. According to the Chief Election Commissioner, it is due to the failure of the law and order machinery of the state concerned, as it is the responsibility of the state to maintain law and order. A disturbing aspect of this pernicious practice is that, ever since it was first indulged in, in 1967, it has been steadily increasing in some states, where it has been happening in successive elections.

Elaborating the point, the Commission observed at a meeting of the Chief Electoral Officers soon after the elections that, both before and during the election process, the government should take special precautions to ensure, and should be seen to ensure, that the official machinery and official positions were not used directly or indirectly in any manner whatsoever for furthering the interests of the party in power. The officials concerned with elections, including the law and order machinery, should not be influenced, pressured or misused in any way. Laws were there for these matters, but they had to be voluntarily observed.

The Election Commission has evolved a model code of conduct in consultation with all political parties, but in quite a few cases this code was violated, particularly by the ruling party. The Commission suggested that the electoral law should be amended to provide that any minister interfering with or influencing the formation of polling parties or the location of polling stations in a clandestine manner should not only be disqualified but also be debarred from holding public office for at least a decade.

Some of the other glaring defects of the present electoral system that prevail in India today also deserve our consideration. The constitution of India prescribes the system of a simple majority of votes polled for the success of candidates seeking elections to Parliament or state assemblies. According to this rule, among the contestants, the one who gets the highest number of votes is declared elected. This provision is best suited to Great Britain, where there are only two major parties, but India is notorious for its multiplicity of parties, besides innumerable splinter groups, with the result that in an election more than two parties or groups besides a number of independents enter the fray. In a large number of constituencies the total number of candidates runs into dozens or even scores. The Indian experience, spanning a period of five decades, with the simple majority system reveals a number of incongruities. For example, under the two-party system, simple majority in effect means absolute majority, because, among the two contestants, the successful candidate gets more than 50 per cent of the votes polled. But under the multi-party system, as there are more than two contestants in a constituency, a candidate who wins by a simple majority obtains only a minority of the votes polled. The elected members of the legislature therefore do not represent the majority opinion of the people. Elections in India show too many of such glaring instances. Table 9.1 shows a breakdown by state of elected candidates who in their respective constituencies polled less than 50 per cent of the votes in the 1989 elections.

Table 9.1 Candidates elected in 1989 with less than 50 per cent of the vote

State	Total number of seats	Candidates elected with less than 50%
Andhra Pradesh	42	9
Arunachal Pradesh	1	1
Bihar	54	25
Goa	2	1
Gujarat	26	1
Haryana	10	5
Himachal Pradesh	4	3
Jammu and Kashmir	6	2
Karnataka	28	13
Kerala	20	13
Madhya Pradesh	40	17
Maharashtra	48	27
Manipur	2	2
Meghalaya	2	—
Mizoram	1	1
Nagaland	1	—
Orissa	21	3
Punjab	13	9
Rajasthan	25	2
Sikkim	1	—
Tamil Nadu	39	7
Tripura	2	1
Uttar Pradesh	85	59
Centrally Administered Territories	13	8
Total	486	209

Thus, out of a total of 528 seats contested, 220 candidates who won the election did manage to win with less than 50 per cent of the votes polled. To illustrate the most glaring examples, in Bihar three candidates won with around 30 per cent of the votes polled and one candidate won with only 27.12 per cent.

The Election Commission recognizes political parties in two categories: national parties and state parties. In the 1989 general election, the Commission had given recognition to eight parties as national parties and 20 parties as state parties. In addition, the Commission had permitted 89 parties to be styled 'recognized parties'. But apart from the political parties, recognized or unrecognized, there has been an enormous number of independent candidates at recent elections. Their number was rather negligible in the first three general elections, in 1952, 1957 and 1962. Thereafter, their numbers began to swell at an almost exponential rate. For instance, there were 2694 and 3746 in 1980 and 1984, respectively. In 1989, their number had further increased, to 3928. In 1984, only one out of 758 independent candidates got elected. In all, only five of them succeeded in getting into Parliament. And for every independent candidate elected, 749 lost their deposits. (Any candidate who fails to poll less than one-sixth of the total votes polled in a constituency will forfeit his deposit.) In one of the constituencies of Tamil Nadu (Palani) there were as many as 49 independent candidates.

A large number of independent candidates makes for serious administrative problems, such as the need for a large number of additional symbols at short notice, ballot papers of considerable length or size to be printed, a large number of polling agents to be accommodated in the booths and the counting centres, and so on. Perhaps there is no other country in the world where democratic elections are conducted with such great numbers of independent candidates entering the poll fray.

There has been no correlation between the votes polled by a party and seats won by it. Under the Indian system of elections, a party may poll a minority of votes and yet get a comfortable majority of seats. For instance, in 1984, the Indian National Congress polled only 48.1 per cent of the votes but won 415 out of 517 seats; BJP, which polled 7.4 per cent of the votes in the same year, won only two seats. In 1989, the same Indian National Congress, with 39.5 per cent of the total votes polled, won only 197 seats. In contrast, Janata Dal, which polled only 17.8 per cent of the votes, won as many as 143 seats. The BJP, with 11.4 per cent of the votes, won 85 seats. Thus it is clear that, between the percentage of votes polled and the percentage of seats won, there is no correlation. In fact, the seats gained give an altogether highly distorted picture.

A characteristic feature of elections in India has been the sizeable number of invalid votes. The percentage of invalid votes has shown no tendency to come down, in spite of the fact that general elections have been a regular political exercise in India for 50 years. In this respect, India can be compared well with any other country where democratic elections form an integral part of its political system. But at the same time, India's electoral system shows its weakness through the number of invalid votes. In 1984, there were 6.41 million invalid votes; the corresponding figure in 1989 was 7.63 million. Why such large numbers? This can be explained only by the very high rate of illiteracy that still prevails in India.

The fact is that a good number of illiterates are unable to exercise their franchise correctly although the voting method is highly simplified by adopting a system with symbols. The literacy rate in India as a whole is still rather low: around 35 per cent, according to a 1981 Census. Although the Census of 1991 has been completed, the final figures are not yet available in detail. But it is estimated that the literacy percentage has gone up to around 50. Even so, India has the largest number of illiterates in the world, as the total population of India in early 1991 was around 845 million. In some of the more populous states of India, such as Uttar Pradesh, Bihar and Rajasthan, the percentage of illiterates is far higher than the national average, and the number of invalid votes in those states is much higher than in other states. The least number of invalid votes was in Kerala, a state which has the highest rate of literacy in the country.

All these drawbacks show how much progress India has to register in order to make the general elections a true measure of the democratic will of the people of India. Nevertheless, elections in India, the largest democracy in the world, will continue to be of absorbing concern to all those interested in comparative representation and electoral systems.

Note

This chapter was first presented as a paper at the Fifteenth World Political Science Congress, Buenos Aires, in July 1991.

Bibliography

Butler, A., A. Lahiri and P. Roy (1991), *India Decides (Elections, 1952–1991)*, New Delhi: Living Media India.

Election Commission of India (1989), *Report on the General Elections to the House of the People in India*, New Delhi.

Index

ACHRO *see* Asian Coalition of Human Rights Organization
administration 39, 153, 175
   elections 189
   electronics 137, 149–57, 159–60
Africa 5, 85, 88
Agricultural Produce Cess Fund 100, 102–4, 108–9
Agricultural Scientists Recruitment Board (ASRB) 100
agriculture 15, 31, 37, 72
   gender 88
   research 97–113
Ahmedabad 10
Alexander the Great 32
All India Radio 120
Almond, G. 64–5
Altekar 170
alternative development strategies 75–6
Ambani 122
Ambedkar, B.R. 176
Amte, B. 85
AMTIESA *see* Association of Management Training Substitutes of East and South Africa
Anand, M.R. 90
ancestor worship 32
Andhra Pradesh 84, 177, 186
Antrobus, P. 70, 75
AP *see* Approach Paper
Appico movement 80–1, 90–1
Approach Paper (AP) 76
Arabs 32

Armed Forces (Punjab and Chandigarh) Special Powers Act 120
art silk 11
Arthashastra 88, 169
artisans 81, 88
Ashton-Tate Inc. 126
Asia 85, 88
Asian Coalition of Human Rights Organization (ACHRO) 90
Asoka Mehta Committee 18
ASRB *see* Agricultural Scientists Recruitment Board
Assam 120, 177
assembly lines 1–5
Association of Management Training Substitutes of East and South Africa (AMTIESA) 2
Atomic Energy Commission 144, 154
Atreyi 31
Aurobindo, S. 32–3
automatic shuttle looms 14, 21
automation 128–9
Ayodhya 48

Babari Masjid 48
Baddal 82
Bailadilla iron ore mines 129
Balwant Rai Mehta Committee 177
bamboo 81
Banda 73
banking services 152
Bankura 81
Baratiya Janata Party (BJP) 131
Basham, A.L. 175

Basu, S. 116
Bedthi 84
Beria 82
Besant, A. 33
Bhakra Dam 84
Bhakti movement 33
Bhandara district 81
Bharat Electronics Ltd 127
Bhartiya Janta Party (BJP) 60, 63, 181, 183, 186, 189
Bhasin, K. 71
Bhatt, C.P. 81
Bhattacharjee, A. 126
Bhikhus 171
Bhilai iron ore mines 129
Bhopalapatnam 84
Bhyunder valley 82
big business 5–6
Bihar 84, 177, 186, 188, 190
biomass 73, 81
biosphere 75
biotechnology 137
Birlas 122, 126, 127
BJP see Bhartiya Janta Party
Black, E. 118
black economy 14
BNDE see National Economic Development Bank
Bodo Kacharis 36
Bombay 10, 21, 130
Bonjean, C.M. 48
booth capturing 186
Brazil 137–62
bride price 36
British rule 32, 78, 173
   administration 153
   agriculture 98
   IT 116
Brown, I.R. 75, 85–6
Brundtland Report 86–7, 89
Buddhism 33, 35, 169–72, 175
Building a Sustainable Society 69
bureaucracy 80, 91, 140, 143
   elections 185
   electronics 145, 150, 153–6, 158–60

Cabinet 39
capital 14, 21–2, 118, 122–3, 128, 137
CAPRE 147
careers 53, 59, 60
case studies 47–65
caste system 34, 171, 178, 185
Chakravarty, S. 23
Chamoli district 80, 82
Chanda Commission 132
Chandigarh Disturbed Areas Act 120
Chandrapur district 81
Charter of the United Nations 41
checklists 6
Chenoy, K.M. 122
child marriages 32
China 144
Chipko movement 80–1, 90–1
Christianity 31, 35
Citizens' Manifesto 183–4
Citizens' Report 81–2, 84
CMC see Computer Maintenance Corporation
COBRA 147
Coimbatore 10
Colhando, K. 126
collectivization 2
colonialism 72
   see also British rule
Committee on Public Undertakings 151
Committee on the Status of Women in India (CSWI) 43
communications 10, 38
Communist Party of India (CPI) 181, 183, 186
Communist Party Marxism (CPM) 181, 183, 186
Community Development Programmes 177
Company Act 76
comparative advantage 23
computer industry 110, 129, 142–9
   see also electronics
Computer Maintenance Corporation (CMC) 144, 145, 152, 155
Computer Point India Ltd 126
Concurrent List 177

Conferences on Women 42–3
Congress Party 50, 61–3, 116, 152, 183, 185–6
  see also Indian National Congress
CONIN see National Council for Informatics and Automatization
conservation 69, 76, 81, 87
conservatism 5
Constituent Assembly 175–6, 177
Constitution 41, 50, 179
Constitution (48th Amendment) Act 120
copercenary properties 39
core-periphery links 128–31
corporatism 159
corruption 80, 155, 184–5
cost of elections 182–3
cottage industries 3–4
cotton 10
Cotton Textiles (Control) Order (CTCO) 16, 24
CPI see Communist Party of India
CPM see Communist Party Marxism
credit 15
CSWI see Committee on the Status of Women in India
CTCO see Cotton Textiles (Control) Order
Cullinet Inc. 126

dams 84–5
DARE see Department of Agricultural Research and Education
databases 110
Datamatics 126
DAWN see Development Alternatives with Women for A New Era
Dayabhage system 39
DCM 126
debt 88, 122–3
Decade for Women 43, 70
Declaration of the Right to Development 90
demography 85–8
Department of Agricultural Research and Education (DARE) 99, 101–2, 107

Department of Atomic Energy 155
Department of Electronics 144–5, 154–5
Department of Social Welfare 43
Deshmukh, D. 33
Devadasis 32
development 69–91
Development Alternatives with Women for A New Era (DAWN) 70
Devi, G. 80
Devri 82
Dharampur block 82
Dharma 170
Dharmashastras 169
Digh Nikaya 169
Digital Equipment Corporation 126
Directive Principles of State Policy 176, 177
dirigists 24
Disturbed Areas Act 45
divorce 35
Doordarshan 120
dowries 32, 41
Drafting Committee 176
dual development thesis 23
Dungari-Paitoli 82

Earth summit 69
Earth Week 91
ECIL see Electronics Corporation of India Ltd
ecodevelopment camps 81
Economic and Social Council 42
education 31–2, 35–6, 38
  elections 183–4
  electronics 156
  environment 86–8
  political 47–65
  republicanism 179
  women 44
Election Commission 181–2, 185, 187–9
elections 181–90
  see also voting
electronics 137–62
Electronics Commission 144

Electronics Corporation of India Ltd
    (ECIL) 144–5, 152, 155
electronics revolution 141–9, 160
Electronics Trade & Technology
    Development Corporation 146
Elkin, F. 47
Emergency 119, 152
employment 36–8
energy 5
entrepreneurs 14, 19, 21, 26, 154–5
environment 69–91
essential services 123–4
Estimates Committee 151
Europe 84, 91
evaluation 109–10
exports 12, 19–20, 23, 25
    electronics 142
    IT 123, 125, 130

factories 2–3, 5, 13, 89
family 54–8, 60, 62–3
    environment 73–4
    IT 130
FAO *see* Food and Agriculture Organization
female infanticide 32–4, 41, 44, 73
Femia, J.V. 121
FERA *see* Foreign Exchange Regulations Act
fertility rates 86–7
feudalism 32, 124, 153, 178
finance 108–9, 118, 122–3
fisheries 81, 87, 91, 99–100
    research 113
    research planning 107
flexible specialization 138, 139–40
Food and Agriculture Organization
    (FAO) 102
Ford, H. 3, 5
Fordism 138–9, 140
foreign exchange 118
Foreign Exchange Regulations Act
    (FERA) 127
Forest (Conservation) Act 78–9
forests 78–84
France 127

franchise 171, 181, 190
free trade zones 127
French Regulation School 138
funding 122–3

Gan 170
Gana-Rajya 170
Gandhi, I. 119, 152
Gandhi, K. 33
Gandhi, M.K. 33, 49–50, 55, 57, 173
    republicanism 174–5
Gandhi, R. 185–6
Gandhiism 1–2, 16, 23, 25
    environment 85
    IT 116
    republicanism 176
Ganges 90
Gargi 31
Garos 35
gender 69–91
    see also women
General Assembly 90
General Motors 5
Ghosa 31
Global Assembly of Women 69
goals 3–4, 81, 97–113, 172
Gopeshwar 80
governance forms 169–79
Government of India Act 98
Gram Panchayats 177
Gram Sabha 178, 179
Gram Swaraj 173
Gramani 175
Grameen Mahila Shramik Unnayan
    Samiti 81
grassroots women's movements 78–84
greed 80
green revolution 97, 117–18
Greenstein, F.I. 48
growth economics 6
Gujarat 84, 85, 177, 186
Guptas 175
Gwalior 73

hand looms 14
hand-crafted work 1, 3–5

Handel, G. 47
handlooms 1-2, 10-11, 13-18, 21-2, 25
Haryana 186
health 53, 70, 73-4
   environment 84, 86, 88-90
   IT 130
Himachal Pradesh 80, 82, 177
Himalayas 80, 82
Hinditron Computers 126
Hindu Personal Law 35
Hindu Succession Act 39
Hinduism 31-2, 34-5, 53
   IT 131
   Panchayati Raj 170, 171
   women 57, 61
history of textile industry 10-13
home industry 3-4
housewives 38, 56
human resources 109
humanism 33, 173
Huns 32
Hutchinson, E. 74

IAEA *see* International Atomic Energy Agency
IARI *see* Indian Agricultural Research Institute
IAS *see* Indian Administrative Service
IBM 144-9, 152, 157
ICAR *see* Indian Council of Agricultural Research
ICL 144-5
ICSSR *see* Indian Council of Social Science Research
IDA *see* International Development Association
IDRC *see* International Development Research Centre
Ila Bhatt Report 74
Ilchman, W.F. 118
IMF *see* International Monetary Fund
imports 10, 20, 127, 145, 148
Inchampali 84
Independence 10-11, 16, 22, 33
   agriculture 97-8

elections 181, 185
environment 72, 78
IT 116
political socialization 50, 59, 61
republicanism 173, 175
women's rights 33, 36, 44
Indian Administrative Service (IAS) 153
Indian Agricultural Research Institute (IARI) 93
Indian Council of Agricultural Research (ICAR) 97-113
Indian Council of Social Science Research (ICSSR) 44
Indian National Congress 116, 181, 183, 189
   see also Congress Party
Indian Oil Corporation (IOC) 122
Indira Sagar Project 85
industrial policy 1-6
Industrial Policy Resolution 15
Industrial Policy Statement 116
Industries (Development and Regulation) Act 16
infanticide 33-4, 41, 44, 73
informal sectors 9-27
Informatics Council 151
informatics industry 139
Informatics Law 150
information technology (IT) 115-33
inheritance 39
integrative paradigm 75
inter-caste marriage 32, 39
interest rates 14
International Atomic Energy Agency (IAEA) 100
International Development Association (IDA) 100, 108
International Development Research Centre (IDRC) 100, 108
International Monetary Fund (IMF) 71, 88
International Women's Year 42
IOC *see* Indian Oil Corporation
Islam 31-2, 35, 53
   republicanism 173

women 57
IT *see* information technology

Jainism 31, 35
Jaintias 35
Jammu 177
Janata Dal 181, 183, 186, 189
Janpad 170
Japan 2, 4–5, 23–4
   environment 84
   IT 122, 126–7
Jayaswal, K.P. 169, 170, 172
Jhansi 73
Jharkhand Mukti-Morcha movement 91
Jindal group 122
JK Group 126
Joshi Commission 132
Joshimath 80

Kalase forest 81
Kalinga integrated steel plant 122
Kangle, R.P. 169
Kanpur 10, 90
Kanungo Committee 17, 18
Karkhanas 15
Karnataka 81, 84, 177
Karve Committee 17
Kashmir 120, 177
Kautilya 88, 169, 172
Keol-karo 84
Kerala 84, 177, 190
Kernal Refinery Project 122
Keynesianism 139
Khadeen 82
khadi cloth 14, 16
Khana 31
Khasis 35
kit culture 127
Kripalani, S. 33
Krishi Vigyan Kendras (KVKs) 110
Krishnamachari, T.T. 118
kshatriyas 171
Kurien, C.T. 117
KVKs *see* Krishi Vigyan Kendras

Lab to Land programme 111

labour pool 128–31
Lakha, S. 125
Lal, D. 24
Lalpur 84
Lancashire looms 14
Langton, K.P.L. 48
Latin America 85, 88
leadership 184
levies 16, 26
liberalism 5, 33
Licchavis 171
licences 14
Lilabati 31
Lim, L.Y.C. 130
Limits to Growth 69
literacy 34, 53, 55
   agriculture 110
   elections 181–2, 189–90
   environment 74, 86
   republicanism 179
   women 60, 62
living standards 97
lobbying 79
local self-government 169–79
Lopamudra 31
Lotus Development Corporation 126
Lucknow 90

MAB *see* Man and Biosphere Programme
Madhya Pradesh 73, 84, 85, 177
Madras 78
Magalore Refinery 122
Mahabharata 32, 121, 169, 171
Mahalanobis model 17, 23
Mahalingam, S. 128
Maharashtra 81, 84, 177
Majumdar, R.C. 172
Malaysia 127
Man and Biosphere Programme (MAB) 69
management of electronics 141–9
Mandal, D.G.S. 81
manifestoes 63, 183
Manikpur 73
Manu 32, 35

Mao Ze-dong 23
market reserve policy 147
market reserve strategy 149
marriage 35, 38, 39, 56–7, 87
   political socialization 51, 53
mass media *see* media
master weaver system 14, 15
materialism 172
matrilineal system 31, 35, 39
Medhi, K. 31–45
media 55–7, 120–1, 123
   elections 184
   IT 127, 131–2
Medical Termination of Pregnancy (MTP) 34, 41
mega-dams 84–5
Megasthenes 171
Meghalaya 35
menstruation 35
Mexico 129
MFP *see* minor forest products
Microsoft Corporation 126
Middle Ages 32
middle class 49–50, 55, 57, 89
migrants 14, 74, 87–90
military 147, 150, 153, 156
mills 1, 3, 10–22, 25–6
mining 129
Ministry of Agriculture 100, 107
Ministry of Community Development 177
Ministry of Defence 144
Ministry of Environment and Forests 76, 85
Ministry of Food 99
Ministry of Health and Education 86
Ministry of Informatics 155
Ministry of Planning 154
Ministry of Science and Technology 148
minor forest products (MFP) 83
Misra, S. 9–27
Mitakshara system 39
mixed economies 24
Mizoram 120
MNCs *see* multinational corporations

Mody, B. 124
monitoring 109–10
monogamy 39
monopolies 121–4, 127, 131, 137
Monopolies and Restrictive Trade Practices Act (MRTP) 127
mother goddess 31, 49
Motorola 126
Motwanis 126
MRTP *see* Monopolies and Restrictive Trade Practices Act
MTP *see* Medical Termination of Pregnancy
Mughals 32
multinational corporations (MNCs) 72, 122, 127
   electronics 147, 157
   IT 130
Munnar 84
Murdock, G. 127
Murphy, B. 124
Muslims *see* Islam

NAARM *see* National Academy of Agriculture Research Management
Nagaland 120
Nagel, S.S. 1–6
Naidu, S. 33
Nalagarth block 82
Naoriji, D. 32
Narayan, J.P. 173
Narmada Bachao Andolan 84, 85
Narmada Valley Project 84–5, 90
NARS *see* National Agricultural Research System
National Academy of Agriculture Research Management (NAARM) 100
National Agricultural Research Project 108
National Agricultural Research System (NARS) 104–7, 109
National Conference on Women and Development 44
National Council for Informatics and Automatization (CONIN) 148

National Economic Development Bank (BNDE) 146, 153–4
National Forest Policy (NFP) 78–9
National Front 123
National Informatics Law 147
National Information Service (SNI) 147, 156
National Panchayat 174
National Security Council 148
National Wasteland Development Board 78, 82–4
Navy 147
Naxalism 185
New Delhi 183
newly industrialized countries (NICs) 23, 130
newspapers 55, 56
NFP see National Forest Policy
NGOs see non-governmental organizations
Nibedita, Sister 33
NIC see newly industrialized countries
Nimmo, D.D. 48
Nitis 169
nomads 81, 87, 91
non-automatic shuttle looms 14, 20–1
non-governmental organizations (NGOs) 82–3, 85, 132
non-zero-sum games 6
Norma Rae 2
North Carolina 1–2
Norway 179

Oldenberg, H. 169
oligarchy 117
operational research projects (ORPs) 110
Oracle Corporation 126
organization 13–15
Orissa 177, 186
ORPs see operational research projects
Our Common Future 69, 86–7
outreach services 110–11
overcrowding 89
ownership see property rights

Panchayat Samiti 177
Panchayati Raj 169–79
Panchayats 79, 82, 118, 170–4, 176–8
Pandit, V.L. 33, 47–65
Parliament 39, 54, 61
  agriculture 100
  elections 181–2, 185, 187, 189
  electronics 140, 150–2
  IT 119–20
Patkar, M. 85
patriarchy 32, 71
patrilineal system 38
patronage system 153
pay rates 15, 25, 89, 130
Pedersen, J.D. 137–62
Petrobrás 153
Philippines 127
piecework 3
planning 107–8
Planning Commission 76, 98, 104, 107–8, 177–8
Planning Ministry 147
politics 39–41, 143
  education 47–65
  elections 183–9
  self-government 169–79
  structures 149–57, 159
polygamy 32, 35
population 85–8
positivism 75
post-Fordism 138–9, 140, 158
post-graduate students 38
power looms 11–15, 17–22, 26
Prajapati 175
Prashar Bharathi Bill 124, 132
price controls 20
private sector 122
privatization 123–4
productivity 1–5, 11–12
property rights 32, 35, 39, 41
  electronics 144
  environment 79
  IT 127
  republicanism 171
protectionism 117
Public Accounts Committee 151

public policy evaluation 1, 6, 15–26
Punjab 83, 84, 118, 120
Punjab Disturbed Areas Act 120
purdah 32, 53
putting out system 14
Pylee, M.V. 181–90

QRTs *see* quinquennial review teams
quality of life 3, 5, 74
quinquennial review teams (QRTs) 108
Quoran 35

radio 56
Rajasthan 35, 177, 186, 190
Rajput, R. 69–91
Rama Rajya 50
Ramayana 32, 64, 121, 169
Rampur Phata 80
rayon filament yarn 11
refugees 87, 88–90, 91
registration 14, 19, 181–2
regulation 138–9
rehabilitation 84–5
Reliance 126
religions 31–45, 48, 51–2, 53
remarriage 32, 39
Reni 80
republicanism 169–79
research 97–113
Research Institute for Social Development 43
research institutions 104, 105–7, 109
Rhys Davids, J.W. 169, 171–2
Rogers, E. 125
Rosav, I. 47
Roy, R.R.M. 32
Royal Agricultural Society 98
Royal Commission on Agriculture 98
rural areas 74, 76, 173–4
  agriculture 98
  elections 185
  IT 117
  republicanism 178
Russia 2

Sabhas 170

Samitis 170
Sangh 170
Sanghas 171
Sankhdher, M. 169–79
Santa Cruz Electronic Export Processing Zone (SEEPZ) 130
Santhanam, K. 177
Sanyal, K.K. 117
Saraswati, S.D. 32
Sardar Sarovar Project 85
Sarin, M. 82
Sarpanch 175
Sarvodaya 173
Satellite Instructional Television Experiment (SITE) 121, 124
Sati 32, 35
Scandinavia 172
schools 55–6
Schumacher, F. 174
science 97–113
secessionist movements 120
SEI *see* Special Secretariat of Informatics
self-government 169–79
service sectors 123–4
Seychelles 2
Sharma, O.P. 97–113
Shiva, V. 71
Shram Shakti 74
shuttle looms 14
SIDA *see* Swedish International Development Authority
Sikhism 31, 35
Silent Valley 84
Silkani forest 81
Singh, J. 120
Singh, N.K. 129
Singh, V.P. 186
Singhal, A. 125
Sirsi district 81
SITE *see* Satellite Instructional Television Experiment
Sivaraman Committee 18
slums 88–91
small businesses 5–6
Small is Beautiful (Schumaker) 174

Smiritis 169
SNI *see* National Information Service
social sciences 106–7
socialization 35, 38, 47–65
socialism 24
Societies Registration Act 98
socioeconomic issues 106, 111, 179
socioreligious perspective 31–45
sociosphere 70
software 6, 125–8, 142, 145, 155–7
SOS *see* super-optimizing solutions
South Asian Association for Regional Co-operation 33
Southeast Asia 23, 127, 129–30
Soviet Union 24
Special Secretariat of Informatics (SEI) 147–8, 151
spinning 10, 14, 17
spinning mills *see* mills
squatters 88–91
SRC *see* Staff Research Council
Stacy, B. 47
Staff Research Council (SRC) 110
state 115–33, 138–9, 144
    elections 182, 187
    electronics 148, 151, 155–6
    management 20
    republicanism 170, 179
stereotypes 57
structural adjustment policies 87–8
Sukhomajri 83
super-optimizing analysis 1–6
super-optimizing solutions (SOS) 3–6
Supreme Court 44, 182
Surat 11
survival levels 73–8, 80–1
sustainability 69, 72, 90
suttee 32, 35
Swarup, H. 69–91
Swedish International Development Authority (SIDA) 100, 108
Syndicate 119

Tamil Nadu 177, 189
Tata Consultancy Services 126, 127
Tata Unisys 126, 127, 128

Tatas 122, 126–7, 146
technoeconomic paradigm 139, 141
technology 97–113
Tehri 84
telecommunications 110, 125–7, 139
television 56, 57, 121, 124
Terrorist and Disruptive Activities (Prevention) Act 120
Texas Instruments 126
textiles 9–27, 90
Thailand 127
Therborn, G. 140
Third Review Team 98–9
Thomas, P. 115–33
Tilak, B.G. 32
TNCs *see* transnational corporations
transnational corporations (TNCs) 123, 126, 130, 137
transport 38
tribal communities 79, 81
    environment 84–5, 87, 91
    religions 35–6
tribunals 76
trickle-down theory 124
Tulpule, B. 128
Turks 32
TVS Group 126

underclass 89
underground economy 14, 15
Union Territories 177
unions 15, 42, 130, 152
Unisys Ltd 128, 146
United Kingdom (UK) 98
United Nations Development Programme (UNDP) 100, 102, 108
United Nations (UN) 41–3, 70–1, 90
United States Agency for International Development (USAID) 100
United States (US) 84, 91, 98, 102
    agriculture 108
    electronics 146, 153
    IT 118, 128
Universal Declaration of Human Rights 41
universities 99–101, 104–6, 108–9, 111

Upadhyaya, D. 173
Upanishads 31, 169
upstream research 112
urban areas 41–2, 49, 74
   environment 76
   self-government 173
   society 38
urbanization 88–91
USAID *see* United States Agency for International Development
utopianism 183
Uttar Pradesh 73, 80, 84, 90
   elections 186, 190
   self-government 177

Vedanta 33
Vedas 31–2, 169, 175
Verba, S. 64–5
Verghese Commission 132
video 132
Vidyasagar, I.C. 32
Vindhyachal 73
Vishnuprayag 84
Voelcker, J.A. 98
voting 58–9, 61–3, 181–90
Vyasulu, V. 127

wage rates 15, 25, 89, 130
Wang Laboratories 126
waste disposal 89

water 89
weaving 10–11, 14–15, 17, 19–21, 24–5
Weber, M. 138, 140, 150, 153
welfare state 139, 171–2
West Bengal 177
Western Ghats 81
Whitney, E. 3
WHO *see* World Health Organization
widows 32, 35, 39
win-win dispute resolution 6
women
   see also gender
   elections 183, 186
   IT 130–1
   politics 47–65
   property rights 171
   rights 31–45
Working Group on Employment of Women 44
World Bank 21, 71, 84, 100
   agriculture 108
   IT 117, 127
World Health Organization (WHO) 89
World War II 10, 16, 19, 50
World Women's Congress for a Healthy Planet 69

Zenana 53
Zila Parishad 177
Zoroastrianism 31